SOLARO

STUDY GUIDE

lish 9

emic (ENG1D)

SOLARO Study Guide is designed to help students achieve success in school. The content in each study guide is 100% curriculum aligned and serves as an excellent source of material for review and practice. To create this book, teachers, curriculum specialists, and assessment experts have worked closely to develop the instructional pieces that explain each of the key concepts for the course. The practice questions and sample tests have detailed solutions that show problem-solving methods, highlight concepts that are likely to be tested, and point out potential sources of errors. **SOLARO Study Guide** is a complete guide to be used by students throughout the school year for reviewing and understanding course content, and to prepare for assessments.

Publisher
Gautam Rao

Rao, Gautam, 1961 –
SOLARO Study Guide – English Language Arts 9 Academic
Ontario

1. English – Juvenile Literature. I. Title

Published by
Castle Rock Research Corp.
2410 Manulife Place
10180 – 101 Street
Edmonton, AB T5J 3S4

2 3 4 FP 13 11 10

Redeeming Your Free 14-Day Trial

Congratulations on your purchase of a *SOLARO Study Guide*!

As a thank you from us, we are pleased to offer our book
customers a free 14-day trial of SOLARO.com, our online study
tool for math, science, and English language arts for 3rd to 12th
grades.

Please visit http://www.solaro.com/trial2013 to redeem your
free trial now!

Dedicated to the memory of Dr. V. S. Rao

SOLARO STUDY GUIDE—English Language Arts 9 Academic

SOLARO Study Guide consists of the following sections:

Key Tips for Being Successful at School gives examples of study and review strategies. It includes information about learning styles, study schedules, and note taking for test preparation.

Class Focus includes a unit on each area of the curriculum. Units are divided into sections, each focusing on one of the specific expectations, or main ideas, that students must learn about in that unit. Examples, definitions, and visuals help to explain each main idea. Practice questions on the main ideas are also included. At the end of each unit is a test on the important ideas covered. The practice questions and unit tests help students identify areas they know and those they need to study more. They can also be used as preparation for tests and quizzes. Most questions are of average difficulty, though some are easy and some are hard—the harder questions are called *Challenger Questions*. Each unit is prefaced by a **Table of Correlations**, which correlates questions in the unit (and in the practice tests at the end of the book) to the specific curriculum expectations. Answers and solutions are found at the end of each unit.

Key Strategies for Success on Tests helps students get ready for tests. It shows students different types of questions they might see, word clues to look for when reading them, and hints for answering them.

Practice Tests includes one to three tests based on the entire course. They are very similar to the format and level of difficulty that students may encounter on final tests. In some regions, these tests may be reprinted versions of official tests, or reflect the same difficulty levels and formats as official versions. This gives students the chance to practice using real-world examples. Answers and complete solutions are provided at the end of the section.

For the complete curriculum document (including specific expectations along with examples and sample problems), visit www.edu.gov.on.ca/eng/curriculum/secondary.

SOLARO Study Guide *Study Guides* are available for many courses. Check www.castlerockresearch.com for a complete listing of books available for your area.

For information about any of our resources or services, please call Castle Rock Research at 1.800.840.6224 or visit our website at http://www.castlerockresearch.com.

At Castle Rock Research, we strive to produce an error-free resource. If you should find an error, please contact us so that future editions can be corrected.

TABLE OF CONTENTS

Key Tips for being Successful at School

KEY TIPS FOR BEING SUCCESSFUL AT SCHOOL

KEY FACTORS CONTRIBUTING TO SCHOOL SUCCESS

In addition to learning the content of your courses, there are some other things that you can do to help you do your best at school. You can try some of the following strategies:

- **Keep a positive attitude:** Always reflect on what you can already do and what you already know.

- **Be prepared to learn:** Have the necessary pencils, pens, notebooks, and other required materials for participating in class ready.

- **Complete all of your assignments:** Do your best to finish all of your assignments. Even if you know the material well, practice will reinforce your knowledge. If an assignment or question is difficult for you, work through it as far as you can so that your teacher can see exactly where you are having difficulty.

- **Set small goals for yourself when you are learning new material:** For example, when learning the parts of speech, do not try to learn everything in one night. Work on only one part or section each study session. When you have memorized one particular part of speech and understand it, move on to another one. Continue this process until you have memorized and learned all the parts of speech.

- **Review your classroom work regularly at home:** Review to make sure you understand the material you learned in class.

- **Ask your teacher for help:** Your teacher will help you if you do not understand something or if you are having a difficult time completing your assignments.

- **Get plenty of rest and exercise:** Concentrating in class is hard work. It is important to be well-rested and have time to relax and socialize with your friends. This helps you keep a positive attitude about your schoolwork.

- **Eat healthy meals:** A balanced diet keeps you healthy and gives you the energy you need for studying at school and at home.

HOW TO FIND YOUR LEARNING STYLE

Every student learns differently. The manner in which you learn best is called your learning style. By knowing your learning style, you can increase your success at school. Most students use a combination of learning styles. Do you know what type of learner you are? Read the following descriptions. Which of these common learning styles do you use most often?

- **Linguistic Learner:** You may learn best by saying, hearing, and seeing words. You are probably really good at memorizing things such as dates, places, names, and facts. You may need to write down the steps in a process, a formula, or the actions that lead up to a significant event, and then say them out loud.

- **Spatial Learner:** You may learn best by looking at and working with pictures. You are probably really good at puzzles, imagining things, and reading maps and charts. You may need to use strategies like mind mapping and webbing to organize your information and study notes.

- **Kinesthetic Learner:** You may learn best by touching, moving, and figuring things out using manipulatives. You are probably really good at physical activities and learning through movement. You may need to draw your finger over a diagram to remember it, tap out the steps needed to solve a problem, or feel yourself writing or typing a formula.

SCHEDULING STUDY TIME

You should review your class notes regularly to ensure that you have a clear understanding of all the new material you learned. Reviewing your lessons on a regular basis helps you to learn and remember ideas and concepts. It also reduces the quantity of material that you need to study prior to a test. Establishing a study schedule will help you to make the best use of your time.

Regardless of the type of study schedule you use, you may want to consider the following suggestions to maximize your study time and effort:

- Organize your work so that you begin with the most challenging material first.

- Divide the subject's content into small, manageable chunks.

- Alternate regularly between your different subjects and types of study activities in order to maintain your interest and motivation.

- Make a daily list with headings like "Must Do," "Should Do," and "Could Do."

- Begin each study session by quickly reviewing what you studied the day before.

- Maintain your usual routine of eating, sleeping, and exercising to help you concentrate better for extended periods of time.

CREATING STUDY NOTES

MIND-MAPPING OR WEBBING

Use the key words, ideas, or concepts from your class notes to create a mind map or web, which is a diagram or visual representation of the given information. A mind map or web is sometimes referred to as a knowledge map. Use the following steps to create a mind map or web:

1. Write the key word, concept, theory, or formula in the centre of your page.

2. Write down related facts, ideas, events, and information, and link them to the central concept with lines.

3. Use coloured markers, underlining, or symbols to emphasize things such as relationships, timelines, and important information.

The following mind map is an example of one that could help you develop an essay:

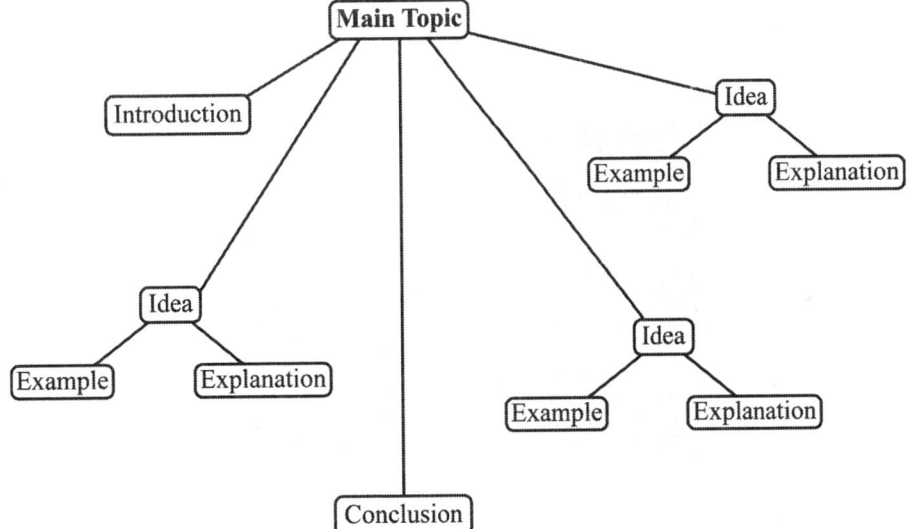

INDEX CARDS

To use index cards while studying, follow these steps:

1. Write a key word or question on one side of an index card.

2. On the reverse side, write the definition of the word, answer to the question, or any other important information that you want to remember.

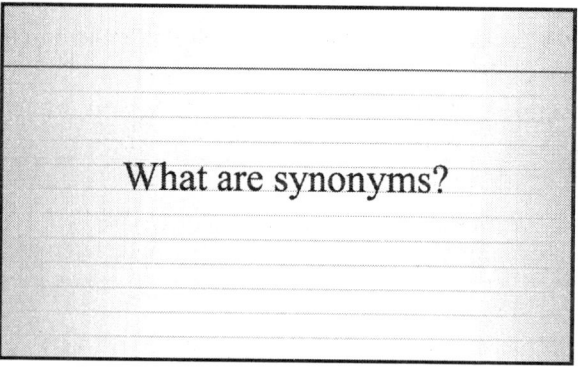

SYMBOLS AND STICKY NOTES—IDENTIFYING IMPORTANT INFORMATION

Use symbols to mark your class notes. The following are some examples:

- An exclamation mark (!) might be used to point out something that must be learned well because it is a very important idea.

- A question mark (?) may highlight something you are not certain about

- A diamond (◊) or asterisk (*) could highlight interesting information that you want to remember.

Sticky notes are useful in the following situations:

- Use sticky notes when you are not allowed to put marks in books.

- Use sticky notes to mark a page in a book that contains an important diagram, formula, explanation, or other information.

- Use sticky notes to mark important facts in research books.

MEMORIZATION TECHNIQUES

- **Association** relates new learning to something you already know. For example, to remember the spelling difference between dessert and desert, recall that the word *sand* has only one *s*. So, because there is sand in a desert, the word *desert* has only one *s*.

- **Mnemonic** devices are sentences that you create to remember a list or group of items. For example, the first letter of each word in the phrase "Every Good Boy Deserves Fudge" helps you to remember the names of the lines on the treble-clef staff (E, G, B, D, and F) in music.

- **Acronyms** are words that are formed from the first letters or parts of the words in a group. For example, RADAR is actually an acronym for Radio Detecting and Ranging, and MASH is an acronym for Mobile Army Surgical Hospital. HOMES helps you to remember the names of the five Great Lakes (Huron, Ontario, Michigan, Erie, and Superior).

- **Visualizing** requires you to use your mind's eye to "see" a chart, list, map, diagram, or sentence as it is in your textbook or notes, on the chalkboard or computer screen, or in a display.

- **Initialisms** are abbreviations that are formed from the first letters or parts of the words in a group. Unlike acronyms, an initialism cannot be pronounced as a word itself. For example, GCF is an initialism for **G**reatest **C**ommon **F**actor.

KEY STRATEGIES FOR REVIEWING

Reviewing textbook material, class notes, and handouts should be an ongoing activity. Spending time reviewing becomes more critical when you are preparing for a test. You may find some of the following review strategies useful when studying during your scheduled study time:

- Before reading a selection, preview it by noting the headings, charts, graphs, and chapter questions.

- Before reviewing a unit, note the headings, charts, graphs, and chapter questions.

- Highlight key concepts, vocabulary, definitions, and formulas.

- Skim the paragraph, and note the key words, phrases, and information.

- Carefully read over each step in a procedure.

- Draw a picture or diagram to help make the concept clearer.

KEY STRATEGIES FOR SUCCESS: A CHECKLIST

Reviewing is a huge part of doing well at school and preparing for tests. Here is a checklist for you to keep track of how many suggested strategies for success you are using. Read each question, and put a check mark (✓) in the correct column. Look at the questions where you have checked the "No" column. Think about how you might try using some of these strategies to help you do your best at school.

Key Strategies for Success	Yes	No
Do you attend school regularly?		
Do you know your personal learning style—how you learn best?		
Do you spend 15 to 30 minutes a day reviewing your notes?		
Do you study in a quiet place at home?		
Do you clearly mark the most important ideas in your study notes?		
Do you use sticky notes to mark texts and research books?		
Do you practise answering multiple-choice and written-response questions?		
Do you ask your teacher for help when you need it?		
Are you maintaining a healthy diet and sleep routine?		
Are you participating in regular physical activity?		

Analyzing for Meaning

ANALYSING FOR MEANING

TABLE OF CORRELATIONS		
Specific Expectation	**Practice Questions**	**Unit Test Questions**
By the end of this course, students will:		
General Outcome		
9R1.1 read student- and teacher-selected texts from diverse cultures and historical periods, identifying specific purposes for reading		
9R1.2 use several different reading comprehension strategies before, during, and after reading to understand both simple and complex texts		
9R1.3 identify the most important ideas and supporting details in both simple and complex texts	4, 12, 13, 17, 19, 21	7, 8, 10, 12, 20, 24
9R1.4 make and explain inferences about both simple and complex texts, supporting their explanations with stated and implied ideas from the texts	3, 6, 10, 14, 15, 18	4, 5, 13, 22, 23
9R1.5 extend understanding of both simple and complex texts by making connections between the ideas in them and personal knowledge, experience, and insights; other texts; and the world around them	11, 16	6, 15, 17, 19
9R1.6 analyse texts in terms of the information, ideas, issues, or themes they explore, examining how various aspects of the texts contribute to the presentation or development of these elements	1, 2, 8, 9, 22	1, 14, 21
9R1.7 evaluate the effectiveness of both simple and complex texts, using evidence from the text to support their opinions	5, 7, 20	3, 11, 16
9R1.8 identify the perspectives and/or biases evident in both simple and complex texts and comment on any questions they may raise about beliefs, values, and identity		2, 9, 18
9M1.1 explain how both simple and complex media texts are created to suit particular purposes and audiences		
9M1.2 interpret simple and complex media texts, identifying and explaining the overt and implied messages they convey		
9M1.3 evaluate how effectively information, ideas, issues, and opinions are communicated in both simple and complex media texts and decide whether the texts achieve their intended purpose		
9M1.5 identify the perspectives and/or biases evident in both simple and complex media texts and comment on any questions they may raise about beliefs, values, and identity		

ANALYSING FOR MEANING

The main function of writing is to communicate meaning. Finding out the meaning of the text you are reading is not always easy, and it is important to find different strategies for finding meaning in a variety of texts. Analysing the meaning of a poem will involve different techniques than analysing the meaning for a research essay. The following section of your study guide will show you how meaning is communicated in different forms of writing and will give you some strategies for analysing meaning. This section will also show you how best to communicate the meaning you intend in your own writing.

ON 9R1.2   *Use several different reading comprehension strategies before, during, and after reading to understand both simple and complex texts*

READING COMPREHENSION STRATEGIES

Reading comprehension strategies help you make sense of what you read. The following section provides some specific reading strategies, explanations, and examples that highlight the importance of being a thoughtful reader, and shows you how to use these strategies for reading prose, poetry, and visual texts.

PREVIEWING

Previewing means taking a brief overview or glance at the parts of the text that stand out to you. When previewing, take a look at the reading selection and think about what stands out. Are there headings or titles? Are there graphs or charts? Are there any pictures? Are there captions describing the pictures? If the passage has any of these things, make a note in your mind to pay close attention to them as you read.

It is an excellent idea to preview a new text, such as a textbook, before you receive any reading assignments. You can learn helpful information about a course and its content before you even begin. Here are some possible previewing activities to try with textbooks or other books:

• Look at the publication date. Is it important that this particular text is current?

• Look over the table of contents. How is it organized?

• Does the text have a glossary?

• Is there an index?

• Leaf through the text to check the graphics: pictures, diagrams, charts, maps, and so on. How will these aid your learning?

• Skim through at least one chapter:

  – How is it organized?

  – Are vocabulary terms listed at the beginning?

  – Are the subheadings in a larger, bolded font?

  – Are key words bolded?

  – Are there questions or comments in the sidebars to help you understand the text as you read?

  – Is there an overview paragraph at the beginning of the chapter?

  – Is the chapter summarized at the end?

  – Is there a chapter review?

  – Does the text include an answer key?

USING PRIOR KNOWLEDGE

- Build on your background knowledge and experiences to help you understand any text you read. Take your time reading and use what you already know about something to make the text you are reading clearer. To do this, make connections between what you know and what you read by asking yourself the following questions:

- Does this story remind me of any other stories or texts?

- What do I already know about the topic I am reading about?

- Is there something in this text that is similar to something I already know?

PREDICTING AND QUESTIONING

As you read, try to predict what you will learn or what will happen next. Using your background knowledge and clues from the text, you can form hypotheses (predictions) as you read. You should be able to support your predictions with facts from the text.

The following steps form an example of how you can predict what will be in a text:

1. Before you start reading, ask "I wonder…" questions.

2. Predict story will be about what the perhaps based on its title.

3. If there are headings or chapter titles, think about what ideas or subjects are being touched upon before reading further.

4. As you read, stop and predict what might happen next.

5. When you are finished reading, ask yourself if your predictions were correct. If they were not, consider why.

A PURPOSE FOR READING

As with the strategies discussed earlier in this section, what you do before you start to read can add to your reading experience. One of the most important steps to take before reading is to establish your purpose. The reason you are reading a text can help you decide how to read it. Are you reading to research information for an essay, to answer questions for an assignment, or to locate the phone number, hours of operation, and address of a new clothing store? How you go about reading for any of these different tasks will change with your purpose.

When you have a purpose for reading, you can keep a closer eye on your progress. You know when to stop and reread. Sometimes, you need to revisit your purpose; at other times, your purpose changes.

MONITORING FOR MEANING

Monitoring for meaning means checking your understanding of the material you read. Think about whether or not the text makes sense to you and think about the broader meaning of the story. Keep in mind that it is perfectly acceptable to have difficulty with or be confused about some part of a text. Monitoring for meaning means thinking about what you understand as well as what you do not understand.

To practise monitoring for meaning, you can ask yourself the following questions as you read:

- Do I understand what I just read?
- What is happening in the story?
- How do the important ideas and details relate to each other?

When you are finished reading, think about any questions you still have. These questions can help you pinpoint parts of the text you may have had trouble with.

VISUALIZING

Visualizing is a process in which reading can become like watching a movie. Writers convey information with words. As you read, you can use these words to create pictures in your mind that show what is happening in the text. Usually, visualizing is something natural that happens for the reader. Visualizing in this way can help you remember information more easily and can deepen your understanding of the text. Through visualization, you can create images of the characters, settings, and events in a story.

To practise visualizing while reading, try the following techniques:

- Pause frequently and think about what you have read.
- After reading a passage, create an image in your mind of what has been described.
- Work backward. This could include looking at a wordless picture book and creating a story to match the pictures.

INFERRING

Inferring is part of everyday life. When you wake up, you make inferences, or assumptions, about what is going to happen throughout the day. You brush your teeth, get dressed, and perform other morning tasks because you infer that you are going to school. Suppose that, in the middle of breakfast, you learn that it is a snow day and school is cancelled. Now you immediately start thinking of what else to do and make inferences about your options for the day. Reading is the same way. As soon as you open up a book, you begin making assumptions about the text based on what kind of book it is, if you know any other books by the writer, and how the cover of the book looks. You will make different inferences about a textbook than you will about a novel or an instructional manual.

The inferences you make are based on your life experiences and what you already understand. Your background knowledge and the information in the text create meaning beyond what is directly stated in the text. Inferences may include conclusions, predictions, and new ideas.

To practise inferring while reading, ask yourself the following questions:

- What do I think this story is about?
- How do I think the character feels?
- Why did I think that would happen?
- How did I know that?
- What does the writer actually say?

IMPORTANCE

Determining what is important in a text is particularly useful for non-fiction and informational texts. You can save time by distinguishing between what is vital information in a text and what may be less important. By identifying important ideas and themes, you can set aside less important information.

To practise determining what information is most important in a text, try the following techniques:

- While reading, look for clues in the format of the text that might indicate importance. Pay attention to the first and last lines of a paragraph, the title, any headings or subheadings, captions, framed text (text with a box drawn around it), quotation marks, font size, and font style (underlined text, italicized text, bold text).
- Pay particular attention to pictures, illustrations, charts, and diagrams; they may provide you with important information.
- As you read, focus on remembering information that appears to be "must-know" information.
- After reading, think about the most important information you learned.

SYNTHESIZING

Synthesizing is the ability to put various elements together to form a whole. It allows you to sort through information to make sense of it.

To practise synthesizing, ask yourself the following questions while reading a text:

- What was the writer's purpose in writing this piece?
- What is the main idea of this story?
- What clues helped me to determine the main idea?
- How do the different parts of this story connect with one another?
- Has my thinking changed after reading this piece?
- Can I think of a different title for this piece?

FIGURE IT OUT

If you are having trouble understanding something you are reading, different strategies can help. As you use these strategies, they will become more and more familiar to you. In time, you will probably use these strategies without even realizing it. The following list describes some strategies that can help your reading comprehension:

- **Reread:** sometimes, a second reading is all it takes. If you cannot make a picture in your mind or you do not understand what you have just read, try reading it again.

- **Skip ahead:** sometimes, you need to move on. If you do not understand something you have just read, skip ahead and continue reading. There may be information later on that helps you to understand the section you are having trouble with. You can always go back and reread difficult sections later.

- **Context clues:** use familiar words surrounding an unfamiliar word to help you determine the unfamiliar word's meaning.

- **Picture clues:** use information from pictures to help make sense of what you have read.

- **Ask for help**: ask a teacher, parent, classmate, or sibling for help when you have tried your own strategies and still do not understand something.

To help you better understand what you read, there are some questions you can ask before, during, and after reading a piece of text.

Before Reading

- Are there headings, charts, graphs, vocabulary, or questions I can preview?
- What is my purpose for reading this text?
- What will I be doing with the information I read?
- What do I already know about this topic?
- What reading strategies should I use to read this text?
- How is the text organized?
- What questions do I have before reading this text?
- Can I turn headings or subheadings into questions?

During Reading

- Am I meeting the purpose I set out for reading?
- Am I making sense of what I am reading?
- Do I have a clear visual image in my mind's eye?
- Is what I am reading what I expected?
- Are some parts different or similar to my predictions?
- What is the main idea of the text so far?
- What kind of graphic organizer would I use to begin organizing the ideas?
- What am I visualizing in my mind about these ideas while I am reading?
- Is the information in the text similar to other passages I have read?

After Reading

- Do I need to reread any parts that were difficult?

- What new information did I learn, and how does it fit into my background knowledge?

- What else do I still need to know about this topic?

- What are my thoughts about what I have read? Do I agree or disagree? Why?

Do I like what I have read? Why or why not?

In cases where you are not permitted to mark the text itself, you can put symbols or reading comments on sticky notes, which can be removed later.

Remember, the purpose of every reading strategy is to help you better understand what you read. Any strategy that becomes an automatic part of your reading contributes to your success in school and in life and allows you to pursue your academic goals with confidence.

ON 9R1.3   Identify the important ideas and supporting details in both simple and complex texts

UNDERSTANDING CONTENT

When you are reading, understanding the main idea of a work is important to help you tie together all of the information you are taking in. A main idea connects the details of a text together. Often, the main idea is in the title or in one or two strong sentences near the beginning or end of the passage. The main idea of a piece of writing is always supported by details that describe or explain the main idea. Look at the two examples below and notice how the details support the main idea in each article.

TSUNAMIS (main idea)

Tsunamis are caused by underwater earthquakes and volcanic eruptions, and they are the largest waves of all (**main idea**). Earthquakes occur when two **tectonic plates** collide or slide past each other. When an earthquake occurs under the ocean, the ocean bottom shakes. This movement causes the water above to become **displaced**. Waves of energy spread out in all directions from the source of the vibrations in ever-widening circles. As the tsunami approaches the shore, the waves rub against the seafloor. **Friction** causes the waves to slow down and build from behind, creating a huge volume of water that crashes onto the shore.

All the other sentences in the passage support the main idea that tsunamis are caused by underwater earthquakes and volcanic eruptions.

ROGUE WAVES (main idea)

Sometimes, groups of large ocean waves caused by a storm slam into a powerful ocean current passing in the opposite direction. (1) When this happens, several storm waves pile up to form gigantic waves called rogue or freak waves. (2) These waves can be more than 100 feet (30 metres) tall and can bury cargo ships beneath the sea. (3) Rogue waves are most common off the coasts of Japan, Florida, and Alaska. (4) Currently, a project known as WaveAtlas monitors the oceans with satellites. (5) Over the next few years, oceanographers hope to analyse these satellite images to help them better understand why freak waves occur. (6)

In this paragraph, sentences 1 and 2 support the main idea by expressing exactly what rogue waves are, while the other sentences give further informative details about rogue waves.

MAIN IDEAS AND DETAILS IN INFORMATIONAL TEXT

There are various strategies for identifying and recording main ideas and supporting details in informational text. Two common methods are to create a chart or graphic organizer or to make an outline. Read the following passage and review the sample outline that follows. Think about how you might use an outline to organize the information in this passage.

CLIMBING THE HIGH PEAKS

If you have ever scrambled up a rocky cliff, followed a trail to the top of a hill, or gasped at the beauty of the Rockies, you can probably understand why people climb mountains. It's difficult, dangerous, and—some say—deranged. But there is a certain kind of person who thinks it's the best adventure of all.

The greatest challenges for mountain climbers lie in Tibet and Nepal. There the Himalayan chain of peaks rises skyward, with Mount Everest the highest at 8 840 m. Traditionally, these remote Asian countries did not allow Europeans to enter, so the first climbers had to disguise themselves as Nepalese herdsmen, Buddhist pilgrims, and Tibetan merchants.

Early in the twentieth century, permission was granted for an occasional British expedition to enter Tibet for the purpose of exploring the Himalayas. From this time on, conquering the high peaks has become the goal of adventurers from around the world.

The mountains themselves, of course, offered their own difficulties to climbers. First of all, there were the steep glaciers. Parties of climbers crossing these stretches of ice had to beware of falling into deep crevasses. They dodged almost daily avalanches. High altitudes caused breathing problems, headaches, and worse. Worst of all, ferocious storms could—and sometimes did—sweep the climbers and their equipment right off the steep ridges.

Essential to the success of most expeditions in the Himalayas has been the assistance of the Sherpas. These mountain people are used to high altitudes, can carry 115-kg loads day after day, and can even walk barefoot in snow. They have earned the nickname of "tiger" from visiting climbers. The most famous of the tigers—Tenzing Norquay (or Norgay)—was one of the first men to reach the summit of Mount Everest.

Hillary of New Zealand and Tenzing Norquay, the Sherpa. They spent the night alone in Camp IX, huddled in their tent at 8 504 m. At 6:30 the next morning, May 29, 1953, they set out on their famous journey. Armed with a nylon rope, ice axes, oxygen tanks, and crampons for walking on snow, they kicked steps across the steep snow slope. At times the ridge was as narrow as a knife-blade, and cornices of snow hung over the edge. As the snow became harder, the men had to cut out each step with their axes. And the oxygen would last less than five hours longer. They had to reach the summit by 11:30 or else turn back. At one point, Tenzing almost stopped breathing as ice clogged his oxygen tubes.

An hour after this incident, Hillary suddenly stopped. Just ahead of him, a tower of rock 12 m high rose straight up from the ridge. He thought they had been beaten. Then he saw a wide crack that led all the way up.

It was the last major obstacle. After pushing and kicking their way to the top, they realized that there was yet more snow climbing, but they were too close to stop. They cut step after weary step into the ice. Finally, at 11:30 exactly, Tenzing and Hillary were standing together on the highest point of the earth's surface—looking down! While Hillary took photographs, Tenzing buried gifts for his Buddhist gods.

The following outline is an example of one you could make for the passage "Climbing the High Peaks." Making an outline can help you identify the main ideas and how they are supported by relevant details.

Outline for "Climbing the High Peaks"

I. Tibet and Nepal greatest challenges to mountain climbers
  A. Himalayas are world's highest mountains
  B. They are in a remote part of Asia
  C. Until early 20th century, no Europeans were allowed to climb

II. Difficulties for climbers
  A. Glaciers and crevasses
  B. Avalanches
  C. High altitude problems
  D. Storms

III. For climbs to be successful
  A. Sherpas were needed
    1. Tenzing Norquay—a famous Sherpa—First to climb Everest
  B. Proper equipment needed
    1. Sunglasses
    2. Oxygen mask and bottle
    3. Down parka
    4. Ice axe
    5. Crampons
    6. Pack
    7. Nylon over boots

IV. 1953 ascent of Everest
  A. Header John Hunt
    1. Arranged equipment to be carried up mountain
    2. Established camps on mountain
    3. Ensured time was spent acclimatizing
  B. Actual attempts at summit
    1. 1st attempt by Bourdillon and Evans failed
    2. 2nd attempt by Hillary and Tenzing succeeded
      a) May 29, 1953
      b) Started at 6:30 a.m.
      c) Reached summit at 11:30 a.m.
      d) Hillary took photos
      e) Tenzing buried gifts for Buddha

Creating an outline of a text you have read will help you remember the facts of the text. An outline will also reveal what parts of the text are most important and show how the text has been structured. Outlines can be arranged in different ways, so find an outline that works best for helping you find the main idea of a text.

MAIN IDEAS AND CHARACTERS IN LITERARY TEXT

If you are able to identify important ideas and supporting details in a text, you will be able to apply the same skills to your study of literature. For instance, when you read about a character in a short story, you make conclusions about that character's appearance and personality. Those conclusions are main ideas supported by stated or implied evidence in the story. Often, main characters are changed by the conflicts they encounter in the story. These changes are also main ideas supported by stated or implied details.

The following is an examination of the main ideas and details of character in the short story "The Diamond Necklace" by Guy de Maupassant. Matilda Loisel and her husband are the major characters in this story. Matilda is the protagonist (the main character), and Maupassant has written the story from her point of view. Madame Forestier is a minor character in this story because she has a fairly insignificant part in the plot.

There are two main aspects of character: personality and appearance. Let's look at how the author has described Matilda Loisel.

Matilda Loisel Before Loss of Necklace		
Personality		**Appearance**
charming	greedy	pretty
unhappy	cunning	beautiful
angry	vain	plain clothes
dissatisfied	flirtatious	no jewelry
materialistic	selfish	

The two excerpts that follow reveal evidence supporting some of the conclusions about Matilda, namely that she is materialistic, greedy, and cunning. It is clear from the excerpts that Matilda does not accept being poor, and that she pictures a much more elegant lifestyle for herself.

When she seated herself for dinner, before the round table where the tablecloth had been used three days, opposite her husband who uncovered the tureen with a delighted air, saying: "Oh! the good potpie! I know nothing better than that—" she would think of the elegant dinners, of the shining silver, of the tapestries peopling the walls with ancient personages and rare birds in the midst of fairy forests; she thought of the exquisite food served on marvelous dishes, of the whispered gallantries, listened to with the smile of the sphinx, while eating the rose-colored flesh of the trout or a chicken's wing.

The husband appreciates simple things.
but:

Matilda's unwillingness to accept a life of poverty is evident.

She reflected for some seconds, making estimates and thinking of a sum that she could ask for without bringing with it an immediate refusal and a frightened exclamation from the economical clerk.

Matilda is scheming to get what she wants.

Because of the circumstances of the story, Matilda has to repay a huge debt to a friend who had loaned her a necklace. The following chart shows the changes to her character resulting from this crisis in her life.

Matilda Loisel After Loss of Necklace	
Personality	**Appearance**
loud-voiced	old-looking
hardworking	commonly dressed
thrifty	stringy hair
uncomplaining	untidy clothes
strong	red hands
hard	
sad	
unselfish	

Mrs. Loisel now knew the horrible life of necessity. She did her part, however, completely heroically. It was necessary to pay this frightful debt. She would pay it. They sent away the maid; they changed their lodgings; they rented some rooms under a mansard roof.

She learned the heavy cares of a household, the odious work of a kitchen. She washed the dishes, using her rosy nails upon the greasy pots and the bottoms of the stewpans. She washed the soiled linen, the chemises and dishcloths, which she hung on the line to dry; she took down the refuse to the street each morning and brought up the water, stopping at each landing to breathe. And, clothed like a woman of the people, she went to the grocer's, the butcher's, and the fruiterer's, with her basket on her arm, shopping, haggling, defending to the last sou her miserable money.

This excerpt from the story provides evidence of some of these changes, particularly for the conclusion that she has become hardworking, thrifty, and commonly dressed. This excerpt shows how a life of poverty affected and changed Matilda.

Based on the information in the two charts, you can see how the loss of the necklace affected Matilda and completely changed her life, personality, and physical appearance. Although Matilda takes on her burden of debt without complaint, she still wonders what life would have been like had she not lost the necklace:

How would it have been if she had not lost that necklace? Who knows? Who knows? How singular is life, and how full of changes! How small a thing will ruin or save one!

The main idea about the virtue of humility and sacrifice is expressed in "The Diamond Necklace" through the changes in Matilda's character. In many texts, main ideas or themes are revealed through characters' actions and changes.

ON 9R1.4   *Make and explain inferences about both simple and complex texts, supporting their explanations with stated and implied ideas from the texts*

ON 9M1.2   *Interpret simple and complex media texts, identifying and explaining the overt and implied messages they convey*

ON 9M1.5   *Identify the perspectives and/or biases evident in both simple and complex media texts and comment on any questions they may raise about beliefs, values, and identity*

MAKING INFERENCES

As you read fiction and non-fiction, you will draw conclusions and make inferences. Your responses to texts should always be supported by relevant aspects of the texts themselves or by your experiences in reading and in life.

The following examples illustrate how you can draw conclusions or inferences using the clues in texts.

IN PROSE

In the following narrative "I Am a Native of North America," by Chief Dan George, you could make several inferences about Chief Dan George and his father using stated or implied ideas in the text. Some questions about possible inferences follow this example.

I AM A NATIVE OF NORTH AMERICA

I am a Native of North America.

In the course of my lifetime I have lived in two distinct cultures. I was born into a culture that lived in communal houses. My grandfather's house was eighty feet [24 m] long. It was called a smoke house, and it stood down by the beach along the inlet. All my grandfather's sons and their families lived in this large dwelling. Their sleeping apartments were separated by blankets made of bull rush reeds, but one open fire in the middle served the cooking needs of all. In houses like these, throughout the tribe, people learned to live with one another; learned to serve one another; learned to respect the rights of one another. And children shared the thoughts of the adult world and found themselves surrounded by aunts and uncles and cousins who loved them and did not threaten them. My father was born in such a house and learned from infancy how to love people and be at home with them.

And beyond this acceptance of one another there was a deep respect for everything in nature that surrounded them. My father loved the earth and all its creatures. The earth was his second mother. The earth and everything it contained was a gift from See-see-am … and the way to thank this great spirit was to use his gifts with respect.

I remember, as a little boy, fishing with him up Indian River and I can still see him as the sun rose above the mountain top in the early morning … I can see him standing by the water's edge with his arms raised above his head while he softly moaned … "Thank you, thank you." It left a deep impression on my young mind.

And I shall never forget his disappointment when once he caught me gaffing for fish "just for the fun of it." "My Son," he said, "The Great Spirit gave you those fish to be your brothers, to feed you when you are hungry. You must respect them. You must not kill them just for the fun of it."

This then was the culture I was born into and for some years the only one I really knew or tasted. This is why I find it hard to accept many of the things I see around me.

—by Chief Dan George

Inference Questions

What kind of environment did Chief Dan George grow up in? How did his environment and his actions affect his beliefs?

What did Chief Dan George's father teach him about life and about nature? What are some words you could use to describe his father's character?

What kind of relationships has Chief Dan George had with spirituality? Has he always thought of nature and his heritage in the same way? What changes have taken place in his mind?

Being curious is the first step in making inferences. You probably know a lot more about a text than you think you do, and asking questions is the first step to unlocking that information.

In Poetry

Inferences can also be made when you read poems. The mood, for instance, can be suggested in the rhythm, as you will see when you read the first few stanzas of "The Highwayman," by Alfred Noyes.

THE HIGHWAYMAN

Part One

The wind was a torrent of darkness among the gusty trees,
The moon was a ghostly galleon tossed upon cloudy seas,
The road was a ribbon of moonlight over the purple moor,
And the highwayman came riding—
Riding—riding—
The highwayman came riding, up to the old inn-door.

He'd a French cocked-hat on his forehead, a bunch of lace at his chin,
A coat of the claret velvet, and breeches of brown doeskin;
They fitted with never a wrinkle: his boots were up to the thigh!
And he rode with a jewelled twinkle,
His pistol butts a-twinkle,
His rapier hilt a-twinkle, under the jewelled sky.

Over the cobbles he clattered and clashed in the dark inn-yard,
And he tapped with his whip on the shutters, but all was locked and barred;
He whistled a tune to the window, and who should be waiting there
But the landlord's black-eyed daughter,
Bess, the landlord's daughter,
Plaiting a dark red love-knot into her long black hair.

—by Alfred Noyes

What stands out to you about this poem? Which parts are striking and which parts are descriptive? What literary devices are used?

Here are some examples of comments and observations about the poem:

- The regular rhythm throughout the entire poem suggests the advancing and retreating hoofbeats of a horse.

- The first stanza of the poem contains some highly descriptive figurative language:

  "The wind was a torrent of darkness" (metaphor)

  "a ghostly galleon tossed upon cloudy seas" (allitcration, metaphor)

  "a ribbon of moonlight" (suggests the mysterious and suspenseful setting of a dark and wind-swept night, with the moon lighting a lonely road across an isolated moor)

The repetition of the words "twinkle" and "jewelled" in the second stanza emphasizes the intermittent flashing or sparkle of light reflected from the highwayman's pistol butts and sword hilt as he rides under a star-studded sky.

The word choice of "clattered and clashed" is both alliteration and onomatopoeia. The words themselves imply the harsh sounds of hooves and steel over uneven cobblestones.

INTERPRETING ADVERTISING

Advertising communicates meaning that is both overt and implied. Advertisers want you to buy their products or services and will use as many techniques as possible to convince you to do so.

Growing up in a world where advertising plays such an important role in your daily life, you need to be aware that you are being persuaded or drawn to a particular viewpoint every time you look at an advertisement in a magazine or watch a commercial on TV.

If you understand some of the strategies behind persuasive advertising, you will be less influenced by its impact. You will be more independent in your thinking. You will make choices based on reason and fact rather than on the sleek images of advertising.

Propaganda is the art of expressing ideas in such a way that a certain group of people are influenced to a particular point of view. Propaganda has been used by political parties to persuade people to adopt their beliefs or give them power. Propaganda can be very dangerous. Advertising is a form of propaganda, and it uses many of the same techniques.

Listed below are some of the more common propaganda techniques used in advertising. These techniques often rely upon tricky ways of using pictures and language.

Propaganda uses:

- **unsupported inferences:** suggestions that sound believable until you look for actual evidence to support the suggested claims

- **fallacious reasoning:** false reasoning. The reasons are incorrect or are missing important information that would make them true.

Propaganda is sneaky because it can influence you without your even knowing it. Think about ads you have seen that play music from artists you like in the background. Do you pay more attention to ads like that? Corporations know to whom they want to sell, so they have probably studied what type of music their target audience listens to. Even though it is just music in the background, it will make you pay special attention to the advertisement and will make you feel that because the ad is playing "your" type of music, maybe what they are selling is "your" type of product.

Advertising is useful to inform you about products and to offer choices. Do not be fooled, though, into letting a company or brand name do your thinking and make your choices for you. Look for tricks in what you see and read so that your reasoning is clear, informed, and logical. Next time you pick up your cereal box, take a closer look at the words, symbols, and images on the box. What messages are implied or conveyed? Now examine the listing of ingredients on the side of the box. How many ingredients do you recognize? How many are of nutritional value? In this case, the information presented in the ingredient list is overt, or obvious, but the overwhelming message you are receiving from the cereal box is covert, or implied. Covert ideas are the lifeblood of advertising. As you train yourself to interpret media texts, particularly advertising, in logical ways, you will become a smart and practical consumer. You will not be tricked into buying things you do not need or even want.

HOW DIFFERENT MEDIA CONVEY MEANING

Interpreting media text involves observation. The creators of media text in all its many forms: cartoons, artwork, photographs, films, newspapers, magazines, and so on, use a variety of techniques and conventions to convey meaning. Some of these media are described below.

Cartoons

Cartoons can be humorous, but they can also present opinions. For example, political cartoons often ridicule and criticize politicians or governments. Cartoons have evolved over the years. Originally, most cartoons were designed as entertainment for children. Nowadays, there are many cartoons aimed at adult audiences. Cartoons have also evolved in terms of how they are created. Today, computer graphics are more popular than conventional animation. Most animated movies use computer animation, and even conventionally animated shows enhance their animation with computer graphics.

Cartoons may be presented in a single frame or in several frames that tell a story. The following elements of illustrated cartoons can be important to understanding their overall meaning:

- characters' appearances (facial features, body, clothing, etc.), which can reveal things like emotion, age, and status
- the body positions of the characters, which suggest actions and emotions
- other details in the cartoon, such as backgrounds and shading
- speech bubbles or captions, which can provide sound effects, dialogue, and information about the setting

Drawings and Paintings

Artists use varying techniques to communicate emotion, mood, and ideas such as composition, distance, and perspective. Composition refers to the arrangement of the subject matter in a drawing or a painting. Artists are able to create a sense of distance and depth by using a line to indicate where the sky and the ground meet. This line is known as the horizon line. Objects in the picture that are closer to the horizon line appear to be in the background and farther away. Objects in the picture that are farther away from the horizon line appear to be closer to the forefront.

Magazines

Magazines are usually lighter reading than novels or non-fiction books. They can include shorter pieces like short stories or news articles, but they also contain a lot of advertising. Notice the differences in the types of ads that appear in different magazines. A magazine designed for teenaged girls will contain very different advertisements than, say, a magazine about fishing. As you look at a magazine or any other kind of print publication, examine its content, graphics, design, layout, and cover. What is effective and what is not? Ask yourself questions such as:

- How are the photos sized and placed?
- What is included in the ads that would appeal to the readers?
- What seems to be important? Where is the emphasis?
- Why did I buy this magazine?
- Is it worth the cover cost? Why or why not?

Think about why you might be drawn to a particular magazine or ad. What is it selling that appeals to you? Is it only the product being sold that appeals to you, or is there something else that attracts you to the ad?

Companies typically try to sell products to a particular audience. This means they want to create an image of the product that will appeal to their intended audience. Answering questions about why you like certain products, magazines, or other forms of media will help you to become more savvy or knowledgeable about the media around you.

Books to Movies

When stories or books are adapted to media-text versions, usually films, one of several outcomes is possible:

- The movie version dramatizes and enhances the original story. The visual interpretation and details make it memorable.

- The movie version supplements and enriches your understanding of a play or novel studied in class.

For example, *A Night to Remember*, a historical novel by Walter Lord, was made into a movie about the sinking of the Titanic. The grainy black-and-white version seems almost like a news documentary and is very realistic.

Plays are also frequently adapted for film. Seeing a play acted out on film can bring the text of the play to life. Shakespearean plays such as *Macbeth* and *Romeo and Juliet* can become clearer after seeing the movie versions.

Canadian Perspective in Television Programming

Many of the programs Canadians watch are actually created and produced in the United States; however, Canadian law requires a certain percentage of what is called "Canadian Content" in television programming. These programs are designed to depict a more Canadian perspective on life. Canadian television writers are particularly good at helping Canadians laugh at everyday predicaments, cultural situations, and political issues. A few examples of television programming with a strong Canadian slant include the following programs: *This Hour has 22 Minutes*, *The Rick Mercer Report*, and *The Royal Canadian Air Farce*. These shows regularly depict national news events and political situations in humorous ways. The program *Corner Gas* makes fun of small-town life on the Canadian prairies. *Little Mosque on the Prairie,* a comedy about a Muslim family making a life for themselves in Canada, entertainingly presents some of the complications and foibles that are unique to Canada's cultural mosaic. Programs such as these help contribute to shaping Canada's cultural identity.

ON 9R1.5   *Extend understanding of both simple and complex texts by making connections between the ideas in them and personal knowledge, experience, and insights; other texts; and the world around them*

Using What You Read Every Day

Books are powerful and have the ability to change your thoughts and actions. When you read a book, you are adding the information and experiences of the writer to your body of knowledge. The information you take in while reading does not stay inside the pages of books; it becomes part of how you interact with the world. After you read a book on pollution, for example, you are likely to begin to look at everyday things differently. If you see someone throwing a pop can into the garbage rather than into the recycling bin, the information you learned in the book will spring to mind. Activities that may not have bothered you before, such as littering or driving a gas-guzzling car, may seem more negative now that you have learned more about the effects of pollution. The knowledge you gain from books allows you to experience the world with a new perspective.

The ultimate goal of most writers, whether they write to inform, explain, persuade, or entertain, is to have their readers connect with and understand what they have written in a personal way. When you make connections in text, you are remembering or internalizing what you read. You make connections by:

- accessing prior knowledge that can help you understand new material
- expressing a new insight or way of looking at an issue by reading a related story, poem, or article
- feeling empathy with a character because of a similar problem or experience in your own life
- remembering a movie, play, or text that has a related plot or theme to what you are reading
- There are several different types of connections you can make while reading: literary connections, connections through character, setting, theme, and life connections.

Literary Connections

Literary connections apply to characters, settings, and themes in literature because they allow readers to find literature relevant to them personally, regardless of when or where the literature was written. Literary connections are connections between the text you are reading and other works of literature you know. In many different works of literature, authors refer to other books through quotations, allusions, or homage.

CONNECTIONS THROUGH CHARACTERS

Throughout your lifetime, you will read and become familiar with many different literary characters from a variety of settings. These characters will face conflicts and challenges in many different situations; however, human nature has remained consistent throughout history. Even in a science-fiction story, you will meet greedy, curious, fearful, and courageous characters: any type of character that exists in the real world. Think about these characters from literature and compare and contrast their motivations as they confront similar situations and conflicts in different historical eras. For example, a character from the past, Oliver Twist, and one from contemporary literature, Harry Potter, can be compared and contrasted.

Similarities between Oliver Twist and Harry Potter:

- both are orphans

- both are mistreated by abusive adults

- both dream of eventually changing their circumstances: Oliver dreams of going to London, and Harry dreams of freeing himself from his stifling home life.

Differences between Oliver Twist and Harry Potter:

- Oliver has physical survival challenges, whereas Harry has emotional survival challenges.

- Oliver is constantly manipulated by people, whereas Harry learns to use his gifts to have power over his enemies.

The connections demonstrated are between two characters from two very different historical periods.

CONNECTIONS THROUGH SETTINGS

Setting is the where and when of a story. The setting is an important part of the work. Short stories have only one setting, but the action in a novel may occur in several different places over an extended period of time. Descriptions of settings help the reader get a sense of the atmosphere or mood of the story. For example, if the writer describes the setting as a dark forest full of strange sounds and trees with jagged branches, the reader will gain a sense that the atmosphere of the story is spooky or creepy.

The setting is made up of more than simply where a story occurs. It also includes aspects such as period in history, cultural customs, and how people dress. For example, consider *Oliver Twist*. If that story had been written today, Oliver would not be living in an orphanage being fed gruel for breakfast. He would have a social worker and a foster home, where foster parents would see to it that he was fed, clothed, and sent to school. Modern times are very different from the Victorian times in which the Oliver story was set.

Historical context also influences how a story unfolds. During the time of the Industrial Revolution in England, it was the deliberate intent of Charles Dickens to make the public, particularly the middle class, more aware of the social problems, such as child labour, caused by the revolution. The story of Oliver Twist ultimately helped change labour laws to protect factory workers and children. You could extend your knowledge and create a connection between your knowledge of the novel and your knowledge of life's realities today by writing a modern version of *Oliver Twist*, showing that children or unskilled workers continue to be exploited around the world.

CONNECTIONS THROUGH THEMES

The theme of any work is its subject. The theme deals with the meaning the writer wants to convey. The theme can be divided into two parts: the subject itself and what is said about the subject.

In a skilfully constructed narrative, all the parts of the story contribute to the theme. The chart below demonstrates how all the elements of a narrative contribute to the theme.

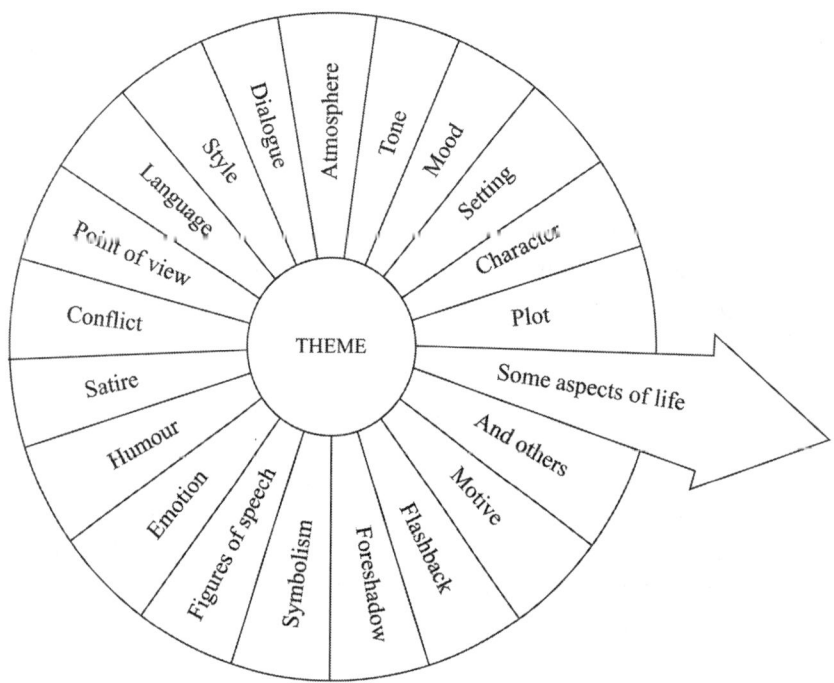

The moral of a story and its theme are connected but are not the same. A moral is a conclusion drawn from events in a story. It is a statement about the best way to behave. A story does not have to have a moral. If a story has a moral, sometimes the writer states it outright. It is more common for the moral to be left for the reader to discover. Recurring themes such as good versus evil appear across traditional and contemporary works of literature.

Example

The Struggle of Good vs. Evil

Traditional	**Contemporary**
Huckleberry Finn	*Star Wars*
Around the World in 80 Days	*Lord of the Rings*

Some common themes in literature include the following:

- survival

- person vs. nature

- triumph over adversity

- rags to riches

- courage and bravery

- heroes

- freedom

- friendship

- loyalty

Recognizing a common theme in a story, poem, or play is a connection that will influence your attitude toward literature. Good literature is timeless and meaningful. Literature can become even more meaningful when you make connections between what you are reading and other knowledge you possess.

LIFE CONNECTIONS

Life connections are connections you find between your life and the literature you are reading. When something you read connects to your real life, it becomes part of who you are as a developing young person. Often, people read books that contain situations or characters that remind them of aspects of their own life. Think about your own favourite books to read: are there any similarities between your life and the lives of the characters in the book? Even fantasy or science fiction works can connect to a reader's life.

ON 9R1.6   *Analyse texts in terms of the information, ideas, issues, or themes they explore, examining how various aspects of the texts contribute to the presentation or development of these elements*

ON 9M2.2   *Identify several different conventions and/or techniques used in familiar media forms and explain how they convey meaning and influence their audience*

ANALYSING TEXTS

Analysing the texts you read involves thinking about how those texts explore or present information, ideas, issues, and themes. Read the following denouement, or final scene, from the story "The Diamond Necklace," where Matilda encounters her former friend 10 years after the incident involving the necklace. Read carefully and see if you can make some observations after reading.

FROM "THE DIAMOND NECKLACE"

One Sunday, as she was taking a walk in the Champs-Elysées to rid herself of the cares of the week, she suddenly perceived a woman walking with a child. It was Mrs. Forestier, still young, still pretty, still attractive. Mrs. Loisel was affected. Should she speak to her? Yes, certainly. And now that she had paid, she would tell her all. Why not?

She approached her. "Good morning, Jeanne."

Her friend did not recognize her and was astonished to be so familiarly addressed by this common personage. She stammered:

"But, Madame—I do not know—You must be mistaken—"

"No, I am Matilda Loisel."

Her friend uttered a cry of astonishment: "Oh! my poor Matilda! How you have changed—"

"Yes, I have had some hard days since I saw you; and some miserable ones—and all because of you—"

"Because of me? How is that?"

"You recall the diamond necklace that you loaned me to wear to the Commissioner's ball?"

"Yes, very well."

"Well, I lost it."

"How is that, since you returned it to me?"

"I returned another to you exactly like it. And it has taken us ten years to pay for it. You can understand that it was not easy for us who have nothing. But it is finished and I am decently content."

Madame Forestier stopped short. She said:

"You say that you bought a diamond necklace to replace mine?"

"Yes. You did not perceive it then? They were just alike."

And she smiled with a proud and simple joy. Madame Forestier was touched and took both her hands as she replied:

"Oh! my poor Matilda! Mine were false. They were not worth over five hundred francs!"

What themes or ideas come out in this final scene? What does the surprise ending reveal about the writer's attitudes toward the characters? The story is written realistically, so the events in the plot can be analysed to reveal something about life in general. A good way to begin searching for a theme in a story is to write out what has happened and how the characters might feel about it. For example, how do you think Madame Forestier feels at the end of the story? She is probably overwhelmed with guilt and sympathy for Matilda. If only she would have told Matilda that the necklace was not real at the time of the incident, Matilda's life would have been very different. Similarly, how do you think Matilda feels? She is likely shocked to hear the truth about the necklace. All of the grief and sorrow she experienced as a result of losing the necklace could have been avoided. Something as insignificant as a piece of jewellery ruined any chance of the life she dreamed of. Can you think of any possible themes after this analysis? What might the writer be trying to say about material goods or about striving for material success?

HOW THEMES ARE PRESENTED AND REINFORCED

As you read through the following poem, an underlying theme becomes evident: a potentially productive life being wasted by someone who is living too much in the glory days of the past. Try to make note of particular phrases in the poem that either suggest or reinforce this theme.

EX-BASKETBALL PLAYER

Pearl Avenue runs past the high-school lot,
Bends with the trolley tracks, and stops, cut off
Before it has a chance to go two blocks,
At Colonel McComsky Plaza. Berth's Garage
Is on the corner facing west, and there,
Most days, you'll find Flick Webb, who helps Berth out.
Flick stands tall among the idiot pumps—
Five on a side, the old bubble-head style,
Their rubber elbows hanging loose and low.
One's nostrils are two S's, and his eyes
An E and O. And one is squat, without
A head at all—more of a football type.
Once Flick played for the high-school team, the Wizards.
He was good: in fact, the best. In '46,
He bucketed three hundred ninety points,
A county record still. The ball loved Flick.
I saw him rack up thirty-eight of forty
In one home game. His hands were like wild birds.
He never learned a trade, he just sells gas,
Checks oil, and changes flats. Once in a while,
As a gag, he dribbles an inner tube,
But most of us remember anyway.
His hands are fine and nervous on the lug wrench.
It makes no difference to the lug wrench, though.
Off work, he hangs around Mae's Luncheonette.
Grease-gray and kind of coiled, he plays pinball,
Sips lemon cokes, and smokes those thin cigars;
Flick seldom speaks to Mae, just sits and nods
Beyond her face towards bright applauding tiers
Of Necco Wafers, Nibs, and Juju Beads.

—by John Updike

The following is an analysis of some lines and phrases in the poem in order to observe how they may suggest or reinforce the theme:

- The quotation "Flick stands tall among the idiot pumps" suggests that Flick is far above what he does for a living, much too talented to be spending his days manning gas pumps. The word "idiot" also expresses the meaningless, mindless futility of Flick's present life.

- The quotations "He was good: in fact, the best … His hands were like wild birds" describe Flick's amazing talent as a player, but the inclusion of the word "once" in the line above and the phrase "In '46" immediately following indicate that his glory days are a thing of the past.

- In the quotation "He never learned a trade, he just sells gas," the words "never" and "just" reinforce the theme of wasted opportunities.

- The lines "Flick seldom speaks to Mae, just sits and nods … toward bright applauding tiers" reinforce the idea that Flick is dwelling on his past athletic achievements and wasting time daydreaming about the days when he was a basketball star performing in front of an applauding crowd.

- The last line, "Of Necco Wafers, Nibs, and Juju Beads," reinforces the theme of the empty reality of a wasted life. Flick is staring off into space at the cheering crowds from his remembered past, while the actual scene above his vacant gaze contains shelves of junk food.

Writers are usually very careful to choose the exact words they want to express a given idea. The next time you are analysing a text, think about how individual words work to convey a message. An analysis like the one above is a helpful way to begin understanding a text's themes and intended meaning. Analysing text in poems allows you to see beyond the words to the images, moods, and themes they express.

HOW ISSUES ARE PRESENTED

Themes are not only present in fiction. It is also important to analyse themes in non-fiction information. Examining articles and letters to the editor in newspapers provides an opportunity to explore several viewpoints on an issue. The following example is a newspaper article objecting to what one person views as an unnecessarily high number of high-sticking violations in the game of hockey. After you read the original article, read the two examples of responses. Three distinctly different views on this issue are expressed by the article and the responses.

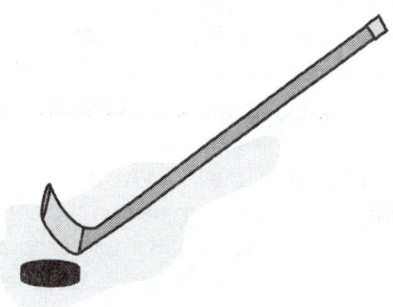

Father Calls Hockey "Game of Butchery"

Toronto (CP)—Norman Neeld, whose son Greg suffered a severe eye injury from a hockey stick last week while playing defence with the Toronto Marlboros says, "Hockey is a game of skill, but butchery has taken over."

Two of his four sons have been hurt by high sticks, he said in an interview Monday, and he feels something ought to be done to prevent such incidents. Neeld, an Air Canada pilot who lives in Vancouver, said "skilled players are subjected to fouls, many of them dangerous high-sticking offences, by the less skilled players."

"My four sons all have been excellent skaters from the time they started to play hockey, and they've all gone through the same thing of fouls against them. This, basically, is where the game falls apart."

Greg Neeld, 18, was hit in the eye by a stick during an Ontario Hockey Association Major Junior A game last Friday between the Marlboros and Kitchener Rangers.

Doctors at Toronto General Hospital say it will be a week before they know whether he will lose the sight in his left eye.

"We have to wait until the swelling in the eye disappears," Neeld said. He added that the doctors are not overly optimistic and do not want to give his son false hope.

Another son, 13-year-old John, was hit on the head by an opposing player in a Vancouver peewee game last year.

Letters to the Editor

Letter 1

I wish to respond to yesterday's editorial expressing the opinion of a parent, Mr. Norman Neeld. I am a 14-year-old junior player from Guelph, Ontario and read the editorial in our local paper. Although I feel sympathy for Mr. Neeld and his injured sons, there is another perspective to consider. Without a doubt, hockey is a rough sport. It is a challenge for referees to call everything they see. Caught in the speed, excitement, and intense emotion of the game, athletes sometimes make impulsive choices that cause unnecessary injuries. I would still choose the organized risk of hockey over the random risk of hanging out with friends outside the arena. One of my friends was injured in a stabbing incident outside our arena. He was not a player. He was a fan, who happened to say the wrong thing to a fan from the town we were playing. I have the utmost respect for referees who are doing their best to keep a physical and emotional game reasonably clean and sportsmanlike.

Lyndon Glassman

Guelph A Rep Team

Letter 2

I read Mr. Neeld's assessment of hockey as a "game of butchery" with interest. I am a parent too, with three sons in hockey. I am involved in the organization, as well as coordinator of an Aboriginal League in our area. We play regularly with other leagues at the various age levels. My goal is to combine skill development with sportsmanlike behaviour on the ice. While infractions do occur, especially with "less-skilled players," as noted by Mr. Neeld, we are constantly addressing the skill/behaviour combination, not only in our coaching clinics, but in our practices and games. When a preventable injury occurs, we review the incident, email all coaches and referees in the organization, and direct the coaches to re-focus on the skill or behaviour that could have prevented the injury. This philosophy has resulted in significant injury reductions in our leagues. We are united here in our view that high-sticking is dangerous and unnecessary and are doing our best
to eliminate the infractions at the grassroots level.

Aaron Lightfeather

High Prairie Aboriginal Hockey Association

Reading all three opinions, which range in objectivity, allows you to explore a variety of viewpoints on the issue. Controversial issues are complex, and there are often valid points to be made on all sides. It is important to gain as much information as you can about these types of issues.

ON 9R1.7   *Evaluate the effectiveness of both simple and complex texts, using evidence from the text to support their opinions*

ON 9M1.3   *Evaluate how effectively information, ideas, issues, and opinions are communicated in both simple and complex media texts and decide whether the texts achieve their intended purpose*

EVALUATING TEXTS

As you evaluate the many different types of texts that you read, both at school and during your personal time, your critical thinking skills will enable you to use text effectively and confidently for a great variety of purposes. You will be asking yourself questions such as the following:

- Why is this story so believable?
- Why is this argument so convincing?
- Why is this poem so appealing?
- Why is this ad so effective?

On the surface, these are simple, direct questions. However, answering them by providing supporting evidence from the text can become fairly complex. Certain elements of a text contribute to a reader finding that text appealing. Following are some explanations of those aspects of text, which will in part explain why some texts appeal to you or convince you more than others.

BELIEVABLE STORIES

A writer's attempt to make a story realistic to readers using real-world details is called *verisimilitude*. This word may remind you of the word "verify." Verisimilitude quite literally means "similar to the truth." An example of verisimilitude would be fiction that deals with current events or real political leaders. A work of fiction that includes details about the city of Paris, such as the Eiffel Tower or the Champs-Elysées, for example, would be verisimilitudinous. By including details about the real world that the reader is familiar with, the writer makes it easier for the reader to relate to the characters and situations in the plot.

Realistic Plot

A believable plotline is very important to the success of a story. If something does not ring true for readers, it is likely that they will not enjoy the text. This is why writers write about what they know. It is easier for them to get all the little details right if they are based on reality. For example, writers for crime television series often come up with plot ideas based on actual events in the news.

Realistic Setting

Having a realistic setting is particularly important in works of historical fiction, such as the Charles Dickens novel *A Tale of Two Cities*. The two cities in this story are London and Paris, and the time of the setting is during the French Revolution. Although the novel is a work of fiction, the story is made realistic and convincing through descriptions of real places, such as the Bastille, and of events that actually took place, such as public executions during the 18th century.

REALISTIC CHARACTERS

Characters are made realistic through descriptions of their appearances, actions, and thoughts. Many writers develop characters with whom readers can identify in terms of age, gender, cultural background, hobbies, religious beliefs, ambitions, motivations, and personality. An example of a popular fictional character is Anne from the novel series *Anne of Green Gables*. She is such a popular character that fans of L.M. Montgomery's series come in droves to visit the inspiration for Anne's house in Prince Edward Island. The house is now a huge tourist attraction. For readers, it supports ideas about the character they have come to know and care about through the books.

REALISTIC SITUATIONS

In real life, not every story has a happy ending. This is true of realistic stories as well. In the novel *The Parent Trap*, identical twin girls try to get their parents back together. With humorous twists and turns in the plot, the girls manage to reunite their parents; however, this is not necessarily a very realistic ending to a story.

CONVINCING ARGUMENTS

How do you know if an argument is logical or true? Many arguments can sound convincing but may not be true. Sometimes, the person writing an argument does not reveal all of the relevant information about the subject so that you will be more convinced by his or her position. There are several aspects to consider when evaluating the level to which an argument or viewpoint is convincing. Never just assume one point of view is correct. Look at all sides of an issue.

Another important part of learning whether or not an argument is reasonable is looking at where the argument comes from and who has written the argument. If the argument is written on a blog on the Internet, it is more likely to have a bias than an article written in a major newspaper.

FACT AND OPINION

Facts are statements that can be proven true. You can use experiments, research, or observations to prove facts. Opinions are statements that express personal beliefs. Opinions cannot always be proven. Sometimes, it is difficult to tell the difference between fact and opinion. At other times, the difference is very obvious. As a reader, you must try to separate the two. Almanacs, encyclopedias, and atlases are examples of books that are usually reliable sources of factual information.

Factual statements are ones that can be proven to be true. Much of what people read is not necessarily verified, but readers usually accept it because it appears to be true or others say that it is true. Sources like magazines, books, newspapers, websites, online bulletin boards, and blogs, for example, should not be trusted entirely until the knowledge and experience of their writers has been verified.

People also often reach faulty conclusions because the evidence they use is based either on faulty observations or on observations that are prejudiced, wishful, or imaginative.

ASSESSING BOTH SIDES OF AN ISSUE

In order to become a skilled debater on any issue, it is an excellent strategy to be equally well prepared to argue or defend either side of an argument. Exploring both sides of an issue also helps you to understand opinions that differ from your own. You will become more confident and comfortable with your own viewpoint if you can support it with evidence.

Consider the following graphic organizer, which presents both sides of the controversial issue "Are zoos moral?" Some people feel strongly opposed to the idea of animals being held in captivity so that people can watch them for entertainment. Others find zoos to be an acceptable source of entertainment and education. Who is right? After looking at the supporting evidence for both sides, notice that your conclusion turns out to be somewhat of a compromise between the two opposing viewpoints. This often happens in real arguments and is an ideal approach to respecting different opinions.

Evidence that Supports		Evidence that Opposes
Help to educate people about different animals in their area		Animals show signs of stress, boredom, and unhappiness
Protect endangered animals	**Should there be zoos?**	Animals belong in their natural habitats
Scientists can study animals up close		Scientists would learn more about animals in the wild
Veterinarians and zoologists can learn how to care for different animals in the wild		Some animals are abused in captivity
Can help injured animals that could not survive in the wild		The natural world is for the survival of the fittest; humans should not interfere
Make money that can pay for animal care in the wild		Do humans have the right to capture animals?
Zoos, wildlife preserves, and aquariums may be the only place for some people to see wild animals and learn about them		Animals are forced to entertain people so parks make lots of money that may not be used for animal welfare

Conclusion

Zoos could be created so that the animals can live in their natural habitats with minimal interference from people. Wildlife preserves help to protect animals from the expansion of towns and cities. These preserves can provide a safe haven for migrating birds and animals.

Reasons

- The welfare of the animals is important, and they cannot choose to be in a zoo.

- People sometimes cause animals' problems in the wild by invading their habitats.

- People should not destroy animals' homes or kill them for fun or for a few body parts. Zoos can help educate people about the importance of protecting wildlife and how to live in harmony with them.

- Videos can be used to show animals in their natural world so that people do not have to capture animals and put them on display.

DETERMINING THE RELIABILITY OF SOURCES

Not everything that is stated with authority is really fact. Generally, you would tend to think that information you find in encyclopedias is fact. There are many other resources available, however, such as eyewitness accounts, newspaper accounts, supermarket tabloid accounts, and the Internet, that are often less reliable than the reference materials you find at the library. Information found on the Internet often has errors or biases.

How do you determine what makes a resource reliable as a source of information? When is the information valid and authentic? What kinds of sources will mostly provide accurate information?

It is important to be critical of what you read, particularly when the information you are reading claims to be factual or truthful. Evaluate the facts stated carefully. Decide what evidence is convincing and what might need verification. Look for biases that suggest a particular viewpoint or opinion, even when the bias is not directly stated. If a newspaper, for example, reports mostly stories and articles that cast a particular politician or political party in a negative light, you could probably draw the conclusion that the paper does not support the policies of that politician or party. It is a good idea to either avoid reading a newspaper that has a strong bias, or, if you do read it, to balance your knowledge of issues by reading a variety of other sources on the same subjects.

EYEWITNESS ACCOUNTS

An eyewitness account is a first-hand description of events from the point of view of an eyewitness who was present at the event as a participant or bystander.

> Responding to a reporter's question about the deadly blast detonated by a terrorist group in the London Underground in 2005, a subway commuter who was there that day might say something like, "The deafening sound of the explosion made me sure we would all die. Then I saw the clouds of smoke and dust. I kept running, but I couldn't find the escalator or the lift."

Usually an eyewitness tries to provide an accurate description of the event, but they may be hampered by faulty memory, location perspective, and subconscious creative twists to the story. Some eyewitnesses deliberately misrepresent the situation or mislead the listener, particularly in cases of crimes or motor vehicle accidents. If possible, it is a good idea to verify any facts reported by eyewitnesses.

NEWSPAPERS

Newspaper sources, both print and electronic, such as the *Ottawa Citizen*, *Montreal Gazette*, and the *Edmonton Journal* are major city newspapers and are usually reliable sources of local, national, and international news. If they make a mistake, the paper will typically print a correction the next day or as soon as the fact is verified. City newspapers tend to deal with "hard news": local, national, and international events that impact large numbers of people. News reporters are expected to be objective and impartial, leaving opinions for the editorial page. The owners of major newspapers have no desire to lose their credibility or be sued for publishing lies. They must be credible, or they risk losing sales and advertising revenues. Newspapers do, however, often display a slant or perspective known as a *media bias*. Even a newspaper must be read critically. Letters to the editor sometimes convey strong disagreement with articles or photos that some readers feel to be misleading or inappropriate.

SUPERMARKET TABLOIDS

Tabloids sell papers with sensational front-page headlines and photos. They spend thousands of dollars on hot tips, celebrity gossip, and photos taken all over the world. Embarrassing or scandalous stories sell well, and celebrities are sometimes forced to issue denials through their publicists or to demand apologies or retractions from the tabloid. Costly, high-profile lawsuits often happen over incorrect or unfair portrayals of well-known people. Journalism like this is known in the industry as "soft news," and it mostly should not be taken too seriously.

INTERNET

For many people, the Internet is a primary source of both hard and soft news. In some respects, the Internet is invaluable because it can be corrected or updated so quickly. The global spread of cellphone use has also added a public dimension to the news, as anyone with the technology can record and share eyewitness footage of events. Access to such public views of the news is changing how news is reported and received. Pictures recorded by bystanders can be very useful, especially when they provide objective accounts of important events.

You have to look at news reported on the Internet even more critically than you would read a newspaper. When using the Internet for research, be sure that the information you are using is accurate. A simple checklist for verifying the credibility of Internet sources should include the following actions:

- Is the writer or contributor mentioned on the site? Are the writer and publisher recognized as reliable authorities on the topic?
- Do you detect any bias? Does the reporting seem fair and objective?
- Can you check the accuracy of the information with other sources?
- What subtopics are covered? Are there links to more extensive coverage?
- How current is the coverage? Has it been revised or updated? How old is the information?

SUPPORTING YOUR OPINIONS

Teachers are usually receptive to opinions that are different from or that disagree with what is being taught, as long as support for a different opinion is given with valid and convincing evidence. You can support your opinion using:

- significant quotes from the text, especially statements by respected experts on the topic or issue
- well-known or proven facts
- statistics
- examples from the text that support your point. You should always use specific examples from a story, for instance, to support your conclusions about a character. When you write about a poem, you should quote phrases or words that illustrate the poet's use of imagery to achieve a special mood or particular effect.

As you can see, one of the most important parts of succeeding at supporting your opinions is using facts or ideas that come from other sources. An argument or opinion is more convincing when it is supported by evidence.

PERSONAL CRITICISM OF LITERATURE

What you enjoy reading is important. Knowing why you enjoy what you read is also important. The reasons you like some texts and dislike others is somewhat elusive and hard to define. What you like has to do with the details of your identity and personal tastes. However, as a critical reader and thinker, you should be able to explain why you feel a certain way about a piece of literature.

Take a look at a few stanzas from "The Highwayman" by Alfred Noyes. Why is this poem memorable and appealing? Think about that question as you read the concluding lines to the tragic love story of a beautiful young woman who sacrifices her life in order to warn her outlaw lover that he is riding into a trap.

> Tlot-tlot, in the frosty silence! Tlot-tlot in the echoing night!
> Nearer he came and nearer! Her face was like a light!
> Her eyes grew wide for a moment; she drew one last deep breath,
> Then her finger moved in the moonlight,
>   Her musket shattered the moonlight,
> Shattered her breast in the moonlight and warned him—with her death.
>
> He turned; he spurred to the West; he did not know who stood
> Bowed, with her head o'er the musket, drenched with her own red blood!
> Not till the dawn he heard it, his face grew grey to hear
> How Bess, the landlord's daughter,
>   The landlord's black-eyed daughter,
> Had watched for her love in the moonlight, and died in the darkness there.
>
> Back, he spurred like a madman, shrieking a curse to the sky,
> With the white road smoking behind him and his rapier brandished high!
> Blood-red were his spurs in the golden noon; wine-red was his velvet coat,
> When they shot him down on the highway,
>   Down like a dog on the highway,
> And he lay in his blood on the highway, with the bunch of lace at his throat.
>
> And still of a winter's night, they say, when the wind is in the trees,
> When the moon is a ghostly galleon tossed upon cloudy seas,
> When the road is a ribbon of moonlight over the purple moor,
> A highwayman comes riding—
>   Riding—riding—
> A highwayman comes riding, up to the old inn-door.
>
> Over the cobbles he clatters and clangs in the dark inn-yard;
> He taps with his whip on the shutters, but all is locked and barred;
> He whistles a tune to the window, and who should be waiting there
> But the landlord's black-eyed daughter,
>   Bess, the landlord's daughter,
> Plaiting a dark red love-knot into her long black hair.
>
> —*by Alfred Noyes*

The following example is one student's explanation of why she finds this poem appealing. After reading it, think about what you might agree or disagree with.

I like this poem because of the rhythm—the rhythm is like the beating of a horse's hooves and gives the poem a lovely atmosphere. The descriptions are very good. They give polish to the poem. I also really like the wording—the specific words, like the rhythm, add atmosphere. It is written in a kind of bold romantic style that makes the story it is telling more vivid. The poem is well written—the poem is written in a very sensitive way. The tension is built up very well.

ON 9R1.8   *Identify the perspectives and/or biases evident in both simple and complex texts and comment on any questions they may raise about beliefs, values, and identity*

CRITICAL LITERACY

Being able to identify perspectives and biases in texts will strengthen your critical literacy skills. You will be better equipped to comment on issues related to beliefs, values, and identity. After perspectives and biases are explained, you will find some examples that illustrate how they apply to texts that you read.

PERSPECTIVE OR POINT OF VIEW

Point of view or perspective is the lens through which a writer writes a text. A writer writing a story is similar to a person using a camera to shoot a video. The person shooting the video decides where to stand and what to capture. A writer chooses what kind of character is going to tell the story and how the story is going to be told. There are three main points of view: first person, second person, and third person.

First Person

In first-person point-of-view writing, the writer chooses one of the characters in the story to narrate events. The pronouns *I, me, my, mine, we*, and *us* are used. When first-person point of view is used, the reader usually only knows the thoughts and feelings of the narrator and not the other characters in the story. The following passage is written in first-person point of view.

> I was terrified. After all, there were only three straws left. I would crumple into a heap of misery if I picked the short one. I can't imagine being stuck with all of the cabin's chores for a week. Devon and Maggie's laundry? No thanks!
>
> "Come on, Katie," Trisha snapped, "Don't dawdle. It's your turn to pick." Trish was probably only irritated because she was last to draw and was getting nervous herself. I figure that since I never win draws or contests that maybe my luck is getting saved up for this very moment in time. Yeah, right.

As you can see from the example, the reader has access to the narrator's thoughts and feelings, but not to the thoughts and feelings of any of the other characters. The narrator guesses as to what other characters might be feeling, but in first-person narration, the point of view is limited to the narrator's inner thoughts and observations.

Second Person

A writer using second-person point of view speaks directly to the reader. The pronouns *you* and *your* are used. This point of view can be used in choose-your-own-adventure stories, texts that give directions to the reader, and some forms of poetry.

> When you are baking, you need to make sure you have all the ingredients ready before you start."

Third Person

Stories written in third-person point of view are told from the viewpoint of a narrator. The pronouns *he, she, his, her, they*, and *their* are used. When third-person point of view is used, the narrator can tell you what is happening in many different places and from any number of different points of views. A third-person narrator can access the thoughts and emotions of all of the characters in a story.

In the following excerpt from *To Touch the Mammoth*, which is written in the third person, you can feel some of the suspense Zol experiences as he and the mammoth face each other.

> Then she took a step toward Zol, stretching out her hairy trunk. Zol closed his eyes and held his breath. Something touched his hair. A tingle zapped through Zol's body like lightning. Then he felt a blast of her warm, smelly breath on his face.
>
> A blaring cry split the air so suddenly that Zol screamed, too. He clapped his hand over his mouth, wild-eyed with fear. The young mammoth tossed her head, trumpeted an answering call, and lumbered off to follow the herd. Zol collapsed like a skin without bones. He crawled to the stream and splashed water on his face. Drinking from cupped hands, he felt the sun on his back.
>
> "I did not touch the mammoth," he said to the chuckling stream, "but the great mammoth touched *me*." A smile of wonder stretched across Zol's face. "And I did not run away!"

The point of view a writer chooses to use affects how readers feel about the characters. Perspective or point of view is more precisely defined in the following definitions.

Limited

First-person narration is usually limited because the narrator is personally involved in the story, often as a main character. The narrator's perspective is limited to what he or she sees and knows in the story.

Omniscient

"Omni" means "all," and "science" means "knowing." An "all-knowing" or omniscient point of view is usually third-person (he, she, they) narration. This type of narration allows the narrator to give a much broader perspective from outside of the story. The narrator is capable of describing the circumstances and motivations of all the characters.

SUBJECTIVE AND OBJECTIVE VIEWPOINTS

Subjective

A subjective point of view can be directly affected by a personal or emotional bias. For instance, if you received a poor mark on a math test, your mother might have a subjective view of that mark because she knows you were not feeling well the night before the test. Sometimes, first-person narration can be quite subjective because it is so personal.

Objective

An objective view reports the facts of a situation without emotional overtones or bias. Newspaper reporters, for example, should report the news objectively, without inserting their own opinions.

HISTORICAL PERSPECTIVE IN A SHORT STORY

Social norms and values evolve and change through time. Historical perspective is a very important aspect of a story and its setting. It provides an emotional and philosophical background for the characters, who are usually guided in their actions and choices by the customs, traditions, and beliefs that dominate their society. These conflicts may drive the actual plot of the story. Historical perspective can show a reader how aspects of history affect people and how history can repeat itself. Historical works often show a reader how little things have changed over time. In a short story, a writer has to include details that allow the reader to quickly understand where and when the story is taking place. Many historical novels go into great detail about the setting of the story. The writer of a short story must be very efficient at describing these same details using far fewer words.

BIAS AND STEREOTYPING

Biases and stereotypes are both rooted in prejudice. It is very important to recognize bias and stereotyping in text and to analyse them from a balanced point of view.

Biases

A bias is a subconscious or natural tendency to adopt a preferred view of something. It may be unspoken, but it is often expressed in attitude or behaviour. It can certainly be positive, as in having an inner pride in being Canadian, which would be a pro-Canada bias, or having a bias to cheer for your home team no matter what. Biases can also be negative, however. For example:

- **anti-youth bias**, which refers to assumptions and misconceptions about young people
- **anti-aging bias,** which refers to assumptions and misconceptions about older people
- **anti-authority bias**, which makes a person view teachers, parents, policemen, and other authority figures with hostility and suspicion
- **racial prejudice,** which makes a person dislike or hate anyone who looks different from their own ethnic group

Other biases include political biases, gender biases, economic biases, and religious biases. Negative biases prevent people from being tolerant of other people and different viewpoints.

Stereotypes

Stereotypes are overly generalized beliefs about individuals or groups. These generalizations are based on preconceived notions that may be the result of a personal bias or from being misinformed. Stereotypes paint a whole group of individuals with the same brush and do not acknowledge uniqueness and individuality. They create mistaken assumptions; for example, that tall people must be good basketball players, people wearing glasses must be smart, or unemployed people must be lazy.

Stereotypes of any kind may, unfortunately, be passed on to younger generations by adult family members. It is important to be mindful of stereotypes when you read texts of any kind. Advertising and editorial writing often include stereotypes. Watch for biases or slants no matter what type of medium is being presented to you. Bias can occur through omission: when an advertiser or a reporter deliberately chooses to include some facts and omit others. The bottom line is that stereotyping and bias come from opinions based on fear, not fact. The best action you can take is to read as much as you can about a topic in order to get a lot of information. Different sources will probably have different opinions and feature different facts. When you read as much as you can about a topic, you are giving yourself a balanced picture of that topic. It is also important to keep in mind that many writers will intentionally expose you to stereotypes and biases in order to educate you about respecting individuality, tolerating differences, and forming your own (hopefully unbiased) opinions.

To wrap up this section on perspectives and bias, enjoy the poem "The Blind Men and the Elephant." This poem shows in just a few stanzas why making an assumption too quickly about anything is a mistake.

THE BLIND MEN AND THE ELEPHANT

It was six men of Hindostan,
    To learning much inclined,
Who went to see the elephant,
    (Though all of them were blind):

That each by observation
    Might satisfy his mind.
The *first* approached the Elephant,
    And happening to fall

Against his broad and sturdy side,
    At once began to bawl:
"Bless me, it seems the Elephant
    Is very like a wall."

The *second*, feeling of his tusk,
    Cried, "Ho! What have we here
So very round and smooth and sharp?
    To me 'tis mighty clear
This wonder of an Elephant
    Is very like a spear."

The *third* approached the animal,
    And happening to take
The squirming trunk within his hands,
    Then boldly up and spake:
"I see," quoth he, "the Elephant
    Is very like a snake."

The *fourth* stretched out his eager hand
    And felt about the knee,
"What most this mighty beast is like
    Is mighty plain," quoth he;
"'Tis clear enough the Elephant
    Is very like a tree."

The *fifth* who chanced to touch the ear
    Said, "Even the blindest man
Can tell what this resembles most;
    Deny the fact who can,
This marvel of an Elephant
    Is very like a fan."

The *sixth* no sooner had begun
About the beast to grope,
Than, seizing on the swinging tail
That fell within his scope,
"I see," cried he, "the Elephant
Is very like a rope."

And so these men of Hindostan
Disputed loud and long,
Each in his own opinion
Exceeding stiff and strong,
Though *each was partly* in the right
And all were in the wrong.

—*by John Godfrey Saxe*

The poem shows how looking at only one part of an issue can lead to the formation of a very mistaken point of view. People often choose to look only at one part of an issue. The best way to avoid developing biased opinions is to try and find as many viewpoints and as much information as possible about any given subject. Analysing all sides of an issue will help you form rational, balanced opinions.

Analysing a text is a complex process. Finding meaning in a text often means relating that text to your life and to information you have already read, and examining smaller parts of the text. One of the great things about literature is that a single text can mean many different things to many different people. This section of your study guide has shown you how using a variety of methods to analyse a text can ensure that the meaning you find in it is balanced and enriching.

PRACTICE QUESTIONS—ANALYIZING FOR MEANING

Read the following passage to answer questions 1 to 7.

ON THE WAY TO THE MISSION

They dogged him all one afternoon
Through the bright snow,
Two white men, servants of greed;
He knew that they were there,
But he turned not his head;
He was an Indian trapper;
He planted his snow-shoes firmly,
He dragged the long toboggan
Without rest.

The three figures drifted
Like shadows in the mind of a seer;
The snow-shoes were the whisperers
On the threshold of awe;
The toboggan made the sound of wings,
A wood pigeon sloping to her nest.
The Indian's face was calm,
He strode with the sorrow of fore-knowledge.
But his eyes were jewels of content

Set in circles of peace.
They would have shot him;
But momently in the deep forest,
They saw something flit by his side;
Their hearts stopped with fear.
Then the moon rose.
They would have left him to the spirit,
But they saw the long toboggan
Rounded well with furs,
With many a silver fox-skin,
With the pelts of mink and otter,
They were the servants of greed;
When the moon grew brighter
And the spruces were dark with sleet.
They shot him.

When he fell on a shield of moonlight
One of his arms clung to his burden;
The snow was not melted:
The spirit passed away —
Then the servants of greed
Tore off the cover to count their gains;
They shuddered away into the shadows,
Hearing each the loud heart of the other,
Silence was born.

There in the tender moonlight,
    As sweet as they were in life,
Glimmered the ivory features
    Of the Indian's wife.

In the manner of Montagnais women
    Her hair was rolled with braid;
Under her waxen fingers
    A crucifix was laid.

He was drawing her down to the mission,
    To bury her there in the spring,
When the blood root comes and the windflower
    To silver everything.

But as a gift of plunder
    Side by side were they laid,
The moon went on with her setting
    And covered them with shade.

—by D.C. Scott

1. Choose phrases from the poem in which the underlying theme of greed is **best** shown.

   ① "a silver fox-skin", ② "To silver everything" and "a gift of plunder"
   The word silver is used as an adjective and verb, both relating
   to money (silver), valuable. So does "a gift of plunder"
   That phrase implies the theme of greed with the word
   "plunder" and "gift"

2. What does the repetition of the phrase "servants of greed" help to contrast?

   The repetition of the phrase "servants of greed" is
   written to contrast the Indian man and the 2 white
   men. It implies the innocent character of the Indian
   trapper and the greedy, careless characters of
   the 2 white men.

3. Although the trapper was aware of the presence of the white men, the **most likely** reason he paid them no heed is that he

   A. had never trusted white men

   B. was focused on his final goal

   C. did not suspect their evil motive

   D. was too tired to worry about others using the same trail

4. The length of time covered by the events in the poem is

   A. one afternoon and into the early evening

   B. early morning and into the afternoon

   C. early morning and into the night

   D. one afternoon and into the night

5. What type of mood is created as a result of the fact that the two pursuers missed their first chance to shoot the trapper?

   The mood that is created is suspense. Given the visualization that they were planning on shooting the trapper but then didn't leaves the reader questioned and in a mood of suspense, and fear for the Indian. Though the men may have greedy anticipation, the Indian feels otherwise.

6. The men following the trapper intended to shoot him because they

   A. found him trapping on their line

   B. wanted to get their stolen furs back

   C. were motivated by greed for his furs

   D. were angry with him for tricking them

7. The **predominant** element of the poet's style in this poem is

   A. repetition

   B. stanza pattern

   C. rhyme scheme

   D. figurative language

Read the following passage to answer questions 8 and 9.

THE COMING OF MUTT

During my lifetime we had owned, or had been owned by, a steady succession of dogs. As a newborn baby I had been guarded by a Border collie named Sapper, who was one day doused with boiling water by a vicious neighbour, and who went insane as a result. But there had always been other dogs during my first eight years, until we moved to the west and became, for the moment, dogless. The prairies could be only half real to a boy without a dog.

I began agitating for one almost as soon as we arrived and I found a willing ally in my father—though his motives were not mine.

For many years he had been exposed to the colourful tales of my Great-uncle Frank, who homesteaded in Alberta in 1900. Frank was a hunter born, and most of his stories dealt with the superlative shooting to be had on the western plains. Before we were properly settled in Saskatoon my father determined to test those tales. He bought a fine English shotgun, a shooting coat, cases of ammunition, a copy of the *Saskatchewan Game Laws*, and a handbook on shotgun shooting. There remained only one indispensable item—a hunting dog.

One evening he arrived home from the library with such a beast in tow behind him. Its name was Crown Prince Challenge Indefatigable. It stood about as high as the dining-room table and, as far as Mother and I could judge, consisted mainly of feet and tongue. Father was annoyed at our levity and haughtily informed us that the Crown Prince was an Irish setter, kennel bred and field trained, and a dog to delight the heart of any expert. We remained unimpressed. Purebred he may have been, and the possessor of innumerable cups and ribbons, but to my eyes he seemed a singularly useless sort of beast with but one redeeming feature: I greatly admired the way he drooled. I have never known a dog who could drool as the Crown Prince could. He never stopped, except to flop his way to the kitchen sink and tank up on water. He left a wet and sticky trail wherever he went. He had little else to recommend him, for he was moronic.

Mother might have overlooked his obvious defects, had it not been for his price. She could not overlook that, for the owner was asking two hundred dollars, and we could no more afford such a sum than we could have afforded a Cadillac. Crown Prince left the next morning, but Father was not discouraged, and it was clear that he would try again.

My parents had been married long enough to achieve that delicate balance of power which enables a married couple to endure each other. They were both adept in the evasive tactics of marital politics—but Mother was a little more adept.

She realized that a dog was now inevitable, and when chance brought the duck boy—as we afterwards referred to him—to our door on that dusty August day, Mother showed her mettle by snatching the initiative right out of my father's hands.

By buying the duck boy's pup, she not only placed herself in a position to forestall the purchase of an expensive dog of my father's choice, but she was also able to save six cents in cash.
She was never one to despise a bargain.

When I came home from school the bargain was installed in a soap carton in the kitchen. He looked to be a somewhat dubious buy at any price. Small, emaciated, and caked liberally with cow manure, he peered up at me in a near-sighted sort of way. But when I knelt beside him and extended an exploratory hand he roused himself and sank his puppy teeth into my thumb with such satisfactory gusto that my doubts dissolved. I knew that he and I would get along.

—by Farley Mowat

8. One way that the narrator's mother is shown to be different from his father is that she is

   A. more practical

   B. less willing to compromise

   C. less aware of a young boy's needs

   D. more aware of the responsibilities of owning a pet

9. Which of the following statements expresses the **main** theme of this narrative?

   A. The true value of things is not based on their price.

   B. Society should try harder to protect abused animals.

   C. Marriage is a difficult journey of constant compromise.

   D. People often become pet owners for the wrong reasons.

Read the following passage to answer questions 10 and 11.

THE GHOST TOWN

Margaret picked up the old yellowed photograph that was lying on top of the pile. It was in black and white. It was better that way, aged, like her memories. Color photographs capture the image, but black and whites capture its soul; it was the soul of this picture that captured her attention now.

It was a simple picture of children playing. A woman, her mother, was standing at the bottom of the slide, her arms outstretched, ready to catch a little girl with pigtails and laughing eyes, her sister. An older boy and a girl of about eight were climbing on the teeter-totter. In the background, she could see the jungle gym filled with walkways and monkey bars. She remembered the squeak and groan of the teeter-totter as it crashed up and down. Oh how she loved teeter-tottering!

She reached for another picture, this one taken only a few weeks ago. Her brother had taken it on his last visit to Fireside. It was a black and white of the playground, overgrown and forgotten. Weeds grew up around the base of the equipment. The bar from the teeter-totter was lost in long grasses and climbing flowers. The sand was blown smooth with nary a footprint was left in the sand. If she looked hard enough at the picture, she could almost see the ghosts of the children who used to play there. She could almost hear their laughter echoing off the old jungle gym with its rusting bars and rotting wooden posts.

The next picture, this one in color, was of the old hotel with its windows boarded up, locking the world out and the memories in. Like the playground, green tangles of weeds and grasses grew unchecked along the walls, the green contrasting sharply with the faded red paint. The glass-framed phone booth was tucked away near the side door. She didn't remember a glass phone booth. They changed that after she left. The phone itself still worked; she knew because her brother had used it two weeks ago when he phoned. She was sure the lights still worked too. One flip of the switch would illuminate the layers of dust and cobwebs of the dining room and the stage where the dance hall girls used to perform.

She closed her eyes, remembering. She was eight. Her sister was a little older. They were sneaking up to the windows to peer inside. They stretched up on tiptoes, pressing their faces tight against the glass. They could see the girls in their sparkling dresses dancing while the miners sat in groups around the tables drinking and playing cards. The girls were so beautiful. They never got to watch for long. As soon as Mr. Uchanko saw them, he shooed them away. "Not for the eyes of little girls," he told them as they scurried away.

She unfolded the letter. Her brother's messy handwriting was scrawled across the crisp white surface. Dear Margaret, he wrote, I hope this letter finds you well. The next few words were scratched out as if he was trying to say something, but the words weren't coming out right. She knew what was coming. She forced herself to read on:

I know you have heard about the new interstate highway. It will run straight through the middle of Fireside. All the buildings will be torn down and moved. The playground and the school will be paved, the hotel dismantled. You know what is beneath those floorboards. You know what is inside that hotel. Margaret, I need your help. We can't let them destroy Fireside. John.

She re-read the note three times before folding it up and tucking it back in the shoebox full of pictures. She wasn't ready to open up the past, not now, not ever. There were too many demons lurking in those shadows.

She pulled her old shawl tight around her shoulders. Why couldn't the secrets have stayed lost for just a few more years? Why couldn't it have waited until she was dead and no one was left to remember? Why—the word hung in the evening air like a herald of doom.

10. Margaret's brother **most likely** sent her a black-and-white photograph of the playground because he

   A. knows how much she likes black-and-white photos

   B. is emphasizing the importance of the playground

   C. is comparing the present to the past

   D. is preying on her memories

11. The sentence "You know what is beneath those floorboards" suggests that

   A. Margaret and her brother hid something in the hotel

   B. the hotel is very important to them

   C. there is gold under the floors

   D. the hotel might be haunted

Read the following passage to answer questions 12 and 13.

HECTOR, THE STOWAWAY DOG

Second Officer Harold Kildall of the *Hanley* noticed the dog first. The *Hanley*, a freighter, was one of five ships loading at the Government Dock in Vancouver, British Columbia, on April 20, 1922. Checking chain lashings, Kildall glanced up to see a large smooth-haired terrier, white with black markings, coming abroad by the gangplank. Once aboard, the dog stood absolutely still, looking and listening all about the deck. He sniffed at the deck cargo of fresh-sawed timbers and at the sacks of grain being loaded into the last hatch. Then he returned ashore, only to board the next ship, which was loading apples, flour and fir logs for England. Here the terrier again sniffed at the cargo and about the decks and living quarters, then slowly went ashore.

The dog's strange actions made Kildall curious. Now he watched the dog board a freighter loading paper pulp for East Coast ports. The dog boarded the other ships in turn, examining each in the same careful fashion. After that, busy getting ready for sea, Kildall forgot the whole thing. And at noon the *Hanley* got under way for the long trip to Japan.

Early the next morning the dog was found lying on a mat outside the cabin of the *Hanley's* captain. Unseen, he had come aboard again and stowed away for the voyage. The captain, who loved dogs, tried to be friendly, but the terrier would not warm up to him. Kildall and others tried, too, to win him over. To all of them he remained distant and cool. He just walked about the captain's deck, sniffing the salt air.

Late that first morning, when Kildall went below to eat, the dog followed him and stood at the galley door, waiting expectantly. The cook gave him his best leftovers. When Kildall climbed to the bridge to take over the watch, the dog followed close behind, walked through the pilothouse, took a turn through the chartroom, then ran up the ladder to the flying bridge and stood beside the compass housing. Seeming to be satisfied, he lay down in a comfortable corner and went to sleep. Obviously this stowaway was an old sea dog.

For 18 days the *Hanley* sailed across the northern rim of the Pacific. Day after day her officers and men tried to make up to the dog but he remained aloof. He allowed his head to be patted but showed no return of affection. When not "on watch" with Kildall he remained at the captain's door, going below decks only for his meals.

When the coast of Honshu was signed, the stowaway sniffed the land breeze and stared straight ahead as the land came in sight. His interest grew as the *Hanley* moved through the Yokohama breakwaters to its anchoring place near some other ships unloading cargos.

While directing cargo work, Kildall noticed that the dog was very alert, his tail switching from time to time and his nostrils quivering nervously as he stared at the other ships. The nearest of these, the Simaloer, was, like the *Hanley*, unloading squared timbers into the harbor.

Soon the *Hanley* swung with the tide so that her stern pointed in the direction of the Simaloer, now some 300 yards away. At once the dog's attention centered on her. He ran to the rear of the ship, as close to her as possible, and sniffed the air with rising excitement. While Kildall watched, a sampan came alongside the Simaloer, took two sailors abroad, and set off for shore on a course that carried the boat close under the *Hanley's* stern.

Whining softly, the dog watched. Suddenly he began running back and forth in wild excitement, barking madly. This caught the attention of the passengers in the sampan. Shading their eyes against the sun, they stared at the *Hanley's* stern.

Suddenly one of them jumped to his feet and began shouting and waving his arms, motioning to the sampan man and slapping the other sailor on the back. His excitement matched the dog's. Now, as the sampan came alongside the Hanley's boarding ladder, the dog became so worked up that he jumped into the water. The shouting man pulled him aboard the sampan and hugged him close, wet coat and all. The dog whined with joy and licked his face. Obviously a dog and his master had been reunited.

The reunion of the stowaway and his happy owner became the talk of the crews of both ships. The dog's name, it turned out, was Hector. His owner, W.H. Mante, second officer of the Simaloer, had the same duties and the same watches to stand as Kildall had on the Hanley. At Government Dock in Vancouver, the Simaloer had changed its position to take on fuel while Hector was off for a last run before the long voyage. Mante searched the waterfront wildly but failed to find Hector in time – and the Simaloer sailed without him.

What mysterious sense could have guided Hector's careful search for the one ship out of many that would carry him across an ocean to rejoin his master? Did the kind of cargo the Hanley carried and perhaps other signs tell him that the Hanley was headed for the same port as his own ship? Did he then attach himself to the officer whose duties were like his master's? Any answers would be the guesswork of men, who know only that it happened.

—*by Kenneth Dodson*

12. The reason Hector missed sailing with his own ship was that

   A. the captain had decided to sail earlier

   B. he boarded another ship to watch the cargo being loaded

   C. he had mistakenly followed someone aboard a different ship

   D. his ship was in a different position when he returned to the loading dock

13. Where did Hector board the *Hanley*?

   A. Vancouver

   B. Yokohama

   C. Honshu

   D. Japan

Read the following passage to answer questions 14 and 15.

AN ENCOUNTER UNDER THE LAMPPOST

The lamppost stood tall and straight in the evening shadows. There was a little rust around its base, and its light had dimmed with age, but it was still the same beautiful lamppost it had been all those years ago when oil lamps first lined the city streets. Those were the days before kerosene when whale oil was still popular and the whales were not extinct. The lamp had been converted to burn kerosene, but even that was becoming rare as the wasteful age of fossil-fuel energy was finally stalling out.

Preserved by city decree, the lamp stood as a testimonial to forgotten years when men wore tall hats and women wore elegant dresses and exchanged smiles of goodwill and gestures of kindness. Those were the days when a handshake still sealed a deal and men honored their word. All that had changed now. Smiles were tightlipped mockeries of the original thing. People hid behind deceptions, insinuations, lies, and half-truths, shaking hands as a leftover formality from bygone years.

Zachariah felt like the lamppost. He did not fit in with the bustle and hustle of the modern world. He did not understand computer games and car racing games. Instead, he learned to whittle wood. Sometimes he thought he had inherited more than just his great grandfather's name. Sometimes he thought his great grandfather was in him, a part of him, guiding his hands as he cut and carved until the soul of the wood was set free in beautiful ornate carvings.

It was late evening. The harsh light of day had been replaced by the soft glow of the city lamps. Zachariah sat with his back pressed against the lamppost eyeing his latest carving. It was a bear. The proportions looked all right, although it was hard to tell for sure. He used pictures to guide his carving. Somewhere behind him, he heard the sound of footsteps cracking on the old, cobblestone courtyard. Time to go, he supposed, tucking his whittle knife in his pocket.

"Where do you think he got to?" a harsh, guttural voice whispered. Zachariah froze.

"He'll be here," a second voice said.

"But he's late."

"Shhh," the second voice hissed. "People will hear you."

"There's no one here," the first voice complained.

"Shhh," the second voice hissed again. "Your impatience will be your downfall. Remember, you are here to observe only."

"I know, I know," the first voice whined, "I stay hidden in the shadows. I don't say a word. You do all the transactions."

"Good. Now get back. I hear someone coming."

There was a shuffling of feet as the hoarse-voiced man shifted back a few paces. Just as Zachariah was contemplating whether to run or stay, the thick crunching steps of a third person came out of the shadows.

"Have you got the item?" a sinister voice asked. There was a rustling sound of an object exchanging hands. "The scroll?" the voice asked.

"Yes."

"Good. You know what to do next?"

"Yes." The scuffling feet moved off back down the alley.

"What do we do next?" the rough young voice asked, staring after the departing shadow.

"We kill the king," the older voice said with a sigh.

"What? That wasn't part of the deal. You never said anything about killing anyone."

"Do you want to save your sister?"

"Of course but—"

"Then you must accept the consequences of the deal."

"But … "

"Either you are a man and you will go through with this or you are still a sniffling boy from the back alleys of Tyr. Which is it? Decide now." There was a hard edge in the second voice, an edge that showed neither weakness nor sympathy. Zachariah found himself drawn to the voice. Bit by bit, he eased his body around until his chest was pressed against the lamppost. He poked his head out just far enough to see two burly shapes dressed in black.

"Ho, who are you? Who's that?" the smaller figure said, pointing.

14. The **most likely** reason Zachariah uses pictures to guide his carving of a bear is that
   A. bears are extinct
   B. pictures are easy to get
   C. Zachariah lives in a city
   D. bears are imaginary creatures

15. What event is **most likely** to happen immediately after the final sentence of the selection: "'Ho, who are you? Who's that?' the smaller figure said, pointing"?

The two burly shaped people dressed in black will most likely chase away or run after Zachariah as they will probably eavesdropping on their conversation when in reality, Zachariah hearing their conversation was unintentional.

Read the following passage to answer questions 16 and 17.

This cartogram shows how the world would probably look if the number of international visitors to a country determined its size.

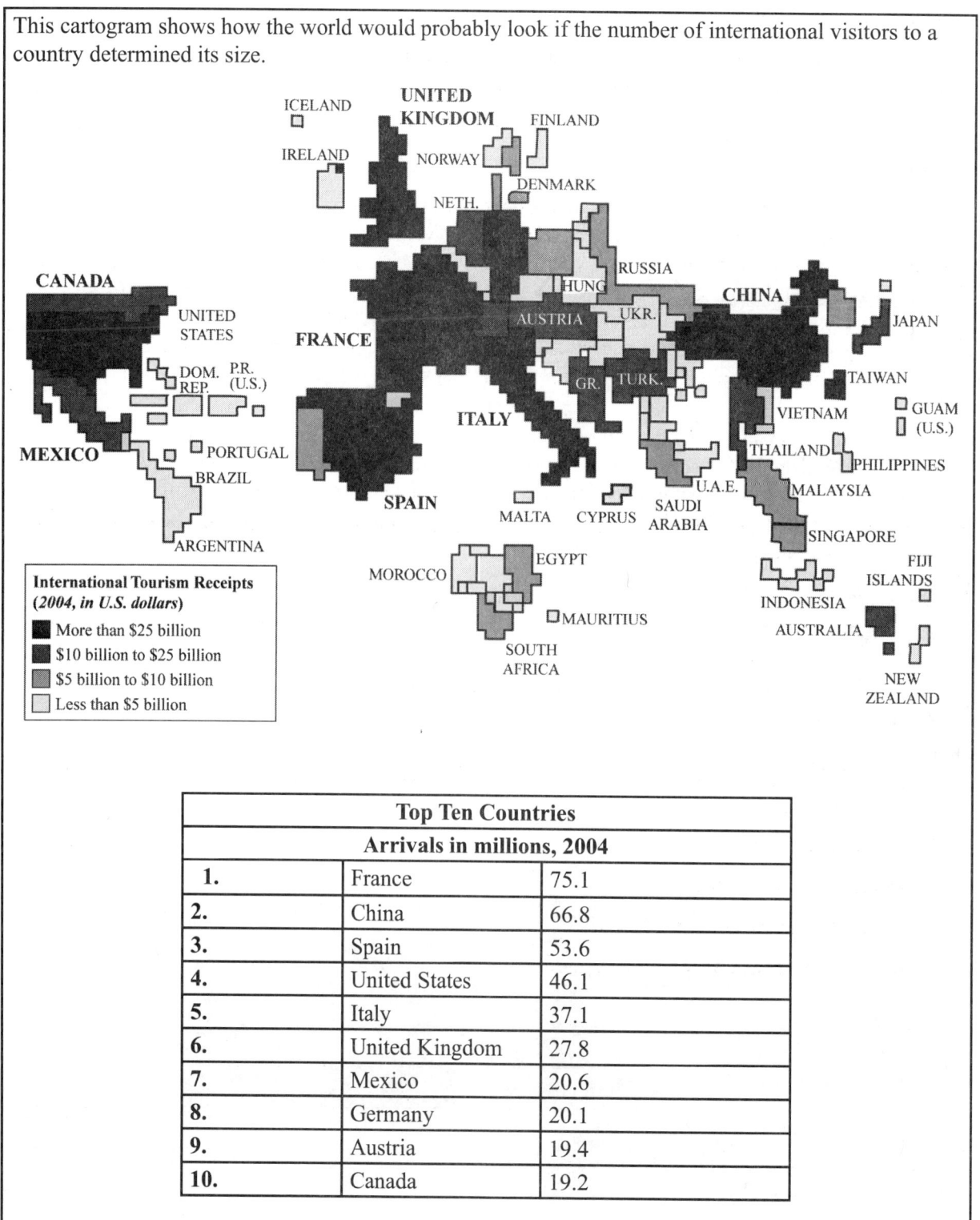

Top Ten Countries		
Arrivals in millions, 2004		
1.	France	75.1
2.	China	66.8
3.	Spain	53.6
4.	United States	46.1
5.	Italy	37.1
6.	United Kingdom	27.8
7.	Mexico	20.6
8.	Germany	20.1
9.	Austria	19.4
10.	Canada	19.2

Fact: Germans spent the most on travel in 2004: 71 billion dollars. Most European countries provide at least 20 days of vacation per year, but Germans receive 24.

Fact: The continent of Africa received 41 million visitors in 2004, 20 million of whom went to sub-Saharan Africa. The conflicts in Sudan kept tourists away.

Fact: Although Asia has faced several disasters: SARS in 2003, the tsunami on December 26, 2004, and the avian flu, its tourism industry is still thriving.

People are travelling more than ever before in history. International tourist arrivals increased from about 540 million in 1995 to 763 million in 2004. Last year, international arrivals worldwide topped 808 million. Tourism decreased briefly due to the devastating 2004 hurricane season in the Caribbean, rioting in France, terrorist attacks in Turkey and the Middle East, and the horrifying Indian Ocean tsunami. Even with all the fear of natural disasters, the desire to travel still wins. Crossings between countries by car, bus, and train have also increased. Low-cost airline flights are also feeding the trend. One carrier recently offered a round-trip ticket from London to Brest, in France, for less than two dollars.

16. Which of the following reasons **best** explains why Africa appears small on the map when compared to the other continents?

   A. Low population

   B. Conflict and war

   C. Fewer number of visitors

   D. Poor national economies in its countries

17. According to the information given in the passage, the **main** reason that international tourism is increasing is because of

   A. low-cost airline flights

   B. easier travel between countries

   C. fewer occurrences of natural disasters

   D. the availability of transportation options

Read the following passage to answer the questions 18 to 24.

MULGA BILL'S BICYCLE

'Twas Mulga Bill, from Eaglehawk, that caught the cycling craze;
He turned away the good old horse that served him many days;
He dressed himself in cycling clothes, resplendent to be seen;
He hurried off to town and bought a shining new machine;
And as he wheeled it through the door, with air of lordly pride,
The grinning shop assistant said, "Excuse me, can you ride?"

"See here, young man," said Mulga Bill, "from Walgett to the sea,
From Conroy's Gap to Castlereagh, there's none can ride like me.
I'm good all round at everything as everybody knows,
Although I'm not the one to talk—I hate a man that blows.
But riding is my special gift, my chiefest, sole delight;
Just ask a wild duck can it swim, a wildcat can it fight.
There's nothing clothed in hair or hide, or built of flesh or steel,
There's nothing walks or jumps, or runs, on axle, hoof, or wheel,
But what I'll sit, while hide will hold and girths and straps are tight:
I'll ride this here two-wheeled concern right straight away at sight."

'Twas Mulga Bill, from Eaglehawk, that sought his own abode,
That perched above Dead Man's Creek, beside the mountain road.
He turned the cycle down the hill and mounted for the fray,
But 'ere he'd gone a dozen yards it bolted clean away.
It left the track, and through the trees, just like a silver streak,
It whistled down the awful slope toward the Dead Man's Creek.

It shaved a stump by half an inch, it dodged a big white-box:
The very wallaroos in fright went scrambling up the rocks,
The wombats hiding in their caves dug deeper underground,
As Mulga Bill, as white as chalk, sat tight to every bound.
It struck a stone and gave a spring that cleared a fallen tree,
It raced beside a precipice as close as close could be;
And then as Mulga Bill let out one last despairing shriek
It made a leap of twenty feet into the Dead Man's Creek.

'Twas Mulga Bill, from Eaglehawk, that slowly swam ashore:
He said, "I've had some narrer shaves and lively rides before;
I've rode a wild bull round a yard to win a five-pound bet,
But this was the most awful ride that I've encountered yet.
I'll give that two-wheeled outlaw best; it's shaken all my nerve
To feel it whistle through the air and plunge and buck and swerve.
It's safe at rest in Dead Man's Creek, we'll leave it lying still;
A horse's back is good enough henceforth for Mulga Bill."

—by A.B. "Banjo" Paterson

18. The **most likely** reason the shop assistant is grinning as he asks, "'Excuse me, can you ride?'" is that
   A. Mulga Bill has just told a joke
   B. Mulga Bill looks funny in his cycling gear
   C. he thinks Mulga Bill is too short to ride a bicycle
   D. he knows Mulga Bill will probably fall off the bicycle

19. Which of the following pairs of personality traits **best** describes Mulga Bill?
   A. Confident and shy
   B. Proud and boastful
   C. Cheerful and modest
   D. Aggressive and uncompromising

20. Which of the following quotations from the text **best** reveals Mulga Bill's high opinion of himself?
   A. "'Twas Mulga Bill, from Eaglehawk, that caught the cycling craze"
   B. "And as he wheeled it through the door, with air of lordly pride"
   C. "'I'm good all round at everything as everybody knows'"
   D. "'But riding is my special gift, my chiefest, sole delight'"

21. Throughout the course of the poem, Mulga Bill's attitude changes from
   A. impatient to sheepish
   B. courageous to tearful
   C. conceited to abashed
   D. confident to angry

22. Which of the following elements of the setting are **most essential** to the plot of this poem?
   A. The date, place, and time of day
   B. The hill, stones, and Dead Man's Creek
   C. The bicycle, the horse, and the shop assistant
   D. The bicycle, Mulga Bill, and Dead Man's Creek

ANSWERS AND SOLUTIONS—PRACTICE QUESTIONS

1. WR	7. D	13. A	19. B
2. WR	8. A	14. A	20. C
3. B	9. A	15. WR	21. C
4. D	10. D	16. C	22.B
5. WR	11. A	17. A	
6. C	12. D	18. D	

1. WRITTEN RESPONSE

Phrases such as "silver fox-skin," "to silver everything," and "gift of plunder" reflect notions of greed. The use of the word "silver" both as an adjective and a verb implies money (silver) and helps to support the underlying theme of greed, as does the word "plunder."

2. WRITTEN RESPONSE

The phrase emphasizes the will of the two men and the innocent purpose of the trapper. This seems to be the implied purpose of the poet, as the entire poem is a study in the struggle between good and evil.

3. B

The strongest inference is that the trapper is focused on his goal of bringing his wife to the mission to be buried there in the spring. There is nothing to suggest that the trapper distrusts white men, and stanza one indicates the trapper steadily goes on without rest. We do not know if the trapper suspects the motives of the white men; however, we do know he is aware that they are behind him.

4. D

In the first stanza, the poet states that the two white men dogged the trapper "all one afternoon," and the action in the poem continues as "the moon went on with her setting." This indicates that the length of time covered by the events in the poem is one afternoon and into the night.

5. WRITTEN RESPONSE

The prolonging of the action in the poem establishes and maintains a mood of suspense. The fear is caused by an imagined movement, which adds to the suspense. Greedy anticipation might be the mood of the white men, but certainly not of the trapper.

6. C

The fact that the white men are greedy is emphasized throughout the poem. There is no evidence to support the idea that the two men found the trapper on their lines or that they are angry with him. Had the trapper stolen someone's furs, he probably would not have just ignored the two men following him.

7. D

The poem is rich in imagery created by verb phrases such as "to silver everything" and numerous examples of simile, metaphor, and personification. The repetition of "servants of greed" is a lesser style element, and the poem often does not rhyme. The two sections of the poem—one with long stanzas and one with short stanzas—could lead to a discussion of why the poet chose that pattern, but this is not as predominant as the imagery.

8. **A**

The narrator's mother is more practical or sensible in sorting out the problem. She does not try to purchase a dog that the family cannot afford, and yet she realizes how important having a dog is to her family. She compromises by buying an inexpensive dog. Her solution is a practical one.

The narrator's mother is not less willing to compromise than her husband; in fact, she may be more willing to compromise. She realizes that a dog is "inevitable" and so finds a way to have one without spending a large sum of money. The father is still expecting to buy an expensively bred hunting dog. She finds a compromising solution to the problem while he is determined to continue on with his objective.

Nothing in the story suggests that the boy's mother is unaware of her son's needs.

The narrator's mother does not seem to be more aware of the responsibilities of owning a pet than other family members.

9. **A**

The title "The Coming of Mutt" suggests the focus of the passage. The ending hints at how important and treasured the dog became to the narrator, even though it was not an expensive or well-bred dog. The contrast of Mutt with Crown Prince emphasizes the idea that greater expense does not guarantee greater value.

The animals in the passage are not abused or in need of protection.

The narrator's main objective is not to comment on the difficulties of marriage. A compromise between the narrator's parents is involved in the coming of Mutt, but the main message comes out of the comparison of the "worth" of the two dogs. The reader is forced to think about what is truly valuable.

The narrator's father does not necessarily want a dog for the wrong reasons. There is nothing to suggest that the expensive hunting dog would not be well-treated. His insistence that expensive, well-bred dogs are more skilled and intelligent is shown to be incorrect, however.

10. **D**

The passage does not explain why one photograph was in colour while the other was in black and white; however, the fact that the photograph of the playground is in black and white suggests that the playground is important. He is using his sister's memories to solicit her help in protecting a secret.

11. **A**

The passage does not reveal what is under the floorboards, but the fact that Margaret's brother is soliciting her help, stating that she knows "what is beneath those floorboards," and Margaret's reference to a secret suggest that Margaret and John hid something there.

12. **D**

The answer to this question is found in the second-last paragraph: "At Government Dock in Vancouver, the *Simaloer* had changed its position to take on fuel while Hector was off for a last run before the long voyage."

13. **A**

The correct answer is clearly implied both in the opening paragraph and in the second-last paragraph of the story.

14. **A**

This story is set in some future time when whales are extinct, an event that has not happened in our time. Given that bears are becoming rare today, it is likely that in a future where whales are extinct, bears are also extinct.

15. **WRITTEN RESPONSE**

If the smaller man is pointing and asking who is watching them, the next likely event is that the larger man will turn around to see who is watching them. Zachariah will likely try to run away from the two men, who will probably be unhappy about having a witness to their activities.

16. C

Africa appears smaller on the map because it receives fewer visitors than other places on the map. The writer speculates in the passage that Africa has fewer international visitors than other parts of the world because of conflicts in Sudan and other parts of Africa.

17. A

Easier travel between countries, including more relaxed passage between borders, has increased travel in European countries. However, cheap airfare is the main reason for worldwide increase in travel.

18. D

The assistant grins because even though Mulga Bill is very confident and has an "air of lordly pride," the assistant knows that he will most likely fall off the bicycle on his first ride.

19. B

Quotations from the passage such as "with air of lordly pride" (verse one), and "I'm good all round at everything" (verse two), reveal that Mulga Bill is proud and boastful.

20. C

Although he may have a "lordly" air and a special gift at riding, it is Mulga Bill's boast that he is "good all round at everything" that most clearly illustrates his high opinion of himself.

21. C

Mulga Bill's attitude at the start of the poem is one of conceit (full of pride and self-importance), which is evident in his boasting. This changes after his adventure to an attitude of ashamed acceptance of his inadequacy on the bicycle. He felt abashed after falling off of the bike.

22. B

Without a hill to ride on and stones on the road to dislodge the bicycle, Mulga Bill would have ended up in Dead Man's Creek. The hill, stones, and creek have to be part of the setting in order for the plot to unfold as written.

UNIT TEST—ANALYSING FOR MEANING

Read the following passage to answer questions 1 to 9.

WARREN PRYOR

When every pencil meant a sacrifice

his parents boarded him at school in town,

slaving to free him from the stony fields,

the meagre acreage that bore them down.

They blushed with pride when, at his graduation,

They watched him picking up the slender scroll,

his passport from the years of brutal toil

and lonely patience in a barren hole.

When he went in the Bank their cups ran over.

They marveled how he wore a milk-white shirt

work days and jeans on Sundays. He was saved

from their thistle-strewn farm and its red dirt.

And he said nothing. Hard and serious

like a young bear inside his teller's cage,

his axe-hewn hands upon the paper bills

aching with empty strength and throttled range.

—by Alden Nowlan

---

1. Explain how the following statement accurately describes the joy and pride experienced by Warren's parents:

   The parents are very proud of Warren but their pride blinds them to Warren's goals and desires.

   Warren's parents have always dreamed of Warren going to school and succeeding in life. But once their dreams become a reality, they were too proud of Warren to notice what his dreams were. Furthermore, Warren is too much of an obedient son that he does not want destroy his parents happiness and pride. Since Warren's parents are so proud that their life long dream for their son has become real, they are blinded towards Warren's personal goals and desires in life.

2. The final stanza of the poem indicates that Warren Pryor

    A. is shy about speaking aloud

    B. is proud to be working in the bank

    C. feels the work he is doing is boring

    D. does not share his parents' sentiments

3. The reason Warren Pryor's name is given in the title of the poem but never in the body of the poem that

    A. his parents' names are not mentioned either

    B. he has experienced a loss of individuality working in a large institution

    C. his identity was not considered when his parents made their plans for him

    D. it is sufficient to refer to the title character with pronouns like "he" and "him"

4. Warren Pryor says "nothing" because he

    A. cannot find the right words to thank his parents

    B. respects his parents and does not want to hurt them

    C. has been brought up not to speak back to his parents

    D. does not want to speak to his parents now that he works in a bank

5. What is the **most likely** reason that the poet chose the word "milk" to describe Warren's white shirt?

    Prior to working in a bank, Warren worked on a farm alongside his parents. Now that he works in a bank, the poet wants to remind the reader of Warren's previous situations and how his life drastically changed. His parents describe his shirt as "milk white" in relation to their rural background.

6. Warren's parents marvelled "how he wore a milk-white shirt / work days and jeans on Sundays" because

    A. white shirts are so expensive

    B. they appreciate his sense of style

    C. they do not think jeans should be worn on the weekends

    D. it is just the opposite of what he would have worn on the farm

7. Warren's parents send Warren to school because
   A. they do not want him to live with them on the farm anymore
   B. he wants the opportunity to earn more money
   C. he wants to be free of his life on the farm
   D. they believe he wants a better life

8. Choose the quotation from the passage that best indicates that Warren would rather not be working in the bank.

   The quotation "his axe hewn hands..../aching with empty strength and throttled range." Through the author's description, we can understand that Warren doesn't enjoy his job. His hands are weak and empty of strength. At his job, Warren contains a lack of energy because he doesn't see any happiness or enjoyment in his work.

9. The line from the poem that best illustrates the fact that Warren's parents do not like life on the farm is
   A. "his parents boarded him at school in town"
   B. "When he went in the Bank their cups ran over"
   C. "They marveled how he wore a milk-white shirt"
   D. "his passport from the years of brutal toil / and lonely patience"

Read the following passage to answer questions 10 to 12.

from Drift House

After the towers came down Mr. and Mrs. Oakenfeld thought it best that their three children go and stay with their uncle in Canada. Although Susan, Charles, and Murray knew something terrible had occurred, the Oakenfeld family lived high on the Upper East Side, and the children understood very little of what was going on downtown. In the days immediately following the tragedy their parents wouldn't even let them watch television, so it's understandable that the children were mostly concerned—at least at first—with how the move would affect school.

Susan in particular, had just joined the eighth grade debating club, and she was quite annoyed. When she was nine she had decided she would be a lawyer like Mr. Oakenfeld: she had been waiting to start debate for three whole years. Whereas Charles, in fifth grade, was secretly relieved. He was taking special classes at the magnet high school for science, and two days a week had to ride the West Side train all the way up to 205th Street in the Bronx, where the older boys were more than a little intimidating. At five, Murray was only in kindergarten, and so didn't care about all that. But of course he didn't want to leave his mother and father.

"But Uncle Farley has just moved into a gorgeous old house on the Bay of Eternity," Mrs. Oakenfeld told Murray. "He tells me there are pelicans and puffins, and tidal pools with starfish, and the most beautiful sunrises you've ever seen. And the house has rooms and rooms and rooms—an enormous attic, and some kind of tower-gallery-type thingy for showing off his art collection, and every imaginable exotic plant in the solarium."

"Yay, Solar Mum!" Murray yelled, and ran off to pack his suitcase.

As the eldest—and a future lawyer to boot—Susan felt it was her job to be a bit more skeptical.

"The Bay of Eternity? Really, Mum, that's quite the queer name for a place."

"Don't say 'queer,'" Charles said. "It's affected."

I suppose I should explain right off that Susan was Charles and Murray's half sister. Before Mrs. Oakenfeld had come to America and married Mr. Oakenfeld, she had lived in England, only there she had been Mrs. Wheelwright. Lt. Wheelwright had died when Susan was just a baby, and she called Mr. Oakenfeld "Daddy" just as Charles and Murray did, and indeed she thought of him as her father. But some part of her clung to England, for though she had lived in America since she was two years old she insisted on calling Mrs. Oakenfeld "Mum" instead of "Mom." In fact all the children called Mrs. Oakenfeld "Mum," but only Susan said it with an English accent—a habit for which Charles chided her constantly.

"I say, Mum," Susan said again, ignoring her middle brother, (who, as usual, had his nose buried in some boring-looking science magazine). "The Bay of Eternity is a queer name for a place. It sounds positively Victorian."

"Don't say 'Victorian,'" Charles said, drawing out the second syllable somewhat longer than his sister had, then turning a page in his magazine—which, in fact, wasn't a magazine at all, but a catalog that offered replacement parts for old radios. The previous summer Charles had developed a passion for what he called "antiquated technology," and the bedroom he shared with Murray was overrun with half-assembled (or, more accurately, half-disassembled) radios and telephones and one ancient television whose console was nearly as big as his dresser, even though the screen was smaller than the one on his father's laptop. "It's affected," Charles added and flipped another page.

"It does sound a bit qu-quaint," Mrs. Oakenfeld said (though Susan was sure she'd been going to say "queer"). "But I think perhaps you shouldn't mention it to Uncle Farley. He might not see it that way."

Susan stuck out the side of her cheek with her tongue, as she often did when she was considering her options. She had pale thin cheeks and very short dark hair, so the lump her tongue made was quite pronounced.

"Does Uncle Farley have a telly?" she said finally.

"I believe they have television in Canada," Mrs. Oakenfeld said.

"I meant, does he have cable?"

Now Mrs. Oakenfeld understood. In addition to reading copious amounts of English literature—which is where she'd picked up somewhat affected words like "queer" and "Victorian"—her eldest child habitually tuned in to BBC World in order to keep her accent in top polish. She was especially fond of the news, and had been frustrated by not being allowed to watch it in recent days.

"I'll make you a deal," Mrs. Oakenfeld said. "If you go up to Uncle Farley's without any fuss, I'll see that you're provided with all the quality British programming you can watch."

A siren sounded in the street below the Oakenfelds' apartment, and the conversation lulled.

Susan's cheek bulged as though she were sucking on a golf ball. Part of her was contemplating a move to a house she'd never seen inhabited by an uncle she'd never met, and part of her was contemplating just what, exactly, the siren in the street might indicate. It was a boggling proposition, and more than a little frightening, and only the strained expression on Mrs. Oakenfeld's face kept Susan from giving her mother the third degree—although Susan claimed to have been waiting to start debating for three years, it was generally agreed in the Oakenfeld household that Susan had been very actively waiting, frequently annoying her parents and Charles with her cross-examinations.

"I suppose it will have to do," she said eventually. And she shook her mother's hand to seal the deal.

Charles turned a page noisily, but didn't say anything. As the well-behaved middle child, he was all too used to no one asking what he wanted.

—by Dale Peck

10. Susan's relationship with her brother Charles is best described as

A. close and friendly

B. conflicted

C. disturbed

D. loving

11. Which of the following sequences presents events from the passage in the order in which they occurred?

A. A siren sounded in the street below; Murray ran off to pack; Charles turned a page noisily

B. Susan's cheek bulged; Charles turned a page noisily; Murray ran off to pack his suitcase

C. A siren sounded in the street below; Susan shook her mother's hand; the towers came down

D. The towers came down; Murray ran off to pack; a siren sounded in the street below

12. Which of the following titles would also be an appropriate title for this story?

A. Weird Uncle Robinson

B. Pelicans and Puffins

C. A Hard Life

D. Fresh Start

Read the following passage to answer questions 13 to 16.

THEY DIDN'T KNOW HOCKEY

Dan Hawley snagged the goalie's pass-out just inside the blue line and whirled away with the puck. Judge, the opposing centre, swooped in and tried to check him, but Dan hurdled Judge's stick, shot the rubber ahead and snapped it up again a moment later as he raced down the middle lane with Judge hard at his heels.

There was less than a minute to play and the score was tied with the teams nearing the limit of their overtime. The visiting Owls would be well satisfied with a tie, but Dan Hawley knew as well as anyone in the rink that anything but a win on home ice would be almost fatal to the Panthers' chances of grabbing the league title.

He streaked toward the Owl goal with the crowd whooping in a frenzy. There was an imploring, hysterical note in the roar of the mob. The Panther fans were begging for that goal; the one goal that would squeeze out a win; the goal that seemed impossible to get and that must be scored within the next fifty seconds, if it was to be scored at all.

Dan was tired, for it had been a long, grim game, and bush-league amateurs are expected to go the distance. He could hear the click and chop of Judge's skates as the Owl centre tried to overhaul him, but Dan knew he could out-foot Judge. He wasn't worrying about that.

But this next scoring play. It had to click. It had to be perfect. There mustn't be a slip-up. If it missed, there wouldn't be time for another. And both of his wings were covered.

The Owls had a hard-hitting defence. And their goalie was smart. Dan streaked in and fired from the outside.

It was a hard, low, wicked shot, but the high-pitched roar of the crowd changed to a long, deep groan. You couldn't beat the Owl goalie on long shots. Everyone knew that. And this shot, moreover, was wide of the net.

The puck spanked against the rear boards with a thud that could be heard the length of the rink.

The left defenceman swung around. And the Owl left winger, covering his check along the boards, began hotfooting it into the corner to pick up the rebound.

But Dan Hawley was already sifting through for that same rebound. He had shot purposely wide; he knew the exact angle at which the puck would ricochet from the boards; he knew exactly where he could pick it up.

It was perfectly timed. He was in like a streak. He got his stick on the puck as it skimmed across the ice on its rebound from the boards. And in the same motion, he pivoted and laid down a swift pass to his uncovered right winger, Ben Borstall.

The play had pulled all the Owls out of position. Borstall swooped in, went right to the net, saw that Steve O'Hara, the left winger, was uncovered and backing him up. Borstall faked a shot that pulled the goalie over, then banged the puck over to O'Hara.

And O'Hara socked the rubber into the upper corner for the perfect goal.

The crowd went wild. They went stark raving mad with joy, seemed ready to tear down the rink in their enthusiasm. They were still in a frenzy of rejoicing when the game ended a few moments later. A mob of fans carried O'Hara off the ice. And scores of them crowded around Ben Borstall, pounding him on the back.

"Ben deserves credit too, don't forget!" bellowed one of the fans. "O'Hara scored that goal all right, but Ben gave him the pass."

A lot of people had nice things to say to Dan Hawley, too. "Nice game, Dan" "You were sure flyin' out there tonight, Dan." But for that matter every member of the team came in for his share of hero worship.

O'Hara, however, occupied the limelight. Wasn't he the league's leading scorer? And hadn't he banged home the winning goal?

"We won't be able to keep him here very long," said someone. "Some of the pro teams will be after him before we know it. A goal-getter like O'Hara would make good anywhere."

Dan Hawley, getting out of his uniform in the dressing room, grinned cynically. After all, what did the average fan know about hockey strategy? So far as Dan was concerned, he didn't care who got the credit, as long as the Panthers won the game.

—by Leslie McFarlane

13. The statement "'We won't be able to keep him here very long,'" implies that Steve O'Hara
    A. wants to be a top goal scorer
    B. is good enough to play pro hockey
    C. has to think about a college scholarship
    D. would want more money to stay with the Panthers

14. Which of the following statements best illustrates Dan Hawley's character?
    A. "Dan knew he could out-foot Judge"
    B. "he knew the exact angle at which the puck would ricochet"
    C. "'You were sure flyin' out there tonight'"
    D. "he didn't care who got the credit"

15. The highest-skilled hockey player in this passage is most likely

   A. Judge

   B. Dan Hawley

   C. Ben Borstall

   D. Steve O'Hara

16. The mood the writer establishes in this passage is one of

   A. satisfaction

   B. excitement

   C. frustration

   D. happiness

Read the following passage to answer questions 17 to 24.

IN SEARCH OF SANTA

For centuries the world's most heroic scientists have challenged the mystery of Kris Kringle, but none have succeeded in uncovering the location of his secret polar fortress. That's why I considered it a unique privilege to be invited to join a new expedition to uncover the truth at last, captained by none other than scientific giant Sir Davis Thighton – the world's most accomplished corpulent explorer.

Sir Davis is of an ilk rare among today's namby-pamby researchers. He alone has the courage to turn every prevailing theory about Father Christmas on its head. "The North Pole is indeed Kringle's hiding place," Sir Davis told me when I met him in his Sydney office. "However the North Pole is not, in fact, boreal."

His loyal lieutenant Sarabjit placed a compass on the desk between us. "In the business of magnetism," explained Sir Davis, one eye narrowing behind his monocle, "like repels like." Since the north end of a compass needle invariably indicates the Arctic, he reasoned the pole there must be magnetically southern. And, in a leap of intuition that distinguishes geniuses like Sir Davis from the riff-raff of the Hawkings and Newtons of this world, he concluded that the secret compound of Father Christmas must therefore be somewhere in the Antarctic.

"Google Maps has revealed nothing unusual on the surface" reported Sir Davis, indicating his pink iBook, "which is why we now believe our quarry lies beneath the glaciers. Thus, we will descend through a crevasse to the continent itself."

He introduced the platoon of Nepalese sherpas in yak-hair jackets milling by the mantel. It was Sir Davis's theory that the sherpas' renowned mountaineering expertise could be turned to our advantage during our icy descent by inverting their faculties. To demonstrate, Sarabjit affixed devices behind the sherpas' ears designed to rotate the sense of balance by one hundred eighty degrees.

The sherpas fell down, and one of them threw up.

"How does it feel to be part of the noble pursuit of scientific truth?" I asked them, but received nothing printable in reply.

Although reluctant, I was obliged by the trained sense of integrity deep inside my journalistic giblets to remind Sir Davis that not all of his previous expeditions had come off well, including his ultimately unsuccessful attempt to find Aztec gold in a Melbourne shopping mall. "We were close," Sir Davis assured me. "Besides, this is no mere trinket hunt. This time we seek to penetrate the ultimate Christmas enigma!"

No expense had been spared to equip us. Sarabjit gave me a parka that was edible in case of crisis, and a pair of heated mittens that could be powered by my own urine. We were also outfitted with helmets and radios but, due to satellite interference, our test transmissions were overlaid by Swedish pop music. There was some confusion while the sherpas asked why Sir Davis kept threatening to break their hearts.

Then, in gesture worthy of Scott, the great man nodded, and the palpable aura of his tenacious spirit wafted over me in an inspiring funk. "Our icebreaker awaits!"

I asked how we would travel to the harbour.

"We're jumping on a bus, actually," admitted Sir Davis with a cough. "Rather blew the budget with these radio helmets, don't you know."

And so we stand now assembled at the bus stop outside of Sir Davis's office, tapping our toes to Swedish pop, and ready to face the worst that Antarctica can muster in defence of Santa's secret hiding place. Sarabjit struggles to keep the packhorses calm despite the constant flow of traffic a few metres away, which has already claimed two dizzy sherpas. As the expedition's departure looms, I cannot help but find Sir Davis's optimism contagious. Father Christmas: watch out!

—by Matthew Frederick Davis Hemming

17. When he describes Sir Davis Thighton as "corpulent," the writer is implying that he is

    A. extremely wealthy

    B. a well-known explorer

    C. a Santa Claus look-alike

    D. interested in scientific proof

18. By referring to other researchers as "namby-pamby" the writer is suggesting that Sir Davis

    A. is not afraid to face danger

    B. is more scientific in his research

    C. carefully examines every possibility

    D. enjoys the experience of exploration

19. The narrator probably refers to Santa Claus by several different names because he

    A. is relating to an idea

    B. is not sure of his real name

    C. likes all the different names

    D. wants to be politically correct

20. Sir Davis chose sherpas to assist in his expedition to the South Pole because he reasoned that it was possible to

   A. rotate their sense of balance

   B. reverse their sense of direction

   C. teach them to descend crevasses

   D. utilize their mountaineering skills

21. In this story, the character Sir Davis Thighton is **best** described as

   A. spiteful

   B. optimistic

   C. courageous

   D. extravagant

22. Given the ending of this story, it is most likely that Father Christmas will

   A. continue to elude discovery

   B. be discovered in Antarctica

   C. move to another place to live

   D. become friends with the narrator

23. The fact that Sir Davis was looking for "Aztec gold in a Melbourne shopping mall" suggests that

   A. he is not serious about his explorations

   B. the narrator is also looking for Aztec gold

   C. he does not know where to find Aztec gold

   D. his exploration skills are somewhat in doubt

24. The narrator was thrilled to be included in the expedition because

   A. Sir Davis was one of the world's bravest explorers

   B. the expedition was bound to be very exciting

   C. he had never been to Antarctica before

   D. he wanted to find where Santa lives

ANSWERS AND SOLUTIONS—UNIT TEST

1. WR	7. D	13. B	19. A
2. D	8. WR	14. D	20. D
3. C	9. D	15. B	21. B
4. B	10. B	16. B	22. A
5. WR	11. D	17. C	23. D
6. D	12. D	18. A	24. D

1. WRITTEN RESPONSE

The parents have let their own dreams determine what path their son's life will take. When he follows that path, they experience joy and pride at his success. Warren is too obedient a son to disrupt their happiness, although he is very unhappy with the direction his life has taken.

2. D

The parents' pride in Warren's career is not shared by their son. Although he is silent and accepting and says "nothing," the reader is led to understand Warren's unhappiness and feelings of being trapped by the poet's reference to a caged bear. This is further underscored by the image of strong fists clenched in rage. Warren "said nothing," not because he is timid but because he does not wish to hurt his parents. The poet does not suggest that Warren is bored—just unhappy.

3. C

By using mainly pronouns in the story ("he," "him," and "his"), the poet minimizes Warren's identity to show that his desires and goals were never considered by his parents.

4. B

Warren knows how hard his parents have worked, and even though his dream is not theirs, he says nothing in order not to destroy their happiness.

5. WRITTEN RESPONSE

Using the word "milk" references the parents' rural upbringing. A lot can be told about where people come from by their vocabulary and expressions. Using the word "milk" rather than other words like *snow* or *chalk* to describe *white*, the poet indicates yet another reality of the parent's world. The shirt is described from their own perspective, which is limited to the farm on which they have spent their lives.

6. D

For the parents, this reversal of their pattern (jeans on work days and a white shirt on Sundays) is worth marvelling at. It symbolizes the realization of their dream for their son to escape life on the farm.

7. D

After labouring on the farm for so long and feeling that they themselves would like to escape that life, Warren's parents assume that their son wants the same thing. In order for him to be able to get a job that does not involve working the land, they send him to school, at great sacrifice to themselves. They believe this will lead to a better life for their son than the life they have lived.

8. **WRITTEN RESPONSE**

The best quotation to illustrate Warren's dissatisfaction in his job is "his axe-hewn hands upon the paper bills / aching with empty strength and throttled range." The poet waits until the last stanza to give us a glimpse of Warren himself. Until them, the focus of the poem has been on Warren's parents. In the last verse, the reader discovers for the first time how Warren feels about his job. The verb "aching" indicates that he is in pain, and the words "empty" and "throttled" suggest that Warren feels dissatisfied and restrained by his job and would prefer to be working on the farm. He does not want the life his parents have chosen for him.

9. **D**

The negative way in which the poet describes how the parents feel about the farm and the use of the word "passport" suggest that they wish they could have escaped the farm life.

10. **B**

There are several situations in the passage that suggest that Susan's relationship with her brother Charles involves conflict.
He chides her for her accent and vocabulary, and in turn, she ignores him. The relationship as it is depicted in the passage could not be described as friendly or loving, and there is also no suggestion that it is disturbed.

11. **D**

The towers came down, Murray ran off to pack, and a siren sounded in the street below.

12. **D**

"Fresh Start" is the best alternative title for this story. The children are moving out of New York City for a fresh start in Canada.

13. **B**

The statement implies that because he is very good at scoring goals, Steve O'Hara may be recruited to play for a professional hockey team.

14. **D**

The phrase "he didn't care who got the credit" **best** illustrates Dan's character. Dan is an unselfish player who is more concerned about his team's success than about receiving personal recognition from the fans.

15. **B**

Dan's ability to skate quickly and set up goals probably makes him the most highly skilled player.

16. **B**

The mood of a story is the feeling or attitude that is conveyed through the writer's choice of vocabulary, setting, and character descriptions. In this passage, a mood of excitement is established through the use of such phrases as "whooping in a frenzy" and " The crowd went wild."

17. **C**

Corpulent means to have a large, bulky body. The writer is suggesting that Sir Davis has a similar physique to that of Santa Claus.

Sir Davis is a successful explorer, and he appears to be looking for scientific proof that Santa exists, but these do not relate to the fact that he is corpulent. In the story, there is little evidence to support the idea that Sir Davis is wealthy.

18. **A**

When the writer states that Sir Davis "is rare among today's namby-pamby researchers," he is suggesting that he is not afraid to face danger. The description "namby-pamby" means weak or lacking in character.

19. A

The entire story relates to the idea of trying to find Santa. The narrator refers to him by his various names in order to express that Santa has many names that can be used interchangeably, but they all refer to the same man. There is no evidence that the narrator is unsure of Santa's real name, wants to be politically correct, or likes all the different names.

20. D

Sir Davis reasoned that the sherpas' "renowned mountaineering expertise" could be used to the advantage of the expedition by "inverting their faculties." In order to do this, he fixed a device behind their ears that would rotate their balance 180 degrees. The device would assist the sherpas in descending crevasses and would rotate their sense of balance, but these are not the reasons why Sir Davis chose sherpas for his expedition, rather, he was hoping to make use of the their famous mountaineering skills.

21. B

In spite of setbacks in other expeditions, Sir Davis optimistically continues to pursue all avenues in his search for Santa. He has spent all his money in this search, but he has not demonstrated particular courage. Overall, Sir Davis' character can best be described as optimistic, as the narrator suggests when he states, "I cannot help but find Sir Davis's optimism contagious."

22. A

Even though the narrator ends the story with "Father Christmas: watch out!" it is most probable that Father Christmas will continue to elude those trying to find his lair, especially since there is no proof for any specific location where he might live. There is no evidence that Father Christmas lives at the South Pole, so it is unlikely he will be found there, nor is it likely that he will move, or that he and the narrator will become friends.

23. D

Since Melbourne is in Australia and Aztec gold would be found in Mexico, it is unlikely that the gold would be found in Australia. The suggestion that an explorer would be looking for Aztec gold in a Melbourne shopping mall further supports the idea that this piece of writing is satirical and should not be taken seriously.

24. D

The narrator states that he "considered it a unique privilege to be invited to join a new expedition to uncover the truth at last."
Since the narrator wanted to help discover Father Christmas' hiding place, it can be assumed that he wanted to know where Santa lived. The other alternatives give accurate information, but they are not the main reasons why the narrator was excited to join the expedition.

NOTES

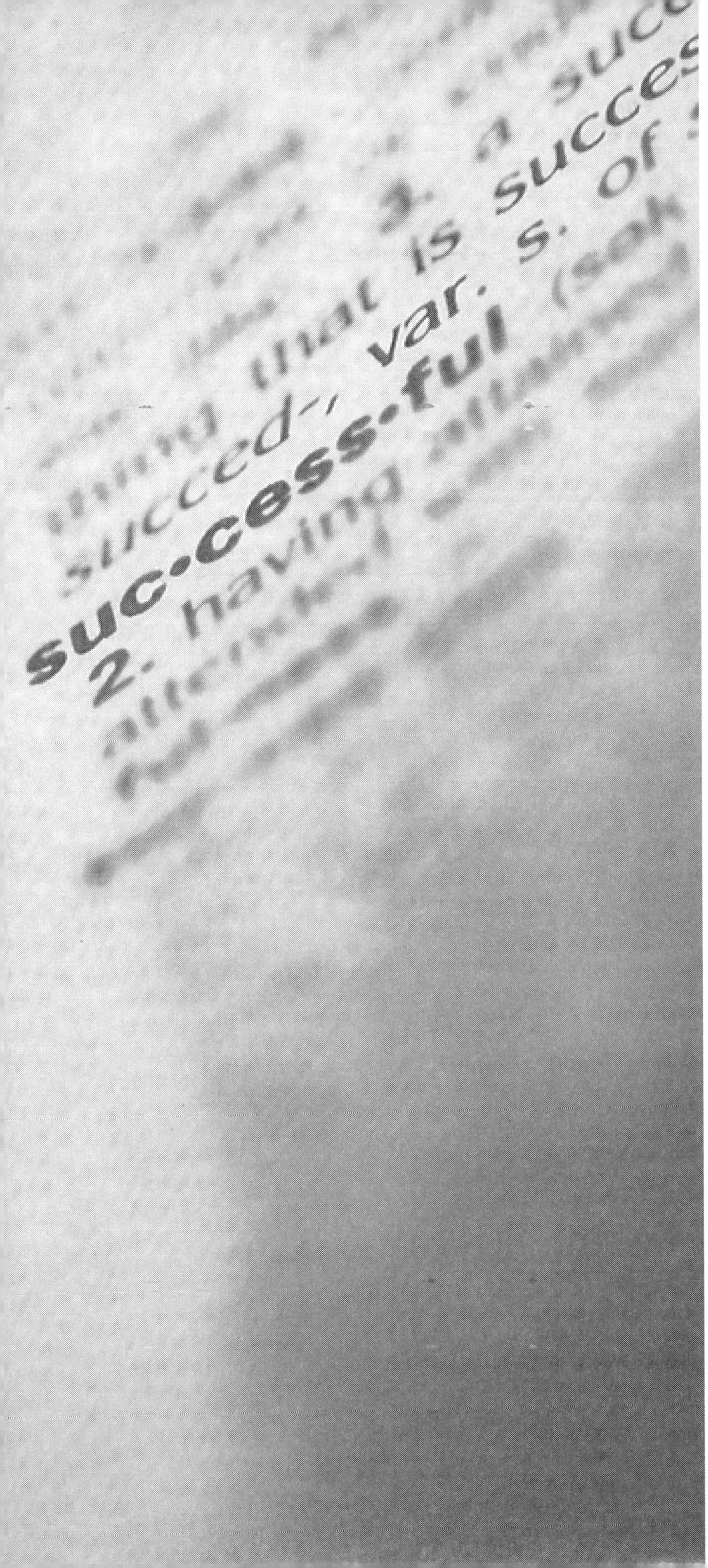

Vocabulary and Grammar

VOCABULARY AND GRAMMAR
TABLE OF CORRELATIONS

Specific Outcome		Practice Questions	Unit Test Questions
General Outcome - Correlations Specific Outcome			
Specific Outomces - Correlations Specific Outcome			
9R3.1	automatically understand most words in several different reading contexts	13, 15, 16, 17, 21	1, 2, 4, 6, 8, 10, 11, 12, 14
9R3.2	use appropriate decoding strategies to read and understand unfamiliar words	11, 14, 19, 22	5, 7, 15
9R3.3	identify and use several different strategies to expand vocabulary	5, 6, 8, 9	9
9W3.1	use knowledge of spelling rules and patterns, several different types of resources, and appropriate strategies to spell familiar and new words correctly	1, 2, 7	19, 20, 21, 22, 23
9W3.2	build vocabulary for writing by confirming word meaning(s) and reviewing word choice, using several different types of resources and strategies, as appropriate for the purpose		3, 13
9W3.3	students will use punctuation correctly to communicate their intended meaning	18, 20	15, 16
9W3.4	use grammar conventions correctly to communicate intended meaning clearly	3, 4, 10, 12	17, 18
9W3.5	students will proofread and correct their writing, using guidelines developed with the teacher and peers		

VOCABULARY AND GRAMMAR

Vocabulary and grammar are both essential for reading and writing. If you have ever tried learning another language, you know how important vocabulary is to understanding what is being said. Learning a different language enables you to communicate with people you would not otherwise be able to communicate with. Each word you learn gives you more power to be able to communicate your needs and wants in that language. Even though you are fluent in English, you are still learning the language, and increasing your vocabulary is an ongoing process. When you increase the number of words you know, you increase the subjects and topics you can understand and discuss.

Grammar is connected to vocabulary. Grammar allows you to use your vocabulary properly. Correct grammar allows you to communicate your ideas clearly. It may seem as though you can be successful at grammar simply by following its rules and guidelines. Following the rules of grammar is important, but it is just important to learn grammar through reading. The more observant you are about the grammar you read in any text, the better you will understand it when the time comes for you to write.

In this section, strategies you can use to expand your vocabulary will be discussed. This section will also show you how to use vocabulary properly by using correct grammar.

ON 9R3.3   Identify and use several different strategies to expand vocabulary

PERSONAL DICTIONARIES

A personal dictionary is a list of words and phrases you encounter at school or on your own. If you keep the list of words and their definitions in a coil notebook or a binder, the list is flexible and can grow as you progress through high school and beyond. Any words you think are important or that you might like to use in your own writing are words that can go into the dictionary. Words your teacher emphasizes are also good words to record in your dictionary. A personal dictionary is great because it is individualized; words you know well and use often do not need to be in the dictionary.

Occasionally you should flip through your list, especially when planning a piece of writing. Try using the words in your dictionary in your everyday speech. The more you use a word, the better you will remember it in the long term. Actually using the words and phrases will help you internalize some of the vocabulary.

Word quizzes and games, crossword puzzles, and game shows that test language knowledge are all useful and fun methods to increase your vocabulary.

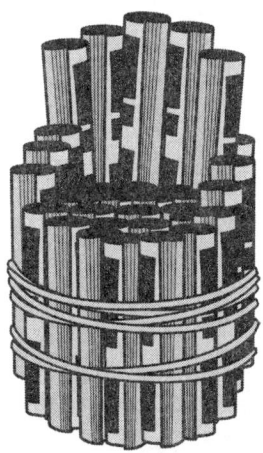

ENGLISH AND OTHER LANGUAGES

English is a language of borrowed words. The majority of English words have been derived from Greek, Latin, or Anglo-Saxon. As the English language spread throughout the world through travel, trade, and settlement, many other cultures contributed words to it.

Phrases

French, Latin, and Spanish phrases have become common in the English language. The following examples are used commonly in everyday speech:

French

à la carte: according to the menu; ordering individual items from the menu as opposed to complete dinners

bon voyage: have a good trip

c'est la vie: such is life

toute de suite: immediately

Latin

e pluribus unum: one from many

ad nauseum: to the point of disgust

mea culpa: my fault

status quo: the way things are

sub rosa: secret or confidential

Spanish

hasta la vista: see you later

mi casa es su casa: my house is your house

EXPLORING WORD FAMILIES USING GRAPHICS

The study of the origin and history of words is called *etymology*. Basic word derivation information is provided in any good dictionary. If you check the front section of the dictionary, you will find an abbreviation key that will explain the abbreviations used in the derivation portion of the entry.

Examples

Gk = Greek

It = Italian

Related words or word families (from the same root) can also be explored as a strategy for expanding your vocabulary. You could use a graphic organizer to track and expand a word, as illustrated in the example that follows.

Word derivation shown in dictionary:

master [L. *magister*: akin to L. magnus great –] 1. a male teacher 2. a person holding an academic degree higher than a bachelor's but lower than a doctor's.

Word family derivation shown in graphic diagram:

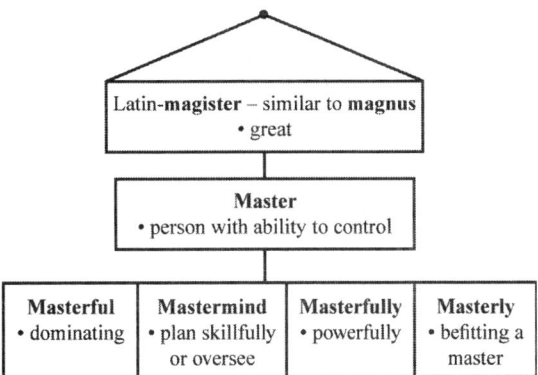

MULTIPLE-MEANING WORDS

Words can have more than one meaning and often have meanings that are quite different from each other. The word *break*, for instance, can be used multiple ways: break the glass, coffee break, "Give me a break," break some news, break the silence, and so on.

Homographs or *multiple-meaning words* are words that share the same spelling but have different meanings. Sometimes the words are pronounced differently, but when you read them, you can determine their meaning from the context.

Example

- *well* (noun): a hole drilled into the ground

- *well* (adverb): in good health

- I was feeling *well* enough to help my father drill a new *well*.

Example

- *sound* (adjective): untroubled, strong, secure, sensible, free from injury

- *sound* (noun): something heard as noise or musical tones

- *sound* (verb): to find out someone's thoughts or feelings

- *sound* (noun): a narrow passage of water

- I was awoken from a *sound* sleep by the *sound* of the distant drums from across   Puget *Sound*.

As these sentences demonstrate, it is usually possible to figure out the meaning of a multiple-meaning word when you see the word in context.

ON 9W3.1   Use knowledge of spelling rules and patterns, several different types of resources, and appropriate strategies to spell familiar and new words correctly

SPELLING

Spelling is one of the most essential aspects of vocabulary and grammar. By Grade 9, you have been introduced to the most common English spelling patterns, have learned basic spelling rules, and have been taught to use spelling resources like dictionaries and the spell-check feature on a computer. Draw upon that knowledge to spell words correctly as you use them in your writing. Keep personal lists for correct spelling, such as:

- words misspelled in writing assignments
- science terms
- math terms
- social studies words

Aim to spell the words you use correctly, and not only when you are doing school assignments. Correct spelling shows that you are a good communicator. The following section will provide some spelling review.

BASIC SPELLING RULES

ei or ie

- If the sound is a long e, put i before e except after c.
- If the sound is a long *a* (as in weigh), reverse this order.

Examples

- long *e*: niece, thief, piece, perceive, receipt, receive
- long *a*: weight, vein, sleigh, veil, neighbour
- exceptions: height, science, either, their, weird

Doubling the Consonant

If the word is one syllable with one vowel and one final consonant, **double** the final consonant before an ending (except when the word ends in *x*).

Examples

- shop + *-ed* = shopped
- wet + *-est* = wettest
- sun + *-y* = sunny
- tar + *-ed* = tarred
- wax + *-ed* = waxed

In words of more than one syllable, follow this rule if the final syllable is stressed.

Examples

begin + *-ing* = beginning

occur + *-ed* = occurred

permit + *-ing* = permitting

e + Ending with a Vowel

If the base word ends in a silent *e*, drop the *e* before adding an ending that begins with a vowel.

Examples

- excite + *-able* = excitable
- love + *-ing* = loving

Exceptions are words that end in *ce* or *ge*; then the *e* stays.

Examples

- courage + *-ous* = courageous
- change + *-able* = changeable
- notice + *-able* = noticeable

Changing *y* to *i*

When the base word ends in *y*, change the *y* to *i* before adding endings.

Examples

- baby + *-es* = babies
- carry + *-es* = carries
- try + *-ed* = tried

Forming Noun Plurals

Generally, you add *-s* to a noun to make it plural. However, there are a few exceptions you need to learn:

If the noun ends in *s*, *ss*, *ch*, *sh*, *x*, or *z*, you add *-es*.

Examples

- glass*es*
- bush*es*
- fox*es*

If the noun ends in *y* with a consonant in front, you change the *y* to *i* and add *-es*.

Examples

- baby to bab*ies*
- sky to sk*ies*

Some nouns ending in *f* are changed to *v* before adding *-es*.

Examples

- leaf to lea*ves*
- dwarf to dwar*ves*

If the noun ends in *o* with a consonant in front of the *o*, you add *-es* unless the noun is a musical term.

Examples

- potato to potato*es*
- tomato to tomato*es*

but

- piano to piano*s* (no *-es*)

Some words change into different words in the plural. These plurals are called *irregular*.

Examples

- mouse = mice
- tooth = teeth

Some words stay the same in the plural.

Examples

- sheep = sheep
- deer = deer
- fish = fish

ROOTS, AFFIXES, AND SYLLABLES

Root: the most basic part of a word

The root word *act* is related to the words *reaction* and *transaction*.

Affix: added to a root word to form a new word

The spelling of a root may change when an affix is added:

- excite*ment*   no change
- excit*ing*   silent *e* dropped

prefix: added onto beginning of word:

- *pro*active
- *re*action

suffix: added onto end of word:

- practi*cal*
- beaut*ify*

Syllable: word part containing a single vowel sound

- beau / ti / fy   three syllables
- con / trast   two syllables

Spelling Tips for Common Prefixes

- -ad sometimes changes to a: amend, arise, ascend
- -ex sometimes changes to e: emission, elastic
- *-in* sometimes changes to
-    il before root words beginning with l: illegal, illogical
-    im before root words beginning with m or p: immovable, immeasurable
-    ir before root words beginning with r: irresponsible

Spelling Rules for Adding Suffixes

Drop the e

Example

- imagine = imaginable
- excite = exciting

Keep the e

Example

- excite = excitement
- notice = noticeable

Double the final consonant (usually when it is preceded by a short vowel)

Example

- admit = admitted
- sag = sagged

Do not double the final consonant

Example

- defeat = defeated
- regret = regretful
- invert = inverting

Change the y to i

Example

- friendly = friendliness
- carry = carried

Do not change the y to i

Example

- enjoy = enjoying
- cry = crying

Using syllables to break a word into natural parts helps you spell correctly.

Example

- dis / ap / point / ment

Syllable rules for diving words into parts:

after a prefix: dis/

between double consonants: ap / point

before a suffix: /ment

Syllables and Inflection

Pay attention to the pronunciation of the word *present* in the following two sentences.

Example

- Sylvia must *present* her report on Tuesday.
- The correct pronunciation is pr‾e-sent′

Example

- The teacher saw that everyone was *present*.
- The correct pronunciation is pr˘e-sent

The word *present* sounds different in each of the sentences, but both words are spelled the same. Another word for different pronunciation is *inflection*.

Word Meaning and Correct Spelling

Being unclear on word meanings can trip up your spelling. The most common examples of this involve homonyms or homophones (words that sound the same) and incorrect usage of a word.

Homonyms (Homophones):

its/it's

- The word *its* is a possessive pronoun and has no apostrophe.
- The cat injured *its* tail.
- The word *it's* is a contraction of the words *it* and *is*.
- *It's* a long way to my house from the school.
- their/there/they're

The word *their* indicates possession of something.

- Tomorrow we are going to *their* new house.

The word *there* refers to the location of something.

- I put your lunch over *there*.
- The word *they're* is a contraction of the words *they* and *are*.
- Beth and Tim said *they're* coming.

to/too/two

The word *to* is a preposition used to indicate direction or contact.

- Are you going *to* the track meet?

The word *too* is used to indicate excess or as another way of saying *also* or *as well as*.

- Last night I ate *too* much candy.

She is able to compete, *too*.

- The word *two* refers to the number *2*.

Gus made *two* lists.

whose/who's

- The word *whose* is used to indicate possession.
- I do not know whose wallet is missing.
- The word *who's* is a contraction of the words *who* and *is*.
- Who's willing to help pick up this litter?

INCORRECT USAGE

The following pairs of words are often confused. Computer spellcheckers will not usually catch these mistakes, so be sure to look out for them in your writing:

accept/except

- Everyone *except* Melody was pleased to *accept* their award.

then/than

- *Then* she told me she would rather go to the movies with me *than* with Susan.
- *Then*: adverb of time
- *Than*: conjunction of comparison

Wrong: She likes me better *then* Susan.

lose/loose

- If your watch comes *loose*, you might *lose* it.

The following sentence will help you remember the difference between *lose* and *loose*:

- You lose the extra "o" when you write "lose" instead of "loose."

FREQUENTLY MISSPELLED WORDS

Certain words in the English language are frequently misspelled, even by people who see themselves as good spellers. Some of these are listed below. Try to master them now. The older you become, the harder it will be to change faulty spelling patterns.

The tricky parts of these words have been underlined for you.

across	experience	possession
argument	foreign	really
calendar	government	relevant
column	grateful	restaurant
committed	height	rhyme
conscience	immediate	rhythm
definitely	lightning	schedule
discipline	mischievous	separate
embarrass	neighbour	until
equipment	occasionally	weird

READING FAMILIAR WORDS

By Grade 9, you are in a position to understand most of the vocabulary you encounter in text, whether it is personal text online, literature you read at school, or the more subject-specific vocabulary used in textbooks and research references. Let's examine the notion of familiar vocabulary under three categories: *slang*, *jargon*, and *subject-specific terminology*.

SLANG

Slang words are words used by a certain group of people, such as teenagers. Slang differs from jargon in the sense that slang is regarded as very casual language, whereas jargon is usually used by professionals to discuss something specific. Slang expressions tend to come and go. For example, in the 1950s, a "hot rod" referred to a powerful car, while today the term is used very rarely and may not be used to refer to a car.

JARGON

Jargon refers to a specialized set of words and phrases commonly understood by a group, such as members of a profession, hobby, or field of study. For example, imagine going to the dentist. If, after examining your teeth and X-rays, the dentist tells you that you have a "cary on your 1-3," you would not know what she is talking about. She is using jargon that is specific to dentists, and she would have to explain to you that she has found a cavity in one of your teeth.

Jargon is common among different professions and can be confusing to someone who does not belong to the special group for whom the jargon has meaning.

ONLINE LANGUAGE

Students in school today are, for the most part, computer literate. The Internet is still a new technology, and Internet jargon is always growing and changing. Take, for example, the blog. Words that have to do with blogs, such as *blogosphere*, *flaming*, and *vlogs* (video blogs), are all Internet-specific jargon words not everyone will understand.

In all forms of online writing, shorthand is frequently used. *Leetspeak* is often used to indicate emotions or actions that would take a long time to type out conventionally. For example, rather than saying "I'm laughing out loud" or trying to indicate laughter by typing "ha ha ha," many people online just type out "lol." This makes online conversation faster and more similar to real-time conversation. Leetspeak has become built in to online communication. It is also easily adapted to text messaging on cellphones. It is strongly discouraged, however, in any formal writing for school or work.

SUBJECT-SPECIFIC TERMINOLOGY

As a student, you are required to read all the time in a variety of subjects. Most of these subjects are presented in units. Most units, no matter what the subject is, will have some terms you will have to learn. Before you can master the unit, you must understand central vocabulary terms. Often, subject-specific terminology is introduced at the beginning of a new unit or chapter.

For instance, before beginning a poetry unit, most English teachers will review terms such as *sonnet*, *lyric*, *metaphor*, *onomatopoeia*, and so on, because these terms are often used with respect to poetry.

Terminology can have totally different meanings from one subject to another. Here are a few examples from math and science:

Word/Term	Math	Science
base	side or face of a polygon from which an altitude rises	chemical compound that acts with an acid to form a salt
formula	equation that shows a general relationship	chemical or physical equation
power	notation of a number with a base and an exponent such as an, where a is called the base and n is called the exponent	mechanical or physical energy
transformation	any mapping of a figure resulting in a change in position, shape, size, or appearance of the figure	the process of metamorphosis, as in caterpillar to butterfly

Subject-specific words that are important are often:

- bolded in math, social studies, and science textbooks
- defined at the beginning of a new chapter
- defined at the bottom of the page or at the back of the textbook
- used by the teacher on the board, overhead, or for assignments
- Learning new words helps you better understand and remember information, ideas, and concepts.

Some strategies for adopting new words are:

- add them to your personal vocabulary list
- learn the meaning of the words in the content area
- practice spelling the words correctly, even if you have to check back in the textbook
- use the words in answers and assignments
- give the words a permanent home in your "mental computer" (brain) so you can retrieve them as needed

It is important to master the subject-specific terminology used in specific content areas if you want to avoid the frustration that goes along with not understanding what the teacher is trying to explain. Take a look at the following tips.

Learn the words first

Before plunging into new learning, learn any terms that will help you comprehend the information better. Use the glossary, see if the term is defined in the text, and list the terms beside their meanings in your notes for quick reference.

Review old words

Learn or review the terms while you are learning the unit. Most subject-specific terminology is not language you use every day, so just learn it as you need it. Refresh your memory as needed during the unit or course, then review the words later when you need them, such as for a final exam.

UNDERSTANDING UNFAMILIAR WORDS

What should you do when you encounter an unfamiliar word as you are reading?

When you read, you automatically decode words. *Decoding* means identifying or understanding meaning. As you read a passage, the familiar words are quite easy to decode because the meaning you know fits appropriately into the sentence or context. If your automatic decoding does not work for a particular word, or if the word is unfamiliar, some of the decoding strategies described below may help you to
understand the word as it is being used in the passage. Understanding the words you read improves your reading comprehension.

DECODING

Read the whole sentence to see if you can guess the meaning of the unknown word. Does your guess make sense, or do the other words in the sentence give you a clue to what the unknown word might be?

- Look for root words. For example, the root word of *simplify* is *simple*.
- Look for compound words. Compound words are made up of two parts; for example, *some* and *thing* becomes *something*.
- Look for word families or chunks within the word. For example, *infatuate* can be broken into easy chunks like *in-fat-u-ate*.
- Sound out the word.
- If possible, look the word up in a dictionary.
- If you are unable to figure out the word, skip the word and try to understand what is being said in the sentence without the word.

The following passages will help you use different strategies in more detail.

WORD ORDER AND PARTS OF SPEECH

Knowing what part of speech a word is can help you understand or recognize how it is being used. The following section lists the basic parts of speech you may be asked to identify.

NOUNS

A noun is a person, place, thing, or idea. There are two types of nouns: *common* and *proper*.

Common Noun: a *general* person, place, thing, or idea. Examples of common nouns are *dog*, *house*, *car*, and *woman*.

Proper Noun: a *particular* person, place, thing, or idea. Examples of proper nouns are *Samuel*, *Europe*, and the *Olympic Games*.

Pronoun: takes the place of a noun. Examples of pronouns are *I*, *we*, *me*, *anybody*, *that*, *this*, and *us*.

Adjective: modifies or describes a noun or pronoun. Examples of adjectives are *red*, *large*, and *loud*.

VERBS

A verb shows action or state of being. There are two types of verbs: *regular* and *irregular.*

Regular Verb: the verb's past tense and past-participle forms end in *-ed*

Example
- played, jumped, hunted

Irregular Verb: the verb's past tense and past-participle forms are modified in different ways

Example
- run (ran), slide (slid), grow (grew)

INFINITIVES

In English, verbs are often listed in their infinitive form; that is, preceded by the word *to.*

Examples
- to run
- to climb
- to seek
- to study

An infinitive can be used as a noun in a sentence.

Example

Sometimes, *to speak* is an unwise choice. (The infinitive *to speak* is used as the noun subject of the sentence.)

PARTICIPLES

A participle is basically a verb used as an adjective. A participle ending in *-ing*, or a present participle, is the most common.

Example

Arriving late, Norma quickly took her seat. (*Arriving* modifies the noun, *Norma.*)

You will also encounter past participles.

Example

Having arrived late, Norma quickly took her seat. (*Having arrived* modifies the noun, *Norma.*)

ADVERBS

An adverb modifies or describes a verb, adjective, or another adverb.

Examples

She ran *quickly*.

I *rarely* eat pizza in the morning.

This is an *extremely* interesting book.

PREPOSITIONS

A preposition is a word placed in front of a noun or pronoun to connect it to another part of the sentence. Examples of prepositions are *to*, *for*, *over*, *by*, *at*, and *from*.

CONJUNCTIONS

A conjunction joins words, phrases, clauses, and sentences. Examples of conjunctions are *and*, *or*, *but*, *either*, and *or*.

INTERJECTIONS

An interjection is a word, remark, or exclamation that expresses some form of emotion.

Examples

Ouch! That hurts.

Oh! I do not know.

Knowing what part of speech a word is and then recognizing its syntax or word order in a sentence pattern can help you to decode a word's meaning. Look at the form of the following words used for different parts of speech:

Verb	Noun	Adjective	Adverb
beautify	beauty	beautiful	beautifully
depend	dependent	dependable	dependably

Now look at how these words might be used in sentences:

The students *beautified* the field behind their new school by planting trees and shrubs.

Figure it out: *Beautified* is a verb, and the suffix *-ified* usually refers to the changing or acting upon of something. The word must mean that the students made the grounds more beautiful by planting trees.

You will be a *dependent* until you turn 18.

Figure it out: *Dependent* is a noun. You know the meaning of the verb *depend*, so *dependent* must mean a person who relics on adults for their care because they are not yet self-sufficient.

In the following excerpt from Lewis Carroll's nonsensical poem "Jabberwocky," you could make some sense of the underlined words just by recognizing the parts of speech and how the words are used. Even though many of the words Carroll uses are not real, you can imagine different meanings for them.

---

from "JABBERWOCKY"

'Twas brillig, and the slithy toves
Did gyre and gimble in the wabe:
All mimsy were the borogoves,
And the mome raths outgrabe.
"Beware the Jabberwock, my son!
The jaws that bite, the claws that catch!
Beware the Jubjub bird, and shun
The frumious Bandersnatch!"
He took his vorpal sword in hand:
Long time the manxome foe he sought—
So rested he by the Tumtum tree,
And stood awhile in thought.
And, as in uffish thought he stood,
The Jabberwock, with eyes of flame,
Came whiffling through the tulgey wood,
And burbled as it came!

—by Lewis Carroll

"Jabberwocky" is a great example of how the context of a word is important. If you saw the word *jabberwock* on its own, you would likely not have any idea of its meaning. Seeing the word in the context of the poem, as in having "jaws that bite," and "claws that catch," you can tell that a jabberwock is probably a kind of monster. The nonsense words Carroll uses do not need to be defined in an exact way. The fun of the poem is in the silly words that sound like they could be real words in English, but which can be interpreted to have any meaning the reader imagines. In many fantasy novels and poems, nonsense words are used when an author wants to refer to new creations of his or her imagination.

USING CONTEXT CLUES TO FIND MEANING

When you are having trouble understanding a word, try looking at the context clues in the surrounding words of the sentence. Often, there will be other words in the sentence that you understand and that add to the meaning of the sentence. There will also be words you are struggling with. Once you have an idea of the context of the word, try substituting a different word into the sentence to see if it makes sense. If the new word agrees with the meaning of the sentence, chances are the word you were struggling with means something similar to the new word you substituted.

Example

Glancing *dispassionately* at his list of instructions, Gordon, with a casual shrug of his shoulders, took his time leaving the office.

Figure it out: The context, especially the words *glancing* and *casual*, suggests that Gordon does not care. Try substituting *carelessly* or *indifferently* for *dispassionately*. Do these words work?

Example

In her white furs, emerald jewellery, and shimmering silver gown, the countess made her *ostentatious* entrance into the Grand Ballroom as the strains of the first waltz wafted from the orchestra pit.

Figure it out: The context of jewels, expensive clothing, and the Grand Ballroom suggest possible substitutions like *showy* or *extravagant* for *ostentatious*. Do these substitutions make sense?

Substituting might not give you the exact definition of a word, but it will get you close. Use the words you know to help you with the words you do not know. Use a dictionary to confirm that your guess is correct. The dictionary will give you a precise answer, but guessing and substituting are important stages of understanding the meaning of a word.

ROOTS, PREFIXES, AND SUFFIXES

Many scholars think that in prehistoric Europe, there may have been a common language called proto-Indo-European; however, as people moved around over many hundreds of years seeking food and grazing lands, they became isolated from each other and, as a result, developed their own languages.

The three main branches of the proto-Indo-European language that have most influenced the development of English are the Germanic, Italic, and Hellenic languages.

The Germanic language branch had the greatest influence on English, but Italian, Latin, French, Spanish, and Greek have all contributed to the development of the English language. To this day, the English language continues to change and grow as it absorbs new words and phrases.

Many English prefixes and suffixes are derived from Greek and Latin. These words become altered and can often lead to new words being invented.

A prefix is defined as one or more syllables added to the beginning of a root word to form a new word. Here are a few examples of prefixes derived from Greek and Latin:

Latin Prefix	Meaning	New Word
ante-	before	anterior, antemeridian (a.m.)
ben-, bon-	good, well	benefit, bonanza
bi-	two	bicycle, binary
mal-	bad, ill	malfunction, malnutrition
migr-	to move, travel	migrate, migration
Greek Prefix	**Meaning**	**New Word**
anti-	against	anticlockwise, anticlimax
auto-	self	automatic, automobile
hemi-	half	hemisphere, hemicycle
tele-	far off	telephone, telepathic
poly-	many	polygon, polygraph

Suffixes have the special job of changing the root word to another part of speech, for example, a verb, a noun, an adjective, or an adverb. Here are a few examples of Latin and Greek suffixes with their purposes:

Latin Suffix	Purpose	Meaning
-age	forms a noun	belongs to (storage)
-ance	forms a noun	state of being (appearance)
-ible, -able	forms an adjective	capable of being (possible)
-ive	forms an adjective	belonging to/quality of (attractive)
-ly	forms an adverb	like/to the extent of (happily)
-ate	forms a verb	to make (alienate)
-fy	forms a verb	to make (simplify)
Greek Suffix	**Purpose**	**Meaning**
-y	forms an abstract noun	state of (e.g., happy)
-ism	forms a noun	act/condition
-ic	forms an adjective	having the nature of (e.g., pathetic)

As you can see, there are more Latin suffixes than there are Greek. As the English language developed, many prefixes, suffixes, and root words from both Latin and Greek were joined together, and the resulting English word is derived from both languages.

Adding a prefix to a root word changes its meaning. For example, the prefixes *pre-*, *post-*, and *ante-* all change the time frame of a root word. *Pre-* and *ante-* both mean "before," while *post-* means "after." Look at the following root words and how their meanings change when a prefix is added:

Root	Meaning	Prefix + Root	New Meaning
Condition	State of person or a thing	Precondition	Something necessary for a result to occur
View	Act of seeing or looking	Preview	An advance showing
Chamber	A room, especially a bedroom	Antechamber	A waiting room
Script	Handwriting	Postscript	A note added to a letter that has already been signed

A *suffix* also adds meaning to a root word or changes it slightly.

The suffixes *-ic*, *-tic*, *-ical*, and *-al* mean "having to do with." When one of these suffixes is added to a root word, the new word takes a different form, including a different spelling. Look at how a suffix affects a root word. Notice also how the spelling of each word is altered, and how each root is changed from a noun to an adjective.

Root	Meaning	Root + Suffix	New Meaning
Economy	Financial system	Economic	To do with the economy
Drama	Plays and theatrical art	Dramatic	Overtly expressive or emotional
Analyse	Examine carefully	Analytical	Logical or reasoning
Structure	A building or other constructed object	Structural	Part of a structure

Root words from Greek and Latin can sometimes appear to be prefixes and suffixes, but they are actually the roots or main parts of the words. Here are some examples of Greek and Latin root words:

Root	Origin	Meaning	Derivations
bio	Greek	life	biography, biology, microbiology
lab	Latin	to work	labour, laboratory, elaborate
phone	Greek	voice, sound	phonograph, telephone, microphone
port	Latin	to carry	portable, transport, transportation

If you take the time to learn the meanings of commonly used prefixes, suffixes, and root words, you can better identify the meanings of words that contain them. This knowledge allows you to break unfamiliar words into meaningful chunks that can be decoded or figured out.

Look at the following examples to help you understand this concept. Remember that prefixes (*pre* = before) are placed before the root word, and suffixes (*suf* = under) are placed after the root word.

atheist = *a-the-ist* = *a* (without), *theo* (God), *ist* (one who) = one who does not believe in God

incredible = *in-cred-i-ble* = in (not), *credibilis* (deserving of belief) = seems to be impossible or unbelievable

circumnavigation = *circum-navigate-ion* = *circum* (around), *navigate* (to travel by ship), *ation* (state of) = the act of travelling around the world

SOUNDING WORDS OUT PHONETICALLY

Another strategy you can use to decode unfamiliar words is to sound words out phonetically by breaking them into smaller parts or syllables. Often, a word will have syllables that are prefixes, roots, and suffixes. Breaking down a word into its smaller parts of meaning is a good strategy for finding the meaning of
that word.

The following example is taken from the poem "The Prelude," by William Wordsworth. Wordsworth is describing the joy and freedom associated with outdoor skating. Because the language of the poem may be unfamiliar to you, some of strategies described earlier in this section will help you understand the more difficult words in the poem, some of which have been underlined to be decoded for meaning after the poem has been read. While you are reading, try and guess the meanings of the underlined words from the context of the poem as well as using the strategies you have learned about prefixes, suffixes, and root words.

"SKATING," FROM THE PRELUDE

—All shod with steel,

We hiss'd along the polish'd ice, in games

Confederate, imitative of the chace

And woodland pleasures, the resounding horn,

The Pack loud bellowing, and the hunted hare.

So through the darkness and the cold we flew,

And not a voice was idle; with the din,

Meanwhile, the precipices rang aloud,

The leafless trees, and every icy crag

Tinkled like iron, while the distant hills

Into the tumult sent an alien sound

Of melancholy, not unnoticed, while the stars

Eastward, were sparkling clear, and in the west

The orange sky of evening died away.

—by William Wordsworth

Word Meanings in "Skating"

Confederate: The word "confederate" is used here as an adjective describing the noun "games." *Con-* as a prefix means *with*, while you might associate *federation* with a group of states or provinces united under one government. Put all that together, and you understand that "games Confederate" means ice games in which all or most of the skaters joined.

Chace: When you read this word in the context of the adjective "imitative," along with the whole propositional phrase "of the chace," and read the next two lines, you understand that the poet is referring to the *chase*, an English foxhunt. The skaters are involved in a *chase*, or probably a form of tag on ice.

Resounding and *bellowing*: These words are being used as adjectives ("resounding horn," "loud bellowing Pack"). When you go back to "imitative of," understand the root words *imitate*, *sound*, and *bellow*, and think about the meaning of the prefix *re-*, you should arrive at meaning. The skaters are sounding pretend horns and baying or barking loudly like a pack of hunting dogs as they chase each other over the ice.

Now try to think of definitions of the next six underlined six words using the clues and questions in the following section.

Din: What does "not a voice was idle" imply about the meaning of the word "din?" What word could you substitute here?

Precipices: What part of speech is this? How is "icy crag" similar to this word? What do the verbs "rang" and "tinkled" tell you about "precipices" and "icy crags?"

Tumult: Could this word be substituted for another underlined word used earlier?

Alien: What part of speech is this? What is the meaning of the word "alien" used as a noun? What would it mean, then, if it were used to describe "sound?"

Melancholy: In the phrase, "alien sound of melancholy," what must be meant by the word "melancholy?" What word suggests it is quite different from the noisy sounds coming from the skaters?

Unnoticed: What is meant by the root word notice? What does the prefix un- do to the meaning of the word? What does placing the word not before the word do to the meaning?

You may use these decoding strategies more consciously at first. Over time, though, you will find that these strategies become an integral part of how you read, and you may find that you use them quickly without thinking about them too much.

SPELLING FOR OTHER PURPOSES

Text messaging, as you probably already know, does not usually promote the best spelling and grammar. The goal in writing a text message is usually to get your message across using the fewest words and letters possible. Never use texting or online language in your formal writing.

VOCABULARY

Expanding your vocabulary has everything to do with using it. The more you use the words you learn, the better they will stick in your head and become part of your everyday speech and writing. Like your reading vocabulary, your writing vocabulary should be a constantly growing body of words that you are incorporating into your writing with increasing confidence.

You should only use words you understand in your writing. If you are looking for a more precise word, check a thesaurus.

The words in a thesaurus are arranged in alphabetical order. Here is an example of an entry for the word "bright."

Example

BRIGHT
Adj (adjectives/synonyms)
1. sunny, fair, mild, balmy; brilliant, vivid, resplendent
2. smart, brainy, brilliant, clever, gifted, talented, sharp, keen
Antonyms
1. dull, flat, dingy, cloudy, faded, leaden, dim, pale, weak, faint
2. slow-witted, dim, slow, thick-headed, bland, desensitized

Do you need a synonym or an antonym? Do you want the literal/denotative meaning ("sunny") or a more connotative (associated) meaning like "brainy?" The thesaurus helps you add variety to your writing, but avoid choosing words simply because they sound more elaborate. A simple word may be your best choice for the situation.

If you are using technical terms or "content" words in something like a research report, do not underestimate the dictionary as a useful reference.

Dictionaries are always a good place to start when you are looking for the meaning of a specialized term. Look for the meaning associated with the specific subject or content area.

BUILDING VOCABULARY

The following list describes different ways to build your vocabulary:

• extensive and varied personal reading

• personal lists of new words and phrases from texts you read

• lists of subject-related words and their definitions

• using new words in conversation

• word games

• classroom word walls

Classroom word walls are interactive and usually involve a weekly or monthly addition to the wall. Each student posts up words they have learned and want to share with the class. Even if word walls are not part of your classroom environment, you can create a mini word wall of your own in the back of your writing or English binder. Jotting words down from different sources in one easy-to-find location may encourage you to actually use the words in your writing.

USING NEW VOCABULARY

It is a good idea to keep personal vocabulary lists at the backs of binders or in separate vocabulary binders. If you learn a new word in any content area, try to remember to add the word and its definition to your list. If the word is an adjective, for instance, record its other forms, too.

Example
- *frugal* (adjective), meaning "reluctant to spend"
- *frugality* (noun form), meaning "a reluctance to spend"

The best way to increase your vocabulary is to start using new words as often as you can after you learn them, in both speaking and writing. This helps you internalize both the words and their meanings.

ON 9W3.3   Students will use punctuation correctly to communicate their intended meaning

PUNCTUATION

Imagine if punctuation did not exist. Reading anything would be extremely tiring. Punctuation ensures that the meaning of the words you have chosen is understood clearly. You can choose your words carefully, but if your punctuation is incorrect, your meaning may be lost or confused. It is a good idea to use the following section to review what you know about punctuation and what you may be unsure about.

APOSTROPHES

Apostrophe with possessives

Most possessives are formed by adding an apostrophe and an -*s*.

Examples
- a girl's smile
- one country's history

The possessive of nouns ending in an "s" sound is formed by adding an apostrophe and an -s.

Examples
- the boss's car

Charles's, Alex's
- The possessive of a plural is formed by adding an apostrophe after the -s of the plural.

Examples

- five girls' smile
- three countries' history

Apostrophe with Contractions

Letters are omitted from common words or phrases such as cannot and does not to become the contractions can't and doesn't. An apostrophe replaces the missing letters.

COMMAS

Commas with Introductory Phrases

Some introductory phrases have previously been mentioned. Other kinds of introductory phrases are also followed by a comma.

Examples

- During the long summer afternoon, we were able to catch up on our work.
- Knowing he was beaten, he conceded defeat.
- Near a small clump of trees, we made our camp.
- As he was running out of money, he cabled home for more.
- In addition, we will need rope and flashlights.

The Serial Comma

Use a comma after all the items in a series.

Examples

- Bring food, extra clothing, a first-aid kit, and matches.
- A dictionary, a thesaurus, and a writing guide may be used for the test.
- A semicolon should be used after each item in the series when the items already include commas.

Example

The men endured a long, hot march; flies, dust, and brackish water; and a raging, howling sandstorm.

Commas to Set Off Appositives

An appositive, a noun or a word or a phrase used as noun, is set off by commas.

Examples

- Our team, the Hornets, is in first place.
- His cousins, the Sinclairs, were all present at the reunion.
- Everyone in Toronto, the home of the Maple Leafs hockey team, is watching the Stanley Cup playoffs.

Commas with Adjectives

When more than one adjective appears in front of a noun, commas are sometimes necessary.

Examples

- fierce, tough dogs
  but
- three fierce, tough dogs
  and
- three fierce, tough old dogs
  and
- three fierce old sheep dogs

Do not put a comma between adjectives that build on each other to modify a noun. Each adjective modifies the noun and adjective group that follows it.

Examples

- four vile yellow plastic figurines
- her beautiful old Georgian townhouse

Cumulative adjectives have a certain order; they cannot be switched around.

- Incorrect: vile four plastic yellow figurines
- Incorrect: beautiful her Georgian old townhouse

Comma to Separate Clauses

When you link two longer independent clauses with a coordinating conjunction such as *and* or *but*, you should use a comma before the conjunction.

Examples

- We completed our tour of the museum by lunchtime, and then we ate lunch in the patio courtyard.
- We enjoyed having our lunch outside, but our picnic came to a sudden stop because of rain.

Other Uses of Commas

Setting off a transition word, phrase, or clause at the beginning of a sentence.

Example

- On my birthday, I expect many presents.
- Separating direct speech from the rest of the sentence

Example

- "I need some new shoes," Paul told his mother.

Before a quotation

Example

- Hamlet's famous speech, "To be or not to be / That is the question" is an example of a soliloquy.

Separating the date and the year

Example

- January 22, 2008

Separating the city and province

Example

- Sudbury, Ontario

Separating the parts of an address

Example

- 2011 Beech Street, Toronto, Ontario

Semicolons

Use to connect independent clauses, rather than creating two sentences, especially when the sentences (independent clauses) are short and related.

Examples

• (two sentences)	Lightning flashed. Thunder shook the valley.
• (compound sentence/two independent clauses)	Lightning flashed, and thunder shook the valley.
• (semicolon)	Lightning flashed; thunder shook the valley.

Colons

Colons can be used in the following situations:

Before a list

Example

- As we made the cake, we added the following ingredients: flour, eggs, sugar, and milk.

Before you use an example that enriches a point or idea you want to make

Example

- I feel that the following point needs to be made: most people do their best at their job.

After the introductory salutation in a formal letter

Example
- Dear Mr. Evans:
- Dear Sir:

Between numbers to tell time

Example
- 7:08 a.m.
- 11:15 p.m.

When used in sentences, a colon must follow an independent clause.
It introduces a list, an explanation, or an appositive (a word or phrase that restates a noun).

Examples
- You should bring the following items: a sleeping bag, a change of clothes, and matches.
- There is only one honest thing to do: admit you made a mistake and apologize.
- His character was summed up in his name: Grad Grind.

The list may be set up in point form. The same rule applies.

Example
- The introductory course will cover three topics:
  algebra
  geometry
  trigonometry

If a list does not follow an independent clause (a complete sentence), no colon is used.

Example
- You must bring a sleeping bag, a change of clothes, and matches. The introductory course will cover
  1. algebra
  2. geometry
  3. trigonometry

Helpful Hint: A simple way of checking colon use is to cover up all the words after the colon. Can the first part of the sentence now stand alone as a sentence? If not, then do not use the colon.

Example
- Incorrect: You must bring: a sleeping bag, a change of clothes, and matches.
- Correct: You must bring the following items: a sleeping bag, a change of clothes, and matches.

QUOTATION MARKS

Use quotation marks at the beginning and end of all words in a direct quotation (someone's exact words). Watch for the use of quotation marks before and after a speech tag. Also notice the use of the comma after the speech tag (Alfred said), as in the first example.

Example

- Alfred said, "We are ready."
- "I'm finished the job," said Alfred. "We can go now."
- "When we are ready," said Alfred, "we will go."

Also notice that the closing quotation mark is placed after a comma or a period.

Closing quotation marks are also used with exclamation marks and question marks. When these punctuation marks belong to the sentence, they are placed outside the closing quotation marks.

Example

- Didn't you hear him say, "I'm in trouble"?
- If the question mark belongs to the quotation, it is placed inside the quotation marks.

Example

- He said sadly, "Why is it always me?"
- The same rules apply to end punctuation used for other purposes.

Periods and commas belong inside the quotation marks.

Exclamation and question marks belong either outside or inside the quotation marks, depending on whether they belong to the sentence as a whole or to the words inside the quotation marks.

Examples

You could say that her acting was "over the top."

I can't believe that's your "best effort"!

Indirect quotations or quotations that do not repeat exact words never require quotation marks.

Examples

- Alfred asked if we were ready.
- Alfred said he had finished the job and we could go.

Quotation marks are also used set off the titles of short stories and poems.

Example

- Marjorie Pickthall wrote "Stars."

Quotation marks indicate that a word is being used in an unusual sense.

Example

- "Housekeeping" on the space station is challenging.

Quotation marks can also show that a word is used ironically. When a word is used ironically, it has a meaning opposite to its literal meaning.

Example

- It seems that your "help" has put this project three weeks behind.

Quotation marks are used to quote the exact words from a source:

- an individual
  "It is not the mountain we conquer, but ourselves." [Sir Edmund Hillary, the first person to reach the Summit of Mount Everest in 1953]

- a published source
  Where the quote will not exceed four typed lines of text:

It was reported in The Guardian of January 22, 2008, that an "investment banker … may face jail after posing as a university under graduate in order to help a student cheat his way through his final year economic exams."

Note that while the exact original words have been quoted, ellipses (…) have been used to show that some wording at that point has been omitted.

Punctuation plays an important role in meaning. Even if the words you use are clear and well chosen, punctuation can determine how your sentence is understood. Always double check to make sure that your punctuation is correct.

ON 9W3.4   Use grammar conventions correctly to communicate intended meaning clearly

GRAMMAR

Like correct punctuation, grammar conventions allow you to communicate your ideas clearly. You can use your understanding of grammar to place the correct form of a word in a sentence and to combine phrases and clauses in a variety of sentence patterns.

CORRECT SENTENCE PATTERNS

1. Simple Sentence: one subject (noun/pronoun) and one predicate (verb)

Example

- O.C. Marsh discovered the brontosaurus.

2. Simple Sentence with a prepositional phrase

Example

- *Like a prehistoric monster*, the gentle brontosaurus lumbered *slowly across the clearing*.

3. Compound Sentence: at least two simple sentences

Example

- *The brontosaurus lumbered slowly*, yet *he was surprisingly agile*.

4. Complex Sentence: main clause and at least one relative/subordinate/dependent clause. A main clause is a simple sentence.

Example

relative adjective clause

The brontosaurus *you study in school* was really a dinosaur discovered earlier called an Apatosaurus.

The gigantic brontosaurus swayed slightly *as it lumbered slowly across the clearing.*
relative adverb clause

Compound-Complex Sentence: at least two main clauses and at least one relative clause

Example

adverb phrase   main clause   adverb phrase
In the cartoon, Fred Flintstone drives his brontosaurus *like a bulldozer*, and
main clause   relative adverb clause
he also downs a few brontosaurus burgers *while he is bowling with Barney.*

Most correct sentences will be a variation of these basic sentence patterns. The variations offer many creative possibilities for you as a writer.

COMMON SENTENCE ERRORS

The most frequent sentence errors involve incomplete sentences, known as sentence fragments, and run-on or comma-splice sentences. These errors are easy to make, but fortunately they are quite easy to fix in most cases.

Complete Sentences

A sentence is a group of words that expresses a complete thought. Each group of words should make sense by itself. Which of the following sentences expresses a complete thought?

A. While Sonia was hurrying to the station.

B. Kevin finished the test early.

If you guessed that the second sentence expresses a complete thought, you are correct. A complete sentence has both a *subject* and a *predicate*. The subject of a sentence tells *what* it is that you are talking about: the person, place, or thing. The predicate tells something *about* the subject. Every complete sentence must have a subject and a predicate.

In the second example, "Kevin" is the subject of the sentence, and "finished the test early" is the predicate. In the first example, we are left wondering what happened while Sonia was hurrying to the station. It is not a complete sentence because it is not a complete thought. While writing, make sure that you write in complete sentences. By maintaining solid sentence structure, you will be able to express your ideas more clearly.

This fragment could be easily corrected in at least two ways:

1. create a simple sentence: Sonia was hurrying to the station.

2. use the fragment as a relative clause: While Sonia was hurrying to the station, she slipped on some ice.

Run-on Sentences and Comma Splices

When writing, avoid run-on sentences. Run-on sentences generally occur when two or more complete sentences are joined together without the proper punctuation. Run-on sentences do not have to be long to be wrong. Consider the following example:

Bobby loves to draw cartoon strips he is a talented artist.

This is an incorrect sentence because the statements "Bobby loves to draw cartoon strips" and "he is a talented artist" can both stand alone as complete sentences. They are both independent clauses. They cannot run together into one sentence without somehow separating them. There are several ways to fix these types of sentences:

• You could separate the two clauses into two sentences.

Example

  • Bobby loves to draw cartoon strips. He is a talented artist.

  • You could use a semicolon to punctuate the two clauses.

Example

  • Bobby loves to draw cartoon strips; he is a talented artist.

  • You could use a coordinating conjunction (and, but, or, for, yet, nor, so) to separate the two clauses.

Example

- Bobby is a talented artist, and he loves to draw cartoon strips.

You could use a subordinating conjunction (after, although, before, unless, as because, even though, if, since, until, when, while) to separate the two clauses.

Example

- Since Bobby is a talented artist, he loves to draw cartoon strips.

You could use a semicolon and transitional word or phrase (however, on the other hand, therefore, otherwise) to separate the two clauses.

Example

- Bobby is a talented artist; therefore, he loves to draw cartoon strips.

A comma splice is similar to a run-on sentence, except that in the case of a comma splice, the writer has used a comma where there should be a period or semicolon.

Examples

- Incorrect: Bobby loves to draw cartoon strips, he is a talented artist.
- Incorrect: We were in the city for a whole day, we shopped in every mall, I could hardly walk when we boarded the subway.

Comma splices can be corrected using the same strategies for correcting run-on sentences.

Verb Agreement

When you are writing, it is important to check that all your verbs agree in number (singular and plural) and tense (past, present, future). Agreement can sometimes be confusing, so take care when you are editing your writing.

Agreement in Number

If the subject is singular, the verb must be singular.

Example

The box full of Christmas decorations is already open. (The box is open).

Agreement in Tense

Make sure that the tenses (time relationships) are properly expressed.

Example

Incorrect: After she moved to Ottawa, she discovered she likes the rain. (The word "like" is in the present tense, while "moved and "discovered" are in the past tense.)

Correct: After she moved to Ottawa, she discovered that she liked the rain. (All three verbs are in past tense.)

Remember to check the time relationships between all verbs in your sentences and paragraphs.

Pronoun Agreement

Pronouns are words used to replace nouns so that you do not end up with sentences that sound like the following statement: Jerry wondered whether Jerry had lost Jerry's wallet at the park. Fortunately, you can replace nouns like "Jerry" with personal pronouns (I, me, you, he, she, it) and their related forms, so the sentence can be written like this: Jerry wondered whether he had lost his wallet at the park.

Pronouns must agree with their antecedents. The antecedent is the noun represented by the pronoun.

Examples

- Julia noticed she had accidentally picked up the wrong camera, so she gave it to the tour leader.

(Julia is the antecedent of the pronoun "she," and camera is the antecedent of the pronoun "it.")

- The contest was disappointing for Hong, who had counted on winning.

(Hong is the antecedent of the pronoun "who.")

- The man in the tower was flashing a signal to proceed when he suddenly disappeared from the tower window.

(Man is the antecedent of the pronoun "he.")

Use a plural pronoun with a plural antecedent and a singular pronoun with a singular antecedent.

Example

- When the highway policemen arrived at the scene of the collision, they immediately put roadblocks in place.
- When the highway policeman arrived at the scene of the collision, he immediately put roadblocks in place.

Use the same gender pronoun as the antecedent.

Examples

- As he stepped into the mineshaft, Marshall listened for sounds below.
- Marian suddenly remembered she had to babysit after school.

It is *not* acceptable to use the pronoun "they" when the gender is not specified. Rather than saying "If **anyone** knew the answer, **they** would share it," you must say "If **anyone** knew the answer, **he** or **she** would share it."

When one singular and one plural antecedent are joined by the words *or*, or *nor*, the pronoun should agree with the nearest antecedent.

Examples

- Either you or your friends should leave their phone numbers.
- Neither the friends nor John left his phone number.

ON 9W3.5   Students will proofread and correct their writing, using guidelines developed with the teacher and peers

PROOFREADING

When you have finished writing the content of a piece of written work (including revising and rewriting), you should proofread and edit it for correct grammar, punctuation, capitalization, and spelling. Though you may have spent a great deal of time organizing and writing your ideas down, your reader's ability to understand and enjoy them will suffer if the final document contains basic errors and inconsistencies.

GRAMMAR

The following list of aspects of grammar can serve as a checklist when you are editing your work.

- Verb Tense
- Subject/Verb Agreement
- Complete Sentences
- Comparative and Superlative Forms of Adjectives and Adverbs
- Subordinate Clauses and Coordinating Conjunctions
- Modifier Placement
- Correct Word Usage

VERB TENSE

The tense of a verb tells the reader when the action happens. The most common verb tenses you will use in your writing are the past tense (before), the present tense (now), and the future tense (later).

Here is an example of the verb to work written in these three tenses:

Past Tense	Present Tense	Future Tense
He worked.	He works.	He will work.

When planning a story, think about when your story will take place: the past, the present, the future, or some combination of these timeframes. You may decide to begin your story in the present but include flashback sequences. Make sure that when you are writing in the present, your verbs reflect the present tense. When you use a flashback sequence, make sure that the verbs are written in the past tense. Whatever you decide, make sure that you use consistent verb tenses in your narrative writing.

Consistent: Her uncle often <u>came</u> to visit her. One day he <u>asked</u> her...

Inconsistent: Her uncle often <u>comes</u> to visit her. One day he <u>asked</u> her...

SUBJECT/VERB AGREEMENT

Most of the difficulties in subject-verb agreement are caused by difficulties in recognizing singular and plural subjects.

When subjects are joined by the words *or* or *nor*, the verb agrees with the nearest subject.

Examples

- Either Miller or Smith is guilty.

- Neither Miller nor Smith wants to confess.

- Neither the speaker nor the listeners are aware of the irony.

When one part of the verb is singular and the other part is plural, write the sentence so that the plural part is nearest the verb.

Examples

Weak: Neither band members nor the conductor is satisfied.

Better: Neither the conductor nor the band members are satisfied.

Nothing that comes between a singular subject and its verb can make that subject plural. Students should not make the verb agree with the nearest noun.

Examples

- Our school basketball team, the Gerbils, is victorious again.

- The prime minister, accompanied by several cabinet ministers, arrives at the airport shortly.

- Either Miller or Jones—both are suspects—is guilty.

- The contestant with the most votes is now on stage.

- One of the girls sings better.

- The ringleader who was at the head of the rebellious miners is sorry.

Indefinite pronouns such as *each, each one, either, neither, everyone, everybody, anybody, anyone, nobody, somebody, someone,* and *no one* are singular.

Examples

- Each of the contestants wins a prize.

- Everybody near the river is in danger.

- No one who wants to be successful in the exams is likely to be late.

Collective nouns are singular unless there is a reason to consider them as plurals.

Examples

- The group works well.

- The company is bankrupt.

- The jury is deliberating its verdict.

- The jury are arguing among themselves.

Using the correct pronoun is often a problem because the form of a pronoun varies depending on how the pronoun is used. Use *I, you, he/she/it, we, you, they, who* as the subject of a sentence or clause and for the complement of a linking verb.

Examples

- You have been chosen.

- We will be the last of the contestants.

- Who is going to be next?

- It is she who will be chosen.

Use *me, you, him/her/it, us, you, them,* and *whom* as direct or indirect objects of verbs or as the objects of prepositions.

Examples

- Give it to me.

- Hit the ball to them.

- Ask them the time.

- The child next to him laughed suddenly.

Use *my, your, his/hers/its, our, their,* and *whose* as adjectives.

Examples

- my car

- your umbrella

- its fur

Use *mine, yours, his/hers/its, ours, theirs,* and *whose* as subjects of sentences or as the complements of linking verbs.

Examples

- Yours is the one on the left.

- This is mine.

- Theirs is next.

The possessive pronouns *my, your, his/hers/its, our, yours, theirs,* and *whose* **never** use an apostrophe to show possession.

COMPLETE SENTENCES

As a general rule, all sentences should be complete sentences.

Example

Incorrect: He went ahead with his plan. Even though it was faulty.

Correct: He went ahead with his plan, even though it was faulty.

Occasionally, an incomplete sentence is used deliberately for effect. Fragments that are used deliberately are sometimes called minor sentences.

Example

Correct: Is anyone in favour of dictatorship? No? Well, of course not.

Dialogue and reported speech are exceptions to the rule about fragments.

Examples

- "Ready yet?"
- "Not yet."
- "Well then—!"

The opposite error is the "sentence" that is really two sentences. Either punctuation between sentences is omitted, or a comma is used to join two sentences.

Example

- Run-on: We went to Toronto we decided to visit the zoo.
- Comma splice: We went to Toronto, we decided to visit the zoo.

These errors can be fixed by correcting the punctuation or by rewriting.

Example

- We went to Toronto. We decided to visit the zoo.
- We went to Toronto. Then we decided to visit the zoo.
- After we went to Toronto, we decided to visit the zoo.
- We went to Toronto, and then we decided to visit the zoo.

COMPARATIVE AND SUPERLATIVE FORMS OF ADJECTIVES AND ADVERBS

Comparatives and superlatives are special forms of adjectives and adverbs. They are used to compare things. When we compare two things, we use the comparative form.

Examples

A car is much more expensive than a lollipop.

Five plus five is greater than four plus four.

When you compare more than two things, use the superlative form.

Example

That was the best movie I have ever seen.

I wanted to buy the largest dog in the window.

The following chart compares the base forms of some adjectives and adverbs with the comparative and superlative forms of the same words.

Base	Comparative	Superlative
fast	faster	fastest
good	better	best
wide	wider	widest
bad	worse	worst
quickly	more quickly	most quickly
harmful	more harmful	most harmful

SUBORDINATE CLAUSES AND COORDINATING CONJUNCTIONS

A clause is a group of words containing a subject and a predicate. A subordinate clause is a group of words that cannot stand alone as a sentence. Using subordinate clauses allows you to create interesting sentences by combining ideas.

Example

- My sister, *who is a doctor*, has four children.

- *While I clean my room*, I like to listen to music.

The clauses "who is a doctor" and "while I clean my room" cannot stand alone as sentences and are therefore referred to as subordinate clauses. Subordinate clauses add information to a sentence, but they are not complete ideas on their own.

Coordinating conjunctions are words used to join two clauses together. Some examples of coordinating conjunctions are for, and, not, but, or, yet, and so. These simple words can be used to join ideas and create complex sentences.

Examples

- Wendy loved to read books *but* did not enjoy magazines.

- John heard the weather report *and* hurried home.

- The sun was shining brightly, *yet* the air was still cold.

MODIFIER PLACEMENT

As a general rule, a modifier, usually an adjective or an adverb, should be placed as closely as possible to the word being modified.

Examples

- Vague: Entering the room, the door was shut by mother.

- Clear: Entering the room, mother shut the door.

- Vague: At six years of age, my parents started me in piano.

- Clear: At six years of age, I started taking piano lessons.

CORRECT WORD USAGE

The following words are frequently confused:

lie/lay	Incorrect: Father would *lay* down for a ten-minute nap after lunch.
	Correct: Father would *lie* down (recline) for a 10-minute nap after lunch.
	Incorrect: I asked Coach if I should *lie* my uniform down on the shelf.
	Correct: We were asked to *lay* (put or place) our uniforms neatly on the shelf.
accept/except	Jeremy will *accept* (receive) the reward on behalf of his brother.
	Everyone in the family *except* (with the exception of) Nolan came down with the flu.
borrow/lend	May I *borrow* your baseball glove?
	Could you *lend* me your text?
	Incorrect: Could you *borrow* me your text?
to/too/two	We need *to* decide whether *two* pies will be *too* much.
their/there/they're	The students will take *their* final exam on Friday morning.
	We decided *there* were enough people present to take a vote.
	The Smith family lived *there* for thirteen years.
	If *they're* arriving Tuesday, someone should meet them at the airport.
its/it's	Although the cat injured *its* left front paw, it's recovering nicely.
	Its: possessive pronoun; no apostrophe needed
	it's: contraction of "it is"
lose/loose	Try not to *lose* your backpack.
	Our mechanic discovered that the engine problem was caused by a *loose* bolt.
	Hint: You "lose" the extra "o" when you write "lose" instead of "loose."
can/may	Most children *can* (are able to) print their own name by the age of five.
	You *may* (are allowed to) eat your lunch outside today.
	Incorrect: You *can* eat your lunch outside today.
in/into	Sara needs the key to get *into* (inside) her house.
	Incorrect: Sara needs the key to get *in* her house.
	All the information is located *in* (within) your portfolio.
whose/who's	I do not know *whose* wallet is missing.
	Who's willing to help pick up this litter?
good/well	It seemed like a *good* idea.
	Terri did not feel *well* after her game.
	Incorrect: Terri did not feel *good* after her game.

different from/ different than	Correct: Lettuce is *different from* cabbage.
	Incorrect: Lettuce is *different than* cabbage.
	The expression "different than" is **always incorrect**.
could have/could of would have/would of should have/should of	Using "of" with these verbs is **always incorrect**. The word "have" is the correct choice. I *could have* spelled that word correctly. I *would have* spelled it correctly, if I had paid closer attention. You *should have* warned me that this test counted.

CAPITALIZATION

Although there are many special rules for capitalization, the following rules are the most important to practice for now:

Capitalize the first words of sentences, including sentences used in quotations.

Capitalize proper nouns, including any specific person, place, or thing. For instance, capitalize Suzie Walker, Happyville School, Pasadena, December, Christmas Day, Doctor Newman, and Artemis Fowl. Do not capitalize common nouns such as the girl, a school, our city, a month, the day, the doctor, or a book.

Always capitalize the word "I."

Capitalize some abbreviations. For example, R.S.V.P., an abbreviation for a French phrase that means "please respond," and Ave., an abbreviation for Avenue, both require capital letters, as do titles such as Mr., Mrs., and Dr.

Capitalization can sometimes be useful when you are trying to emphasize a certain word or create an emotional response.

Example

WOW! I could not believe my eyes. My brother was flying!

Capitalize the main words in a title, such as *The Cat in the Hat* or *My Summer in Mexico*.

The following proofreading checklist can help you make sure that your revised draft is ready for publishing or handing in. Always save your working draft on the computer in case you have to make changes after proofreading. Proofread both silently and out loud.

- Check for smooth flow of ideas, with all of your revision made to the draft

- Sentences: varied lengths, beginnings, types; no run-ons or fragments

- Punctuation: all end marks, commas, quotation marks, etc., are used correctly

- Capitalization

- Spelling: use spell check, dictionary

- Check for agreement: subject/verb/pronoun/antecedent

- Check with your "personal alert" list from your writing binder: (1) your most frequent usage errors, for example, run-ons or verb agreement; (2) your most frequent punctuation and capitalization errors; (3) words you have misspelled this year

- Print or write your final edited copy

PEER CONFERENCES

These can be helpful both at the revision and at the proofreading stages of your writing. At a peer conference, always read your work out loud. Peer conferences work very well in a partner situation.

Tips for Reader	Tips for Listener
1. Show your punctuation through pauses	1. Listen carefully and pay attention to your reader's ideas.
2. Do not rush your reading	2. Make sure to tell the reader what they have done well.
3. Be open to suggestions	3. Be specific in criticism: "That sentence is confusing;" "you need a stronger verb there."
4. Jot notes for changes on your draft.	4. Try to be constructive: "What if you switched those two ideas to make the argument more clear?"
5. Clarify your partner's comments with questions as needed	5. Remember that you are only trying to help. The writer may choose not to follow some of your suggestions.
6. Thank your partner.	
7. Appreciate that your peer is trying to help you improve your writing.	

FIGURES OF SPEECH

Figures of speech make your writing more interesting. A well-chosen figure of speech helps your reader better visualize the setting, object, or action.

A *simile* compares unlike objects or ideas using the words *like* or *as*.

- The train was as fast as a speeding bullet.

A *metaphor* compares unlike objects or ideas without using the words *like* or *as*.

- It was raining cats and dogs.

Personification attributes human qualities or characteristics to inanimate objects.

- The trees waved their branches in the wind.

Idioms are expressions that should not be taken literally.

- She was walking on air when she heard the good news.

Appropriate Modifiers

Adjectives modify nouns by telling what "kind" of person, place, or thing they are.

Example

Wild geese, *high-flying* geese, *honking* geese, *southbound* geese, *excited* geese
(what kind); *those* geese, *that* goose, *my* geese, *six* geese, *some* geese, *your* goose (limit the description
further)

Adverbs modify verbs or other modifiers by telling "when," "where," "how," or "how much."

Example

The wild geese flew *south* (where) *yesterday* (when).

The wild geese flew *noisily* and *swiftly* (how) *in a 'V' shape* (how).

Modifiers can also be phrases that do the work of a single adverb.

Example

The geese flew *toward the south.*

With loud honking and flapping of wings, the geese flew south.

ACTIVE AND PASSIVE VOICE

Active voice is stronger and more direct than passive voice, and it usually makes your writing more
effective. A sentence is written in the active voice when the subject clearly *does* the action; a sentence is
written in the passive voice when the subject of the sentence *receives* the action. Look at these examples
to help you understand how much stronger and direct the active voice is:

Active Voice   My dad packed the car for the trip.

Passive Voice   The car was packed for the trip by my dad.

Active Voice   Sue ate her birthday cake.

Passive Voice   The birthday cake was eaten by Sue.

In the active voice, you see that the subject of each sentence is placed before the object. You can also see
that active language conveys the same ideas in fewer words.

All of the information presented in this section has been included so that you can develop your vocabulary
and grammar skills. Remember that careful reading and writing will help you better understand how
proper grammar works and help you expand your vocabulary. The rules and guidelines you have learned
in this section of your study guide offer tools that are meant to be used when you are reading and writing.
After you have finished reading something, take another look at the text for grammar and vocabulary.
Note how sentences are made, which words are used, and how they are used. Remember that your
vocabulary and grammar will improve not only through knowing and following rules and guidelines:
reading and being curious and observant in your reading will help improve your vocabulary and grammar
as well.

PRACTICE QUESTIONS—VOCABULARY AND GRAMMAR

1. In the sentence "John received a new bicycle for his nineth birthday," the word spelled **incorrectly** is
    A. nineth
    B. bicycle
    C. received
    D. birthday

2. Which word in the sentence "The car trouble ocurred because of faulty brakes" is spelled **incorrectly**?
    A. Because
    B. Ocurred
    C. Trouble
    D. Faulty

3. Which of the following sentences is grammatically correct?
    A. The boy felt good enough to go to school after having been sick.
    B. For a week after being sick, the boy felt well enough to go to school.
    C. After having been sick for a week, the boy felt well enough to go to school.
    D. After having been sick for a week, the boy felt good enough to go to school.

4. Which of the following sentences is written correctly?
    A. In Science; we studied organisms.
    B. In Science, we learnt about many types of organisms.
    C. In Science we learned about many types of organisms.
    D. In Science, we learned about many types of organisms.

Read the following passage to answer questions 5 to 10.

THE COMING OF MUTT

During my lifetime we had owned, or had been owned by, a steady succession of dogs. As a newborn baby I had been guarded by a Border collie named Sapper, who was one day doused with boiling water by a vicious neighbour, and who went insane as a result. But there had always been other dogs during my first eight years, until we moved to the west and became, for the moment, dogless. The prairies could be only half real to a boy without a dog.

I began agitating for one almost as soon as we arrived and I found a willing ally in my father—though his motives were not mine.

For many years he had been exposed to the colourful tales of my Great-uncle Frank, who homesteaded in Alberta in 1900. Frank was a hunter born, and most of his stories dealt with the superlative shooting to be had on the western plains. Before we were properly settled in Saskatoon my father determined to test those tales. He bought a fine English shotgun, a shooting coat, cases of ammunition, a copy of the Saskatchewan Game Laws, and a handbook on shotgun shooting. There remained only one indispensable item—a hunting dog.

One evening he arrived home from the library with such a beast in tow behind him. Its name was Crown Prince Challenge Indefatigable. It stood about as high as the dining-room table and, as far as Mother and I could judge, consisted mainly of feet and tongue. Father was annoyed at our levity and haughtily informed us that the Crown Prince was an Irish Setter, kennel bred and field trained, and a dog to delight the heart of any expert. We remained unimpressed. Purebred he may have been, and the possessor of innumerable cups and ribbons, but to my eyes he seemed a singularly useless sort of beast with but one redeeming feature: I greatly admired the way he drooled. I have never known a dog who could drool as the Crown Prince could. He never stopped, except to flop his way to the kitchen sink and tank up on water. He left a wet and sticky trail wherever he went. He had little else to recommend him, for he was moronic.

Mother might have overlooked his obvious defects, had it not been for his price. She could not overlook that, for the owner was asking two hundred dollars, and we could no more afford such a sum than we could have afforded a Cadillac. Crown Prince left the next morning, but Father was not discouraged, and it was clear that he would try again.

My parents had been married long enough to achieve that delicate balance of power which enables a married couple to endure each other. They were both adept in the evasive tactics of marital politics—but Mother was a little more adept.

She realized that a dog was now inevitable, and when chance brought the duck boy—as we afterwards referred to him—to our door on that dusty August day, Mother showed her mettle by snatching the initiative right out of my father's hands.

By buying the duck boy's pup, she not only placed herself in a position to forestall the purchase of an expensive dog of my father's choice, but she was also able to save six cents in cash. She was never one to despise a bargain.

When I came home from school the bargain was installed in a soap carton in the kitchen. He looked to be a somewhat dubious buy at any price. Small, emaciated, and caked liberally with cow manure, he peered up at me in a near-sighted sort of way. But when I knelt beside him and extended an exploratory hand he roused himself and sank his puppy teeth into my thumb with such satisfactory gusto that my doubts dissolved. I knew that he and I would get along.

—by Farley Mowat

5. Explain what the writer's comment that they "had owned, or had been owned by, a steady succession of dogs" reveals about his family.

This tells us that the dogs they used to own meant a lot to them. They probably owned the dogs for a long time that the dogs became part of their family. Since they think they might've been owned by the dogs, the dogs might have been a guard or protector for them.

6. When the writer describes his father as "a willing ally," he means that his father is someone who

   A. is willing to support him because they share similar goals

   B. has very different ideas but is willing to compromise

   C. shares the same values but has different objectives

   D. wishes to support his cause silently

7. In the quotation "his stories dealt with the superlative shooting to be had," what does the word "superlative" mean?

The word "superlative" in the quotation means that the shooting was extreme. Frank was born a hunter, therefore, majority of his stories dealt with him shooting things in the western plains. As a hunter born, Frank was able to get beneficial advice and tips for shooting at a young age.

8. When the narrator states that his father speaks "haughtily" about Crown Prince, he means that his father is speaking with

   A. tact

   B. humour

   C. arrogance

   D. hesitation

9. The phrase "evasive tactics of marital politics" suggests that the narrator's parents

   A. distract each other by focusing on other issues

   B. keep to themselves until problems work themselves out

   C. avoid direct conflict and pursue their objectives indirectly

   D. openly state their positions as politicians do in public debate

10. Which of the following quotations does not contain a sentence fragment?

   A. The top just kept spinning. It never slowed, and it never stopped.

   B. The top, never slowed and never stopped, just kept spinning.

   C. The top just kept spinning. Never slowing, never stopping.

   D. The top just kept spinning, never slowing, never stopping.

Read the following passage to answer questions 11 and 12.

AN ENCOUNTER UNDER THE LAMPPOST

The lamppost stood tall and straight in the evening shadows. There was a little rust around its base, and its light had dimmed with age, but it was still the same beautiful lamppost it had been all those years ago when oil lamps first lined the city streets. Those were the days before kerosene when whale oil was still popular and the whales were not extinct. The lamp had been converted to burn kerosene, but even that was becoming rare as the wasteful age of fossil-fuel energy was finally stalling out.

Preserved by city decree, the lamp stood as a testimonial to forgotten years when men wore tall hats and women wore elegant dresses and exchanged smiles of goodwill and gestures of kindness. Those were the days when a handshake still sealed a deal and men honored their word. All that had changed now. Smiles were tightlipped mockeries of the original thing. People hid behind deceptions, insinuations, lies, and half-truths, shaking hands as a leftover formality from bygone years.

Zachariah felt like the lamppost. He did not fit in with the bustle and hustle of the modern world. He did not understand computer games and car racing games. Instead, he learned to whittle wood. Sometimes he thought he had inherited more than just his great grandfather's name. Sometimes he thought his great grandfather was in him, a part of him, guiding his hands as he cut and carved until the soul of the wood was set free in beautiful ornate carvings.

It was late evening. The harsh light of day had been replaced by the soft glow of the city lamps. Zachariah sat with his back pressed against the lamppost eyeing his latest carving. It was a bear. The proportions looked all right, although it was hard to tell for sure. He used pictures to guide his carving. Somewhere behind him, he heard the sound of footsteps cracking on the old, cobblestone courtyard. Time to go, he supposed, tucking his whittle knife in his pocket.

"Where do you think he got to?" a harsh, guttural voice whispered. Zachariah froze.

"He'll be here," a second voice said.

"But he's late."

"Shhh," the second voice hissed. "People will hear you."

"There's no one here," the first voice complained.

"Shhh," the second voice hissed again. "Your impatience will be your downfall. Remember, you are here to observe only."

"I know, I know," the first voice whined, "I stay hidden in the shadows. I don't say a word. You do all the transactions."

"Good. Now get back. I hear someone coming."

There was a shuffling of feet as the hoarse-voiced man shifted back a few paces. Just as Zachariah was contemplating whether to run or stay, the thick crunching steps of a third person came out of the shadows.

"Have you got the item?" a sinister voice asked. There was a rustling sound of an object exchanging hands. "The scroll?" the voice asked.

"Yes."

"Good. You know what to do next?"

"Yes." The scuffling feet moved off back down the alley.

"What do we do next?" the rough young voice asked, staring after the departing shadow.

"We kill the king," the older voice said with a sigh.

"What? That wasn't part of the deal. You never said anything about killing anyone."

"Do you want to save your sister?"

"Of course but—"

"Then you must accept the consequences of the deal."

"But … "

"Either you are a man and you will go through with this or you are still a sniffling boy from the back alleys of Tyr. Which is it? Decide now." There was a hard edge in the second voice, an edge that showed neither weakness nor sympathy. Zachariah found himself drawn to the voice. Bit by bit, he eased his body around until his chest was pressed against the lamppost. He poked his head out just far enough to see two burly shapes dressed in black.

"Ho, who are you? Who's that?" the smaller figure said, pointing.

11. The quotation "smiles were tightlipped mockeries" refers to people who are
    A. shallow
    B. unhappy
    C. insincere
    D. preoccupied

12. As it is used in the quotation "shaking hands as a leftover formality," the word "leftover" is an example of a compound
    A. verb
    B. noun
    C. word
    D. adjective

Read the following passage to answer questions 13 to 17.

HECTOR, THE STOWAWAY DOG

Second Officer Harold Kildall of the *Hanley* noticed the dog first. The *Hanley*, a freighter, was one of five ships loading at the Government Dock in Vancouver, British Columbia, on April 20, 1922. Checking chain lashings, Kildall glanced up to see a large smooth-haired terrier, white with black markings, coming abroad by the gangplank. Once aboard, the dog stood absolutely still, looking and listening all about the deck. He sniffed at the deck cargo of fresh-sawed timbers and at the sacks of grain being loaded into the last hatch. Then he returned ashore, only to board the next ship, which was loading apples, flour and fir logs for England. Here the terrier again sniffed at the cargo and about the decks and living quarters, then slowly went ashore.

The dog's strange actions made Kildall curious. Now he watched the dog board a freighter loading paper pulp for East Coast ports. The dog boarded the other ships in turn, examining each in the same careful fashion. After that, busy getting ready for sea, Kildall forgot the whole thing. And at noon the *Hanley* got under way for the long trip to Japan.

Early the next morning the dog was found lying on a mat outside the cabin of the *Hanley's* captain. Unseen, he had come aboard again and stowed away for the voyage. The captain, who loved dogs, tried to be friendly, but the terrier would not warm up to him. Kildall and others tried, too, to win him over. To all of them he remained distant and cool. He just walked about the captain's deck, sniffing the salt air.

Late that first morning, when Kildall went below to eat, the dog followed him and stood at the galley door, waiting expectantly. The cook gave him his best leftovers. When Kildall climbed to the bridge to take over the watch, the dog followed close behind, walked through the pilothouse, took a turn through the chartroom, then ran up the ladder to the flying bridge and stood beside the compass housing. Seeming to be satisfied, he lay down in a comfortable corner and went to sleep. Obviously this stowaway was an old sea dog.

For 18 days the *Hanley* sailed across the northern rim of the Pacific. Day after day her officers and men tried to make up to the dog but he remained aloof. He allowed his head to be patted but showed no return of affection. When not "on watch" with Kildall he remained at the captain's door, going below decks only for his meals.

When the coast of Honshu was signed, the stowaway sniffed the land breeze and stared straight ahead as the land came in sight. His interest grew as the *Hanley* moved through the Yokohama breakwaters to its anchoring place near some other ships unloading cargos.

While directing cargo work, Kildall noticed that the dog was very alert, his tail switching from time to time and his nostrils quivering nervously as he stared at the other ships. The nearest of these, the *Simaloer*, was, like the *Hanley*, unloading squared timbers into the harbor.

Soon the *Hanley* swung with the tide so that her stern pointed in the direction of the *Simaloer*, now some 300 yards away. At once the dog's attention centered on her. He ran to the rear of the ship, as close to her as possible, and sniffed the air with rising excitement. While Kildall watched, a sampan came alongside the *Simaloer*, took two sailors abroad, and set off for shore on a course that carried the boat close under the *Hanley's* stern.

Whining softly, the dog watched. Suddenly he began running back and forth in wild excitement, barking madly. This caught the attention of the passengers in the sampan. Shading their eyes against the sun, they stared at the *Hanley's* stern.

Suddenly one of them jumped to his feet and began shouting and waving his arms, motioning to the sampan man and slapping the other sailor on the back. His excitement matched the dog's. Now, as the sampan came alongside the *Hanley's* boarding ladder, the dog became so worked up that he jumped into the water. The shouting man pulled him aboard the sampan and hugged him close, wet coat and all. The dog whined with joy and licked his face. Obviously a dog and his master had been reunited.

The reunion of the stowaway and his happy owner became the talk of the crews of both ships. The dog's name, it turned out, was Hector. His owner, W.H. Mante, second officer of the *Simaloer*, had the same duties and the same watches to stand as Kildall had on the *Hanley*. At Government Dock in Vancouver, the *Simaloer* had changed its position to take on fuel while Hector was off for a last run before the long voyage. Mante searched the waterfront wildly but failed to find Hector in time – and the *Simaloer* sailed without him.

What mysterious sense could have guided Hector's careful search for the one ship out of many that would carry him across an ocean to rejoin his master? Did the kind of cargo the *Hanley* carried and perhaps other signs tell him that the *Hanley* was headed for the same port as his own ship? Did he then attach himself to the officer whose duties were like his master's? Any answers would be the guesswork of men, who know only that it happened.

—by Captain Kenneth Dodson

13. In the sentence "Did he then attach himself to the officer whose duties were like his master's?" the word "attach" means

   A. search for

   B. follow closely

   C. fasten himself to

   D. adopt as his master

14. In the phrase "Mante searched the waterfront wildly," describe what the word "wildly" implies about Mante.

   After Mante realized that Hector hadn't returned, he became very
   anxious. He searched the waterfront wildly because he was
   worried for the wellbeing and safety of his beloved dog, Hector.
   The word "wildly" implies that Mante cares for his dog and when he
   didn't find him, he began acting frantically under pressure.

15. In the sentence "the dog followed him and stood at the galley door, waiting expectantly," the word "expectantly" means

   A. fearfully

   B. invitingly

   C. in a friendly manner

   D. with an attitude of anticipation

16. In the sentence "At once the dog's attention centered on her," the word "centered" means

    A. focused

    B. ignored

    C. followed

    D. motivated

17. In the quotation "he remained distant and cool," the word "distant" means

    A. wary

    B. unfazed

    C. physically removed

    D. secretly holding anger

Read the following passage to answer questions 18 and 19.

THE GHOST TOWN

Margaret picked up the old yellowed photograph that was lying on top of the pile. It was in black and white. It was better that way, aged, like her memories. Color photographs capture the image, but black and whites capture its soul; it was the soul of this picture that captured her attention now.

It was a simple picture of children playing. A woman, her mother, was standing at the bottom of the slide, her arms outstretched, ready to catch a little girl with pigtails and laughing eyes, her sister. An older boy and a girl of about eight were climbing on the teeter-totter. In the background, she could see the jungle gym filled with walkways and monkey bars. She remembered the squeak and groan of the teeter-totter as it crashed up and down.
Oh how she loved teeter-tottering!

She reached for another picture, this one taken only a few weeks ago. Her brother had taken it on his last visit to Fireside. It was a black and white of the playground, overgrown and forgotten. Weeds grew up around the base of the equipment. The bar from the teeter-totter was lost in long grasses and climbing flowers. The sand was blown smooth with nary a footprint left in the sand. If she looked hard enough at the picture, she could almost see the ghosts of the children who used to play there. She could almost hear their laughter echoing off the old jungle gym with its rusting bars and rotting wooden posts.

The next picture, this one in color, was of the old hotel with its windows boarded up, locking the world out and the memories in. Like the playground, green tangles of weeds and grasses grew unchecked along the walls, the green contrasting sharply with the faded red paint. The glass-framed phone booth was tucked away near the side door. She didn't remember a glass phone booth. They changed that after she left. The phone itself still worked; she knew because her brother had used it two weeks ago when he phoned. She was sure the lights still worked too. One flip of the switch would illuminate the layers of dust and cobwebs of the dining room and the stage where the dance hall girls used to perform.

She closed her eyes, remembering. She was eight. Her sister was a little older. They were sneaking up to the windows to peer inside. They stretched up on tiptoes, pressing their faces tight against the glass. They could see the girls in their sparkling dresses dancing while the miners sat in groups around the tables drinking and playing cards. The girls were so beautiful.

They never got to watch for long. As soon as Mr. Uchanko saw them, he shooed them away. "Not for the eyes of little girls," he told them as they scurried away.

She unfolded the letter. Her brother's messy handwriting was scrawled across the crisp white surface. Dear Margaret, he wrote, *I hope this letter finds you well.* The next few words were scratched out as if he was trying to say something, but the words weren't coming out right. She knew what was coming. She forced herself to read on:

I know you have heard about the new interstate highway. It will run straight through the middle of Fireside. All the buildings will be torn down and moved. The playground and the school will be paved, the hotel dismantled. You know what is beneath those floorboards. You know what is inside that hotel. Margaret, I need your help. We can't let them destroy Fireside. John.

She re-read the note three times before folding it up and tucking it back in the shoebox full of pictures. She wasn't ready to open up the past, not now, not ever. There were too many demons lurking in those shadows.

She pulled her old shawl tight around her shoulders. Why couldn't the secrets have stayed lost for just a few more years? Why couldn't it have waited until she was dead and no one was left to remember? Why—the word hung in the evening air like a herald of doom.

18. In the sentence "Color photographs capture the image, but black and whites capture its soul; it was the soul of this picture that captured her attention now," the function of the semicolon is to

   A. separate two related ideas

   B. separate two dependent clauses

   C. connect two independent clauses

   D. connect a dependant and an independent clause

19. The function of the dash in the sentence "Why—the word hung in the evening air like a herald of doom" is to

   A. explain a word

   B. show hesitation

   C. create emphasis

   D. replace a semicolon

Read the following passage to answer questions 20 and 21.

SAFE WORK PROCEDURES

Working Alone

There may be times when you have to work alone. Here are some procedures to help you deal with this situation.

1. Have someone contact you periodically to ensure that you are okay. The checking procedure must require you to take some predetermined action to confirm that you are all right and do not need help.

2. Contact may be in person, by telephone, or by any other effective means. This may **include** reciprocal agreements with other company locations, adjacent merchants, or security firms. These agreements can include:telephone contact at predetermined intervalsvisual contact or signal to workers in adjacent premises or to security patrols

3. Use personal alarms or monitored video surveillance systems, provided that:they are properly maintained the response to signs of distress is made immediately by qualified personnel

4. Make arrangements with adjacent employers to have employees watch each other's premises.

5. Prominently display notices indicating:that the premises are monitoredthe emergency numbers to call for assistance

6. If possible, do not open back doors or leave them open and unattended.

7. If possible, do not empty the garbage at night, especially if the dumpster is in a secluded spot or back alley.

Assault Prevention Tips

1. If attacked, scream—as loudly and long as possible—and run to a neighbouring store or the nearest well-lit area. Continue calling for help.

2. If someone grabs your purse, deposit bag, or other personal property, do not resist, and do not chase the thief.

3. Call the police immediately after any incident, and record the appearance and mannerisms of the offender.

20. In the sentence "Have someone contact you periodically to ensure that you are okay," the word "periodically" means
    A. quickly
    B. regularly
    C. diligently
    D. occasionally

21. A synonym for the word "prevention," as it is used in the heading "Assault Prevention Tips," is
    A. patience
    B. response
    C. tolerance
    D. avoidance

ANSWERS AND SOLUTIONS—PRACTICE QUESTIONS

1. A	7. WR	13. B	19. C
2. B	8. C	14. WR	20. B
3. C	9. C	15. D	21. D
4. D	10. A	16. A	
5. WR	11. C	17. B	
6. A	12. D	18. C	

1. A

To spell the word "ninth" correctly, the e is dropped before adding the -th ending.

2. B

The word "occur" is spelled with two cs. When the suffix -ed is added, the final r is also doubled.

3. C

The word good is an adjective; the word well is an adverb used to modify an action. In this sentence, the word "well" modifies the verb "felt."

4. D

The word learned is the past tense of the verb to learn. The word learnt is more likely to be used as an adjective. The sentence "In Science we learned about many types of organisms" requires a comma, and the semicolon is incorrectly used in the sentence "In Science; we studied organisms."

5. WRITTEN RESPONSE

The writer's comment that they "had owned, or had been owned by, a steady succession of dogs" illustrates that his family saw their dogs as equal members of their household. The writer is acknowledging that the family may have been controlled in some ways by its dogs. There is confusion about who is really dominant in a pet-owner relationship.

6. A

An ally is a person who cooperates with another for a common purpose. The narrator and his father are allies because their common objective is to get a dog. Their motives and ideas about the type of dog they prefer are different, but their objective is the same, which makes them allies.

7. WRITTEN RESPONSE

In the phrase "his stories dealt with the superlative shooting to be had," the word "superlative" indicates an extraordinary quality. According to Frank, the hunting opportunities on the western plains are exceptional and unparalleled.

8. C

The word "haughtily" means disdainfully proud or arrogant. The narrator's father is offended by his family's criticism of
Crown Prince. He feels he is a superior judge of the dog's value and that his wife and son's assessment is inaccurate. His reaction is one of arrogance, not of tact, humour, or hesitation.

9. **C**

"Evasive tactics" are indirect strategies used to settle a dispute. The narrator's mother realized that getting a dog "was now inevitable," so she snatched the initiative right out of her husband's hands and took action by buying the duck boy's puppy. She did not wait until the problem worked itself out, and the parents never argued the problem directly. The father took back the Irish Setter because he knew it was too expensive, and the mother, realizing they would eventually have to get a dog of some sort, avoided investing a great deal of money by buying Mutt.

The word "evasive" implies that the parents avoided direct confrontation.

10. **A**

The quotation "Never slowing, never stopping," is a sentence fragment because it has no subject. The word "It" provides the subject in the correct alternative.

11. **C**

A mockery is an inadequate imitation. Since normal smiles show goodwill, mockeries of smiles would be poor or insincere attempts to demonstrate goodwill.

12. **D**

A compound adjective joins two unrelated words together to form an adjective. An adjective is a word that describes a noun.
In this case, "leftover" describes the word "formality," so it is a compound adjective.

13. **B**

In this sentence, the word "attach" means that the dog followed the officer very closely.

14. **WRITTEN RESPONSE**

The word "wildly" implies a sense of panic. Mante was desperate when he searched the waterfront for his missing dog. Departure of his ship was imminent, and he did not want to leave without him.

15. **D**

The galley was the location on the ship where the dog was expecting, from past experience, to be fed. The prospect of being fed fills the dog with expectation or anticipation. To be "waiting expectantly" means to be waiting with an attitude of anticipation.

16. **A**

In this sentence, the word "centered" means focused. The dog's attention was directly focused on the incoming ship.

17. **B**

The dog was distant and cool, not because he was afraid, but because he was unfazed by the attention of strangers with whom he had no emotional bond. The dog was focused on being reunited with his master.

18. **C**

A semicolon is used to join two independent but related clauses, which is how it is being used in this example.

19. **C**

The em dash is used here to create emphasis by making a sharp break between the word "why" and a description of the word's significance.

20. **B**

To do something periodically means to do it at regular intervals of time.

21. **D**

The word avoidance is a synonym for the word prevention.

UNIT TEST—VOCABULARY AND GRAMMAR

Read the following passage to answer questions 1 to 4.

THEY DIDN'T KNOW HOCKEY

Dan Hawley snagged the goalie's pass-out just inside the blue line and whirled away with the puck. Judge, the opposing centre, swooped in and tried to check him, but Dan hurdled Judge's stick, shot the rubber ahead and snapped it up again a moment later as he raced down the middle lane with Judge hard at his heels.

There was less than a minute to play and the score was tied with the teams nearing the limit of their overtime. The visiting Owls would be well satisfied with a tie, but Dan Hawley knew as well as anyone in the rink that anything but a win on home ice would be almost fatal to the Panthers' chances of grabbing the league title.

He streaked toward the Owl goal with the crowd whooping in a frenzy. There was an imploring, hysterical note in the roar of the mob. The Panther fans were begging for that goal; the one goal that would squeeze out a win; the goal that seemed impossible to get and that must be scored within the next fifty seconds, if it was to be scored at all.

Dan was tired, for it had been a long, grim game, and bush-league amateurs are expected to go the distance. He could hear the click and chop of Judge's skates as the Owl centre tried to overhaul him, but Dan knew he could out-foot Judge. He wasn't worrying about that.

But this next scoring play. It had to click. It had to be perfect. There mustn't be a slip-up. If it missed, there wouldn't be time for another. And both of his wings were covered.

The Owls had a hard-hitting defence. And their goalie was smart. Dan streaked in and fired from the outside.

It was a hard, low, wicked shot, but the high-pitched roar of the crowd changed to a long, deep groan. You couldn't beat the Owl goalie on long shots. Everyone knew that. And this shot, moreover, was wide of the net.

The puck spanked against the rear boards with a thud that could be heard the length of the rink.

The left defenceman swung around. And the Owl left winger, covering his check along the boards, began hotfooting it into the corner to pick up the rebound.

But Dan Hawley was already sifting through for that same rebound. He had shot purposely wide; he knew the exact angle at which the puck would ricochet from the boards; he knew exactly where he could pick it up.

It was perfectly timed. He was in like a streak. He got his stick on the puck as it skimmed across the ice on its rebound from the boards. And in the same motion, he pivoted and laid down a swift pass to his uncovered right winger, Ben Borstall.

The play had pulled all the Owls out of position. Borstall swooped in, went right to the net, saw that Steve O'Hara, the left winger, was uncovered and backing him up. Borstall faked a shot that pulled the goalie over, then banged the puck over to O'Hara.

And O'Hara socked the rubber into the upper corner for the perfect goal.

The crowd went wild. They went stark raving mad with joy, seemed ready to tear down the rink in their enthusiasm. They were still in a frenzy of rejoicing when the game ended a few moments later. A mob of fans carried O'Hara off the ice. And scores of them crowded around Ben Borstall, pounding him on the back.

"Ben deserves credit too, don't forget!" bellowed one of the fans. "O'Hara scored that goal all right, but Ben gave him the pass."

A lot of people had nice things to say to Dan Hawley, too. "Nice game, Dan" "You were sure flyin' out there tonight, Dan." But for that matter every member of the team came in for his share of hero worship.

O'Hara, however, occupied the limelight. Wasn't he the league's leading scorer? And hadn't he banged home the winning goal?

"We won't be able to keep him here very long," said someone. "Some of the pro teams will be after him before we know it. A goal-getter like O'Hara would make good anywhere."

Dan Hawley, getting out of his uniform in the dressing room, grinned cynically. After all, what did the average fan know about hockey strategy? So far as Dan was concerned, he didn't care who got the credit, as long as the Panthers won the game.

—by Leslie McFarlane

1. In the quotation "bush-league amateurs expected to go the distance," the term "bush-league amateurs" **most likely** refers to

   A. those players who play just for fun

   B. average non-professional players

   C. players under 16 years of age

   D. outdoor hockey players

2. What other words are similar in meaning to the word "ricochet" as it is used in the quotation "the puck would ricochet from the boards"?

   Other words that can replace the word ricochet are: hit off,
   rebound, retaliate, etc.

3. The phrase "grinned cynically" means that Dan Hawley's grin was

   A. sad

   B. happy

   C. sneering

   D. satisfactory

4. The phrase "socked the rubber" contains an example of

   A. slang

   B. simile

   C. alliteration

   D. onomatopoeia

Read the following passage to answer questions 5 and 6.

SPORT

A fisherman steps
to the banks of a river
a comfortable rainbow
lies still in the water
and slides to the surface
to dine on the hatches
the quick eye that follows
makes perfect the target
while seeking—mouth open
finds steel for its dinner
the stillness is broken
by ripples exploding
implacable bamboo
arcs out to the victim
but short is the battle
for scales are uneven
and mesh that is anxious
awaits gleaming silver
soon two pounds of muscle
lies dead in a basket
and fishermen heart-beats
are proud and disdainful
the womb of the mother
is spilled by the angler
and ten thousand children
lie dead in the sand.

—by Kirk Wirsig

5. The lines "while seeking—mouth open / finds steel for its dinner" suggest that the

   A. lake is polluted

   B. fish has been caught

   C. fisherman has failed

   D. fish senses the danger

6. In the quotation "implacable bamboo," the word "implacable" means

   A. trembling or shaking

   B. reaching or extending

   C. relentless or unyielding

   D. overextended or bending

Read the following passage to answer questions 7 to 11.

NEVER LOOK A BABOON IN THE EYE

It was a critical moment—the time to move from planning and discussion to action. For months I had been working with my colleagues at CBC's Science Unit planning the development of ideas and plans for *A Planet for the Taking*, a special, eight-part series on nature, specifically our human place in nature. We had discussed and proposed, read and argued about the best way to present our proposition that humans are just one of many species on this planet, that nature is giving us increasingly strong signals that it will not be continued by us. Now it was time to go out and film.

The series' three producers had already made the plunge. They had left Toronto a month earlier. One was filming in Oman and the other two in southern India. I was writing the elements of my script that needed to be filmed in those locations. I was also waiting for my daughter, Sarika, to be born. My schedule had been carefully organized. Sarika would be born, I would have five days to share her introduction to the world with my wife, Tara, and then I would embark on a whirlwind rendezvous with the three film crews sprinkled across two continents.

But Sarika was late...

All of our plans were waylaid by good old Mother Nature. It was a small, but important, reminder of just how real *A Planet for the Taking*'s message is. Natural events like birth and death are part of an independent network of life, a net worth with much more at stake than our self-serving timetables...

A similar reminder came in Kenya while I was filming a troop of baboons. We had been introduced to the baboons by Dr. Shirley Strum, an anthropologist who has been observing this same troop of baboons for years. Shirley is well acquainted with each individual baboon in the troop. She knows each baboon's age and place on the family tree. One by one, she introduced members of the film crew to the baboons. Because we, like most humans, have had little acquaintance with other animals in anything but dominating and controlling relationships, Shirley had to remind us of some basic inter-species etiquette. We were told not to look the baboons directly in the eye. That's an aggressive statement, arrogant and challenging.

Properly introduced and graciously accepted, we were ready to start filming. One of the things Shirley has discovered in her studies is that baboons are creatures of habit. Their days follow a strict routine of wandering, feeding, socializing and resting. Considerately we planned our day to fit the troop's schedule. We would rise before dawn to join them in their sunrise walk to a feeding spot. There, we would film the first of several items about how our observations of baboon behaviour—and anything else—are determined by what we expect to see.

Our sunrise rendezvous never happened. For some reason, the troop had decided on a different starting location that day. When we finally caught up with them there was a great sense of relief. According to our schedule of their schedule, the troop was due for a one or two hour stop. They found a sunny spot and seemed to settle down. Hastily the crew unloaded cameras and tape recorders. I reviewed my lines, hoping they would still be there in my memory when the cameras were rolling. In less than a quarter of an hour we were ready. So, too, were the baboons. With a fleeting glance at our set-up, they ambled off.

Five or six times that day this same scenario unfolded itself. When the sun finally set we had covered several miles and had not shot even a single foot of film. We still don't know what happened to the baboons' ironclad schedule that day. Perhaps it was their equivalent of a human weekend, or perhaps it was a gentle reminder from their culture to ours that even well-intentioned, passive observers such as ourselves have an effect on whatever they are observing.

—by David Suzuki

7. In the phrase "It was a critical moment," the word "critical" means

   A. trivial

   B. nagging

   C. important

   D. insignificant

8. In the context of this passage, the word "colleagues" refers to the writer's

   A. friends

   B. companions

   C. partners on the project

   D. superiors at the CBC Science Unit

9. Describe in your own words what "inter-species etiquette" means.

Inter-species etiquette is how various species should interact with each other. Since inter- is meaning between and etiquette is meaning proper behaviours and manners, I came to the conclusion that inter-species etiquette is the proper ways to behave, show kindness and respect between species.

10. According to the information in the passage, a group of baboons is called a

   A. herd
   B. troop
   C. family
   D. colony

11. What other words are similar in meaning to the word "ironclad" as it used in the phrase "the baboons' ironclad schedule"?

Ironclad could have similar meanings to what the reporters thought was the baboons' schedule. Other words with similar meanings could include expected, anticipated, and thought.

Read the following passage to answer questions 12 to 23.

from DRIFT HOUSE

After the towers came down Mr. and Mrs. Oakenfeld thought it best that their three children go and stay with their uncle in Canada. Although Susan, Charles, and Murray knew something terrible had occurred, the Oakenfeld family lived high on the Upper East Side, and the children understood very little of what was going on downtown. In the days immediately following the tragedy their parents wouldn't even let them watch television, so it's understandable that the children were mostly concerned—at least at first—with how the move would affect school. Susan in particular, had just joined the eighth grade debating club, and she was quite annoyed. When she was nine she had decided she would be a lawyer like Mr. Oakenfeld: she had been waiting to start debate for three whole years. Whereas Charles, in fifth grade, was secretly relieved. He was taking special classes at the magnet high school for science, and two days a week had to ride the West Side train all the way up to 205th Street in the Bronx, where the older boys were more than a little intimidating. At five, Murray was only in kindergarten, and so didn't care about all that. But of course he didn't want to leave his mother and father.

"But Uncle Farley has just moved into a gorgeous old house on the Bay of Eternity," Mrs. Oakenfeld told Murray. "He tells me there are pelicans and puffins, and tidal pools with starfish, and the most beautiful sunrises you've ever seen. And the house has rooms and rooms and rooms—an enormous attic, and some kind of tower-gallery-type thingy for showing off his art collection, and every imaginable exotic plant in the solarium."

"Yay, Solar Mum!" Murray yelled, and ran off to pack his suitcase.

As the eldest—and a future lawyer to boot—Susan felt it was her job to be a bit more skeptical.

"The Bay of Eternity? Really, Mum, that's quite the queer name for a place."

"Don't say 'queer,'" Charles said. "It's affected."

I suppose I should explain right off that Susan was Charles and Murray's half sister. Before Mrs. Oakenfeld had come to America and married Mr. Oakenfeld, she had lived in England, only there she had been Mrs. Wheelwright. Lt. Wheelwright had died when Susan was just a baby, and she called Mr. Oakenfeld "Daddy" just as Charles and Murray did, and indeed she thought of him as her father. But some part of her clung to England, for though she had lived in America since she was two years old she insisted on calling Mrs. Oakenfeld "Mum" instead of "Mom."
In fact all the children called Mrs. Oakenfeld "Mum," but only Susan said it with an English accent—a habit for which Charles chided her constantly.

"I say, Mum," Susan said again, ignoring her middle brother, (who, as usual, had his nose buried in some boring-looking science magazine). "The Bay of Eternity is a queer name for a place. It sounds positively Victorian."

"Don't say 'Victorian,'" Charles said, drawing out the second syllable somewhat longer than his sister had, then turning a page in his magazine—which, in fact, wasn't a magazine at all, but a catalog that offered replacement parts for old radios. The previous summer Charles had developed a passion for what he called "antiquated technology," and the bedroom he shared with Murray was overrun with half-assembled (or, more accurately, half-disassembled) radios and telephones and one ancient television whose console was nearly as big as his dresser, even though the screen was smaller than the one on his father's laptop. "It's affected," Charles added and flipped another page.

"It does sound a bit qu-quaint," Mrs. Oakenfeld said (though Susan was sure she'd been going to say "queer"). "But I think perhaps you shouldn't mention it to Uncle Farley. He might not see it that way."

Susan stuck out the side of her cheek with her tongue, as she often did when she was considering her options. She had pale thin cheeks and very short dark hair, so the lump her tongue made was quite pronounced.

"Does Uncle Farley have a telly?" she said finally.

"I believe they have television in Canada," Mrs. Oakenfeld said.

"I meant, does he have cable?"

Now Mrs. Oakenfeld understood. In addition to reading copious amounts of English literature—which is where she'd picked up somewhat affected words like "queer" and "Victorian"—her eldest child habitually tuned in to BBC World in order to keep her accent in top polish. She was especially fond of the news, and had been frustrated by not being allowed to watch it in recent days.

"I'll make you a deal," Mrs. Oakenfeld said. "If you go up to Uncle Farley's without any fuss, I'll see that you're provided with all the quality British programming you can watch."

A siren sounded in the street below the Oakenfelds' apartment, and the conversation lulled.

Susan's cheek bulged as though she were sucking on a golf ball. Part of her was contemplating a move to a house she'd never seen inhabited by an uncle she'd never met, and part of her was contemplating just what, exactly, the siren in the street might indicate. It was a boggling proposition, and more than a little frightening, and only the strained expression on Mrs. Oakenfeld's face kept Susan from giving her mother the third degree—although Susan claimed to have been waiting to start debating for three years, it was generally agreed in the Oakenfeld household that Susan had been very actively waiting, frequently annoying her parents and Charles with her cross-examinations.

"I suppose it will have to do," she said eventually. And she shook her mother's hand to seal the deal.

Charles turned a page noisily, but didn't say anything. As the well-behaved middle child, he was all too used to no one asking what he wanted.

—by Dale Peck

12. As it is used in the phrase "the older boys were more than a little intimidating," the word "intimidating" means

    A. loving

    B. studious

    C. vigorous

    D. frightening

13. The words that best express the meaning of the word "skeptical" are

    A. faithful and loyal

    B. worried and anxious

    C. doubting and mistrustful

    D. accepting and approving

14. In the quotation "a habit for which Charles chided her constantly," the words "chided her" express the idea that Charles often

    A. laughed at the things his sister said

    B. showed affection toward his sister

    C. played mind games with his sister

    D. scolded his sister

15. A synonym for the word "contemplating" is

    A. procrastinating

    B. considering

    C. attacking

    D. resolving

16. Which of the following sentences is punctuated correctly?

    A. There are two things I want for Christmas: a skateboard and a game system.

    B. There are two things I want for Christmas; a skateboard and a game system.

    C. There are two things, I want for Christmas a skateboard and a game system.

    D. There are two things I want for Christmas, a skateboard and a game system.

17. Which of the following sentences is a grammatically correct way of expressing the idea that the writer finds math problems impossible to understand?

    A. I can never understand math problems.

    B. I can't never understand math problems.

    C. I can't always understand math problems.

    D. I can only sometimes understand math problems.

18. Which of following sentences is written correctly?

    A. My uncle died last year, who lived in Denver.

    B. My uncle, who died last year, lived in Denver.

    C. My uncle whom lived in Denver died last year.

    D. My uncle, whom died last year, lived in Denver for 50 years.

19. In the sentence "Your just the employee we're looking for," the word that is spelled incorrectly is

    A. your

    B. we're

    C. looking

    D. employee

20. Which word in the sentence "There are to many dandelions on the lawn" is spelled incorrectly?

    A. To

    B. Lawn

    C. There

    D. Dandelions

21. Which word is spelled incorrectly in the sentence "The professor payed little attention to the late students"?

    A. Payed

    B. Students

    C. Attention

    D. Professor

22. In the sentence "The thief quietly dissappeared before the police arrived," the word that is spelled incorrectly is

    A. thief

    B. police

    C. quietly

    D. dissapeared

23. Which word in the sentence "At the begining of a sentence, always use a capital letter" is spelled incorrectly?

    A. Begining

    B. Sentence

    C. Always

    D. Capital

ANSWERS AND SOLUTIONS—UNIT TEST

1. A	7. C	13. C	19. A
2. WR	8. C	14. D	20. A
3. C	9. WR	15. B	21. A
4. A	10. B	16. A	22. D
5. B	11. WR	17. A	23. A
6. C	12. D	18. B	

1.　A

The description "bush-league" means not of the highest quality or sophistication. In this context, "bush-league amateurs" are those players who play mainly for fun.

2.　WRITTEN RESPONSE

In this context, the word "ricochet" refers to the way the puck is deflected off the boards. Words that are similar in meaning to the word "ricochet" are *rebound*, *deflect*, *bounce*, and *glance*.

3.　C

Dan Hawley was grinning cynically, or sneeringly, because he knew the fans did not know enough about hockey to recognize how players often have to be set up in order to score a goal. Dan felt somewhat disappointed that the goal-scorer received the majority of fan credit for the winning goal that Dan had worked so hard to set up.

4.　A

Slang is the use of informal language. When Steve O'Hara "socked the rubber," he shot the puck hard with his stick.

5.　B

These lines suggest that the fish has been caught. The bait at the end of the fishing rod is likely steel bait; when the fish "finds steel for its dinner," it swallows the bait and is caught.

The fish does not sense danger before it is caught; it is described as a "comfortable rainbow" sliding calmly to the surface to dine on hatches. In doing so, it unknowingly swallows the fisherman's bait.

6.　C

The word "implacable" means relentless or unyielding. The fishing pole, made of bamboo, easily defeats the fish. It arcs with the weight of the fish, but it does not yield.

7.　C

In the context of the phrase "It was a critical moment," the word "critical" means important or vital. The words *trivial* and *insignificant* are antonyms of the word "critical." The word "critical" can mean nagging in a different context.

8.　C

The word "colleague" refers to fellow workers or business partners. In the context of this passage, Suzuki's colleagues are his partners on the project, not his friends, companions, or superiors.

9.　WRITTEN RESPONSE

The phrase "inter-species etiquette" means proper behaviour around other species. The word etiquette refers to appropriate conduct or behaviour in social or official situations.

Shirley Strum informed the film crew on behaviour that was appropriate when dealing with baboons. The crew needed to adhere to this behaviour if they wanted to be successful in following and filming the baboons.

10. B

According to the information given in the passage, a group of baboons is referred to as a "troop." The subtitle, for example, is "A troop of baboons turn down the chance to be on television." It is also stated in the article that "Shirley is well acquainted with each individual baboon in the troop."

11. WRITTEN RESPONSE

The word "ironclad" means rigid or inflexible. Words such as *invariable*, *firm*, and *unchanging* are similar in meaning to the word "ironclad." The baboons' daily routine of wandering, feeding, socializing, and resting had been consistent for months. It was so reliable that Dr. Strum and the film crew thought it would easily be able to film the baboons.

12. D

When the writer states that "the older boys were more than a little intimidating," he means that they were frightening or threatening.

13. C

The word "skeptical" is similar in meaning to the words *doubting* and *mistrustful*.

14. D

To chide means to blame or scold someone. Charles regularly scolded his sister about her accent.

15. B

The word *contemplate* means to consider thoroughly. A synonym for the word "contemplating" is *considering*.

16. A

When compiling a list in a sentence, a colon is used to introduce the items. The sentence "There are two things I want for Christmas: a skateboard and a game system." is punctuated correctly.

17. A

Using two negative words (for example, pairing *not* and *never*) in the same sentence creates a double negative. The sentence "I can never understand math problems" correctly expresses the message the writer is trying to convey.

18. B

The sentence "My uncle, who died last year, lived in Denver" is correct.

19. A

The word *your* is spelled incorrectly in this context. The word *your* indicates possession. The sentence should read *You're* (or you are) *just the employee we're looking for*.

20. A

The word *to* is spelled incorrectly in this context. The sentence is expressing the idea of excess, so it should read *There are too many dandelions on the lawn*.

21. A

The misspelled word in the sentence is *payed*. The correct spelling is *paid*.

22. D

The word *disappeared* is spelled incorrectly. The root of the word *disappeared* is *appear* (with two *p*s). When the prefix *dis-* (with one *s*) is added, the word is correctly spelled as *disappear*. The past tense is *disappeared*.

23. A

The word *beginning* is spelled incorrectly in this sentence. The root word *begin* must have its final *n* doubled before adding the suffix *-ing*.

Form and Style

FORM AND STYLE
Table of Correlations

Specific Expectation	Practice Questions	Unit Test Questions
By the end of this course, students will:		
General Outcome		
9R2.1 *identify several different characteristics of literary, informational, and graphic text forms and explain how they help communicate meaning*	5, 7, 11	1, 13
9R2.2 *identify several different text features and explain how they help communicate meaning*	15, 16, 17, 18	7
9R2.3 *identify several different elements of style in texts and explain how they help communicate meaning and enhance the effectiveness of texts*	1, 2, 6, 8, 9, 10	3, 9, 11, 12
9W2.1 *write for different purposes and audiences using several different literary, informational, and graphic forms*	13, 14, 20	2, 14
9W2.2 *establish an identifiable voice in their writing, modifying language, and tone to suit the form, audience, and purpose for writing*		
9W2.3 *use appropriate descriptive and evocative words, phrases, and expressions to make their writing clear and vivid for their intended audience*	3, 4, 12, 19, 23, 24	4, 6, 8, 10
9W2.4 *write complete sentences that communicate meaning clearly and accurately, varying sentence type, structure, and length for different purposes and making logical transitions between ideas*	22	5
9W2.5 *explain how their own beliefs, values, and experiences are revealed in their writing*		
9W2.6 *revise drafts to improve the content, organization, clarity, and style of their written work, using a variety of teacher-modelled strategies*	21	

FORM AND STYLE

When you want to find out how a work has been written, you have to analyse the form and style of that work. Form and style are connected to each other. The form of a text refers to how it has been written from a broader perspective. How a text is structured, whether or not it is poetry or prose, and how long it is are all examples of form. The style of a text refers to how it has been written from a closer perspective. For example, style can refer to the types of words that are used and the tone or mood of the text.

In this section of your study guide, you will learn about the most common forms of writing as well as about different aspects of style. Learning to identify form and style will help you analyse writing on different and important levels.

ON 9R2.1   *Identify several different characteristics of literary, informational, and graphic text forms and explain how they help communicate meaning*

TEXT FORMS

Text is intended to communicate ideas. Text, as you know, comes in a variety of forms designed to suit the ideas a writer wants to communicate. Literary forms of text are published works that are usually in the form of poetry or prose. They can entertain and give readers insight into the emotions and experiences of others.

Text appears in many different forms. The following chart shows three categories of text forms and provides some examples of each. More detail is provided about the items with asterisks beside them in the following sections.

Literary Text Forms	Informational Text Forms	Graphic Text Forms

• poem
• play
  – musical
  – screenplay
• short story
• novella
• novel
	• history
	  – biography
	  – autobiography
	  – memoir
	  – newspaper article
	• essay
	• letter
	• diary
	• journal
	• reference
	  – textbook
	  – manual
	  – consumer document
	  – workplace document
	  – public document
	  – memorandum
		• advertisement
		• poster
		• cartoon
		• comic book
		• graphic novel
		• graphic organizer

LITERARY TEXT FORMS

As you know, literary texts exist in many different forms. The form of a text gives you an idea of the type of ideas you should be looking for. For example, if you wanted to present facts about a current events issue that interested you, you probably would not choose the form of a poem to write about it. Chances are you would choose an essay or an oral presentation. Poems and novels are usually more expressive, whereas essays tend to be more factual or objective. The next section provides definitions and descriptions of some of the different literary text forms you have encountered in class.

Poems

Poems can take a number of different forms, each of which follows pattern guidelines, such as limericks, epics, ballads, odes, and sonnets. What a poet wants to write about and how he or she wants to write it often change the structure or form of the poem.

A sonnet is a poem of 14 lines that follows a set rhyme scheme and has a logical structure. Some sonnets are written as an octave (eight lines) followed by a sestet (six lines), while others are written as 12 lines followed by a couplet. The following example is the octet/sestet combination.

ON HIS BLINDNESS

When I consider how my light is spent
E're half my days, in this dark world and wide,
And that one Talent which is death to hide,
Lodg'd with me useless, though my Soul more bent
To serve therewith my Maker, and present
My true account, lest he returning, chide;
'Doth God exact day-labour, light deny'd?'
I fondly ask; But Patience, to prevent
That murmur, soon replies: 'God doth not need
Either man's work or his own gifts, who best
Bear his milde yoak, they serve him best, his State
Is Kingly. Thousands at his bidding speed
And post o'er Land and Ocean, without rest:
They also serve who only stand and waite.'

–by John Milton

An ode is a lyric poem expressing admiring or enthusiastic emotion. The following example uses vivid imagery to express a love and admiration for the beauty of autumn.

TO AUTUMN

Season of mists and mellow fruitfulness!
Close bosom-friend of the maturing sun;
Conspiring with him how to load and bless
With fruit the vines that round the thatch-eaves run;
To bend with apples the moss'd cottage-trees,
And fill all fruit with ripeness to the core;
To swell the gourd, and plump the hazel shells
With a sweet kernel; to set budding more,
And still more, later flowers for the bees,
Until they think warm days will never cease,
For summer has o'er-brimm'd their clammy cells.

–by John Keats

This excerpt is the first part of three. Traditional odes often follow the structural pattern of poems from ancient Greek and Latin. The first part of the ode is called the strophe, followed by the *antistrophe* and the *epode*. You might notice, as well, the interesting rhyme scheme: ABABCDEDCCE.

Plays

A play is a story that is meant to be acted. Dialogue is a major part of a play, but how a set looks and how the actors look and move are also very important. Plays have different forms, which usually affects their length. A one-act play is typically under an hour long, whereas a full five-act play, such as Hamlet, can take as long as three or four hours to enact.

Short Stories

A short story is a story of 20 000 words or fewer, usually with a limited number of characters and a plot without subplots.

The main plot elements are often outlined in a plot diagram.

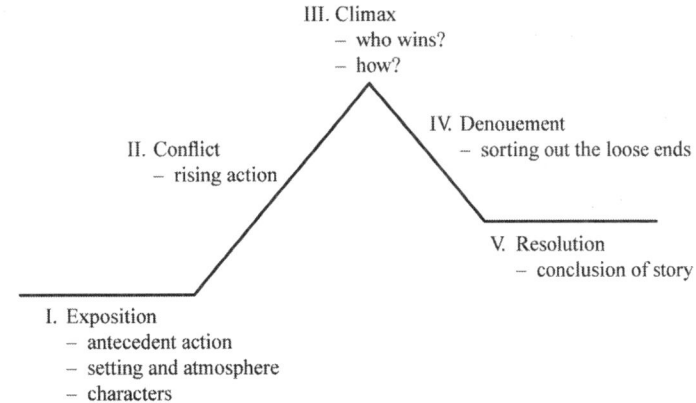

```
                        III. Climax
                          – who wins?
                          – how?

                                      IV. Denouement
                                        – sorting out the loose ends
        II. Conflict
          – rising action

                                              V. Resolution
                                                – conclusion of story

        I. Exposition
          – antecedent action
          – setting and atmosphere
          – characters
```

Either the plot headings or the plot diagram can be used to outline the events that occur in a short story. Short stories can be further categorized into subforms, such as detective, fantasy, or science fiction stories.

Novels

While a novella is longer than a short story (20 000 to 50 000 words), a novel is generally much longer (90 000 to 100 000 or more words) and may contain many characters and multiple plots within the same novel. Some novels, such as the three novels that comprise Tolkien's *Lord of the Rings* trilogy, have so many characters and intertwined subplots that you have to keep backtracking just to keep track of the main plot and characters. Novels come in many forms. Some novels are a combination of forms, like historical romance or the epistolary novel, which is a story told through a series of letters.

INFORMATIONAL TEXT FORMS

Informational texts are non-fiction texts, which means they are based on reality or facts, although they may contain opinions expressed by the writer. They are generally presented in a prose style of writing, which means in sentences and paragraphs. It is important to be careful with non-fiction or informational texts. Although they usually claim to present factual, unbiased writing on a subject, they are not always without bias. Non-fiction can have a writer's slant just as fiction can.

Essays

Essays consist of a thesis, body, and conclusion. An essay attempts to communicate an opinion or idea. Different forms of essays include expository, persuasive, and research essays.

Letters

Letters generally begin with an inside address and date and use conventional greetings and closings such as "Dear ——" and "Yours Sincerely." Letters may be personal and informal (friendly letter) or formal (business letter). Each has a slightly different format. It is common for opinion essays to appear in a newspaper as letters to the editor.

Reference Books

Reference books contain specific non-fiction information. Examples of reference books include encyclopedias, dictionaries, thesauruses, atlases, and almanacs.

Consumer Documents

A consumer document provides important information about products and services. These documents take different forms, such as consumer reports, warranties, recall announcements, and advertisements.

WORKPLACE DOCUMENTS

Most workplaces have specially designed documents suited to that particular workplace. These include application forms, contracts, safety policies, dress codes, emergency procedures, Internet use rules, and email policies.

Public Documents

A public document is often provided through a government office or agency and contains information that supports public safety and welfare. Examples of public documents are acts pertaining to clean air, safe water, and highways, littering laws, driver's handbooks, and library policies.

Memorandums

A memorandum is often brief and is addressed to a limited group such as the employees of a company. It is limited to essential information and is frequently sent in the form of an inter-office email.

GRAPHIC TEXT FORMS

Graphic text forms rely heavily on drawing and illustrations or showing information using graphic organizers such as charts or plot diagrams. There are a variety of forms of graphic text. Some forms are legitimate means of conveying art or entertainment, and other forms are used primarily for organizing statistics or other information. Using visual aids in addition to text to convey meaning gives a work more depth and can often explain information in a way that text alone cannot.

Advertisements

Text advertisements are mostly found in newspapers and magazines or are posted in public places such as buses and on billboards. The Internet is, as you know, full of advertisements ranging from pop-up ads to ads that are built into the design of a website. Companies even pay search engines to have their company's website show up on the first page of a person's search.

Graphic Novels

Graphic novels are also known as picture novels. A graphic novel is a full-length novel where the action and characters have been drawn by an artist to complement the narrative text, which is framed in captions and word balloons similar to a regular comic book. A comic book really differs from a graphic novel only in length.

Graphic novels, in one form or another, have been around since the 1940s. They are not really a new or recent trend. At that time, a series of stories from classical literature were published in a comic-book format called *Classics Illustrated*, with well-known titles such as *Robinson Crusoe* and *Treasure Island*. The intention was to entice young readers to read literature they might be reluctant to read in full-length novel form.

By 1975, graphic novels were gaining broader acceptance as a genre. In 1986, a graphic novel called Maus by Art Spiegelman won the Pulitzer Prize for the category of Letters, Drama, or Music. You may have read a graphic novel or two yourself, such as *5 Shots* by Jemir Johnson or *Diary of a Wimpy Kid* by Jeff Kinney. A selection of graphic novels can be found at your school or local library.

HOW DIFFERENT FORMS COMMUNICATE MEANING

Different forms of text communicate meaning in different ways. A graphic novel, for example, could make use of depictions of facial expressions and illustrations of actions taking place to show emotion and plot progression. Text in the form of a journal, on the other hand, would have to make use of descriptive language to communicate these same ideas. A few text examples are provided in the following section to illustrate aspects of form that communicate meaning.

Journals

Read through "A Pirate's Journal." What aspects of the journal form affect how such a text communicates ideas and information?

A Pirate's Journal

September 17, 1708

Today at dawn, I, Captain Bluenose of the goode shippe Bonnie Doom, berried my tresure on Maryjane Island, so named in honer of my late goode wife and fare frend Maryjane Marlybone. The secretion of the goods was witnessed by my trusted frend and assistent, Matthew Collings. He was also sole dark witness to the plank cerimonie last midnight, by which that black traiter Mossbank Jack went to his watery reward. Those who plan mutinous actions against their captain and his loyal crue must be silenced as an example to those who wuld practice trechery.

September 18, 1708

Perdition and Curses on these high seas! We marked the location of the tresure with care, near a small distinctive tree of a rare veriety at the edge of a grate black rock. The seas were beccoming stormy, so I purposed to stay at anchor for the night. The seas were so high I feered we shuld all be lost forever. This morning, praise Gawd, we are still at anchor, but the island of my treasure has disappeared. Nothing but water as far as the eye can see. My goode Collings is proper distressed, and stays below.

The author's means of communication is limited in journal form by the convention of time. The date is written at the beginning of every journal entry. Because journal entries are typically written in one sitting, a single journal entry might not be able to span a large amount of time. Journal entries tend to stick to specific episodes or events. The author is also limited by personal perspective of the character narrating the journal. The pirate may have insight into another character's feelings, but the narration is limited to one character for any one journal entry.

Travel Narratives

Travel narratives are typically episodic; the writer spends the most time on a brief episode involving a street performer. There is some unpredictability, interest, and suspense created when the writer stops short of describing the entire day in detail. Look for the these characteristics in the following travel narrative.

The organization of the following travel narrative is linear and chronological, beginning at the family's lodging, moving down some streets to St. Peter's Square, to a nearby bus stop, to the Angel Fortress, and eventually on to a sightseeing bus that takes the family on a tour of the city. The series of events seems to unfold mostly in the morning, until the family boards the bus.

ONE DAY IN ROME

Our third day in Rome, we set off to buy a two-day pass on the red double-decker sightseeing bus we had been told was a great (and inexpensive) way to see the city. The #110 is a "hop-on, hop-off" bus which follows a loop route past most of the main monuments and tourist attractions like the Coliseum. You can get off the bus, look around as long as you want, and board another bus to keep going. They are scheduled to arrive approximately every 15 minutes throughout the day and evening.

Our destination was San Pietro, or St. Peter's Square, which was within easy walking distance of our bed and breakfast apartment. We had toured the Vatican Museum, Sistine Chapel, and St. Peter's Basilica the day before, so had explored the Vatican City area quite thoroughly. We were ready to expand our adventure.

As you can see, the structure of the narrative in this passage is very linear and tells the story chronologically. Travel narratives have been a popular literary form for centuries. Travel narratives feature the uniqueness of the traveller's writing style and can be very creative within the structure of the form.

ON 9R.2.2   Identify several different text features and explain how they help communicate meaning

TEXT FEATURES

ORGANIZATIONAL FEATURES OF BOOKS

Informative books are organized with features that help you find information quickly. After you have read a book, these features can also help you recall or find the information that you need again. Here are some features with which you should be familiar.

A **title page** tells you the topic of the book and its writer or editor.

The **table of contents** is found at the front of a book, usually just after the title page. It lists the book's chapters or divisions in order from first to last. The starting page number of each chapter is also given. You can skim a table of contents from top to bottom to find out where a particular chapter begins and how long it is.

Chapter 1 – Under the Sea...........................1
Chapter 2 – Fish, Fish, Fish!............................17
Chapter 3 – Why We Like Diving...............28
Chapter 4 – Underwater Machines...............36

A **preface** or **foreword** is an introduction that sometimes includes helpful or positive features of the book.

The **visual layout** of a book refers to how the book is put together, whether it contains pictures and diagrams, etc.

The appendix is a section found at the back of some information books. It contains extra information to help you understand the material, such as notes, charts, maps, or diagrams.

Index

An index is an alphabetical list of the important topics in an information book. It tells you which pages have information on each topic.

Glossary

A glossary is often found at the back of a non-fiction book. It lists and explains the meanings of words in the book that are important or that you may not already know. While reading a book with a glossary, you can quickly check the meaning of a word without getting out a dictionary.

Chapter organizers are arranged according to the order of the content. Organizing and presenting material using many different styles can help you learn difficult material. These features also help you navigate through a chapter. This is especially useful if you want to read only certain kinds of material from each chapter as you study for an exam.

VISUALS AS AN ORGANIZATIONAL FEATURE

When you read comics, you are interpreting visual clues that convey meaning. Facial expressions and body language contribute to meaning as much as the text in dialogue and thought balloons. When you read the caption under a picture in your social studies text and connect it to the picture, you better understand the meaning that is being illustrated. You can easily recognize the value of visuals in science books, math texts, and manuals. Diagrams make complex systems or processes easier to understand, whether you are trying to solve a problem or are figuring out the functions on your new cellphone.

Visuals enhance communication and convey meaning within text. Whether you are researching a topic or reading in a textbook, do not underestimate the power of any visuals that are included.

TEXT LAYOUT USED TO ENHANCE MEANING

The manner in which text is laid out or presented on a page adds to and can change the meaning of the text itself. Concrete poetry is an example of how text layout affects meaning. Concrete poetry, sometimes called "shape" poetry, uses configurations of words that are related to the subject of the poem. In the following example, the poem is made up of 14 words, all of which reflect on the theme of insolence. Insolence means bold rudeness or open disrespect, usually toward an authority figure. The poet's message becomes more powerful when the poem is read step by step as descending rungs on a ladder, "wrong by wrong" (word play on "rung by rung"), to the bottom. Instead of climbing up toward goals of success, the wrong attitudinal choices follow the words of the poem downward in the direction of probable failure.

INSOLENCE

and
　　the
　　　　young
　　　　　　man
　　　　　　　　laughed
　　　　　　　　　　as he
　　　　　　　　　　　　climbed
　　　　　　　　　　　　　　down
　　　　　　　　　　　　　　　　the
　　　　　　　　　　　　　　　　　　ladder
　　　　　　　　　　　　　　　　　　　　wrong
　　　　　　　　　　　　　　　　　　　　　　by
　　　　　　　　　　　　　　　　　　　　　　　　wrong

–by Nanci Neff

Using such dramatic visual features is usually most appropriate in poetry assignments, but visual tools can be used in less obvious ways in other texts as well. Newspapers, which will be discussed in the following part of this section of your study guide, use many visual tools to keep readers interested.

SPECIALIZED TEXT FEATURES

Certain texts, such as newspapers, have design features that are related to their purpose. Many daily newspapers are designed for rapid reading by people on the go. Large newspapers come in sections so that readers can quickly find the topics they are most interested in. The front page presents an index, similar to a table of contents, of the main sections and daily features, such as the entertainment section, classifieds, and letters to the editor. It also shows an overview of the weather and the newsworthy stories of the day. As you examine the structure of the following news article, you will see how the stories themselves are presented in a design or format that makes the key facts from the news quickly accessible to readers.

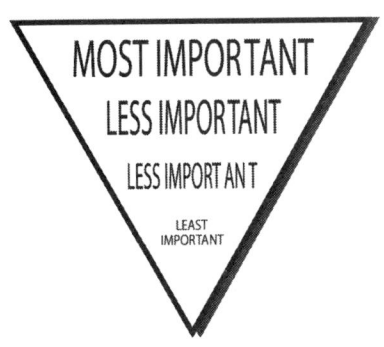

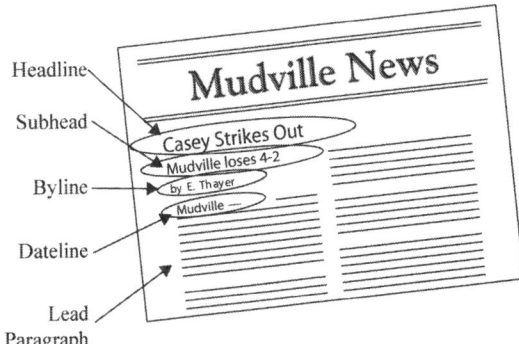

STRUCTURE OF A NEWS ARTICLE

A news article usually consists of a headline, a byline, a dateline, and a body. Writing a news article is very different from writing a narrative. Generally, a narrative will build up to the climax, or most important part, of the story. The news article, on the other hand, begins with the most important information and then proceeds to less important information, leaving the least important to the end. The structure of a news article can be compared with an inverted pyramid. A news article begins with a lead paragraph that contains the most significant information in the story and then continues through the middle paragraphs to the concluding paragraph of the article. The following information is an overview of each part of a news article.

Headline

The headline is the title of the news article. It is a very brief summary of the news article. The headline must grab the reader's attention using exciting and vivid words. It often contains a noun and a verb. All important words are capitalized, and there is usually no punctuation at the end of the title.

Subhead

Sometimes, a subhead, or secondary title, appears immediately after the headline. A subhead provides additional information about the story, but not all stories will have a subhead.

Byline

The byline is positioned after the subhead. As the name suggests, it indicates who has written the article. Often times, the byline will just state the news source rather than an individual journalist. Reuters and The Associated Press are examples of news sources commonly found in news articles.

Dateline

The dateline usually appears at the beginning of an article. It is included at the start of the lead paragraph. It tells the reader where the story happened; it does not tell the date. Usually the byline and the dateline appear in the same line of text.

Lead Paragraph

The beginning of a news article is called the lead, and it introduces the subject of the article. The most important ideas of the article are included in the lead. A good lead usually answers the following questions: Who, What, When, Where, Why, and How.

Who	The subject of the article: the article could be about a person, place, idea, event or object.
What	The action of the article: what has happened or what is currently happening.
When	The time frame of the article: Did the action take place last night, last week, or over the course of a month?
Where	The place the action is happening.
Why	Explains the "what," or the action, of the article.
How	Describes the sequence of events or actions that occurred.

The five Ws and How are usually covered in the first one or two sentences. The rest of the first paragraph may include additional details or important information. The first sentence of the lead is particularly important. It must hook readers and encourage them to continue reading. In most news articles, the first sentence gives answers to as many of the five Ws and How as possible in as few words as possible. The first sentence should provide a good lead-in to the rest of the paragraph and article.

Answer the following questions about the sample front page of the fictional newspaper provided on the next page. Try to answer the questions before looking at the answers that follow the sample. They will help to clarify and highlight some of the text features that are unique to newspapers.

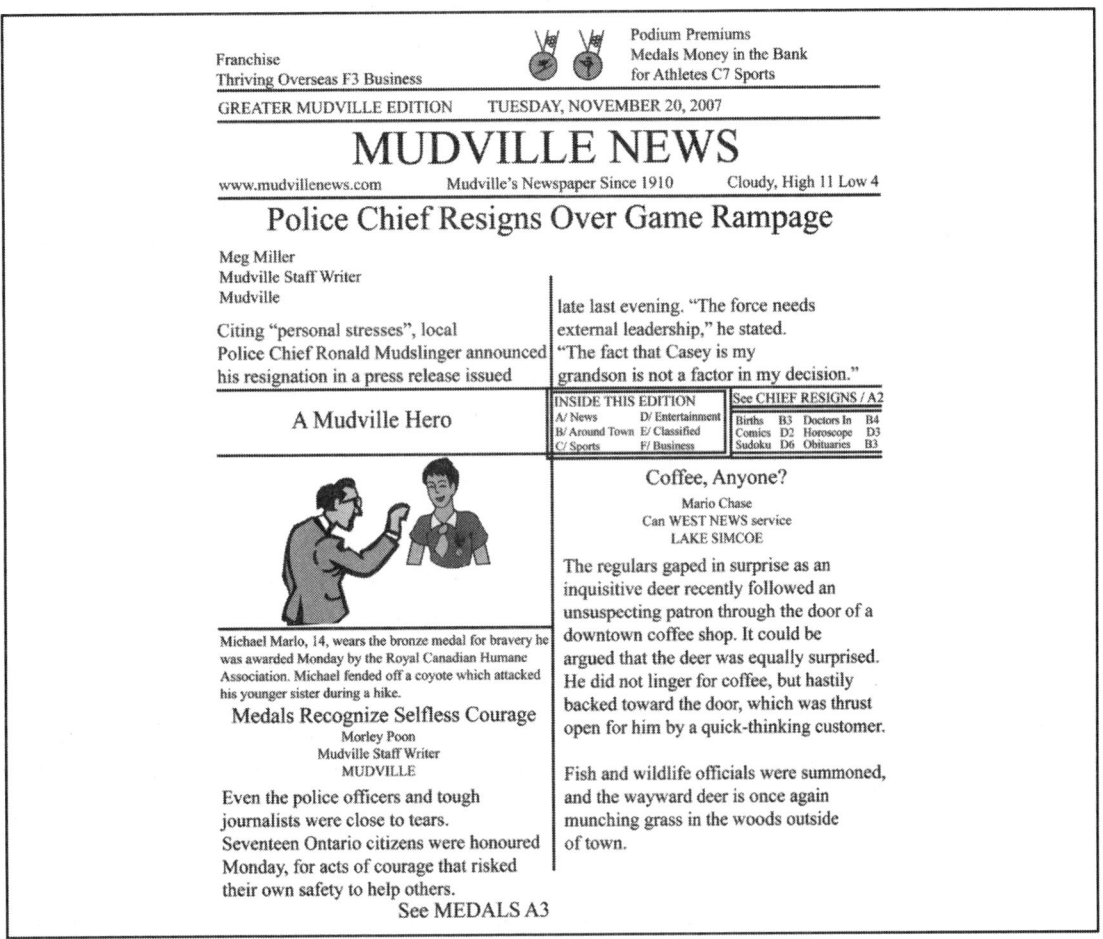

Questions and answers about the front page of the *Mudville News*

Question: What are some text features you recognize on the front page of this newspaper?

Answer: Some text features are the headlines, bylines (Meg Miller, Mario Chase), datelines (Mudville, Lake Simcoe), lead sentences that are good "hooks" and provide key information, boxed text with main sections, and features listed.

Question: What might be the purpose behind the different text fonts and sizes used on this page?

Answer: The largest font is used for the main headline about the police chief. The other two headlines have slightly smaller fonts but are still prominently positioned on the front page. The bylines and datelines are in block letters for easy recognition of the reporter and location of the story. The contents list is in a small font because there is not much room for it, but it is set apart with a boxed-in frame so readers can find it easily.

Question: How do the photograph and caption draw attention to a key story?

Answer: The photograph is large, and it dominates the front page because it is also the only picture. The caption draws attention to the story about the medals immediately below the photo.

Question: What features help readers navigate through this newspaper?

Answer: The features that help readers navigate through the paper are the text box entitled "Inside This Edition," the section follow-up locators by the last sentence of continued stories, and the section locator for an article of interest to the business community ("Franchise Thriving Overseas F3 Business").

ON 9W2.1 Students will write for different purposes and audiences using several different literary, informational, and graphic forms

WRITING WITH PURPOSE

Your topic, purpose for writing, and audience can all play a part in determining the form that you will choose for your writing piece. When writing a cover letter to a prospective employer about a summer job, for example, you would probably choose to write a business letter rather than some other form of text.

Once you have a topic or a purpose for writing, you can choose the best form according to what you want to say, how you want to say it, and who your audience will be.

The following chart displays some writing forms and the motivation you might have for using them.

Personal Letter	**Letter to the Editor**
• to a friend who has moved	• to express your viewpoint on a community issue
• to thank a relative for a gift	• to comment on a news item
• to a parent while away at summer camp	• to express public appreciation for something
Review	**Poem**
• a book you have read	• to express feelings
• a movie you have watched	• to describe something
• an event you have attended	• to celebrate a special occasion
Report	**Narrative**
• to share research	• to relate a personal experience
• to explore an assigned topic	• to create a short story
• to hand in to a social studies or science teacher	• to write a journal entry
Comic Strip	**Trading Cards**
• to depict scenes from a story for young children	• to describe mythological figures
• to portray an issue	• to describe characters in a novel
• to summarize chapters in a novel	• to make mini-biographies of inspirational people

The following methods can be used to help you apply your knowledge of form to specific writing projects.

WRITING PERSUASIVE COMPOSITIONS

If you are writing a persuasive composition, the opening paragraph requires close attention. The introductory paragraph is crucial to keeping your reader's attention. Persuasive writing appeals to a reader's emotional faculties. The logic you use must be stated clearly to ensure your reader will understand. You must use examples drawn from an emotional source in order to fully convince your reader of the plausibility of your position.

Both logical arguments and emotional appeals are useful to persuade your reader, but try to create a good balance between the two.

Type of Appeal	Examples
Emotional	1. Gives personal anecdotes
	2. Asks questions
	3. Appeals to readers' emotions
	4. Uses emotional words
Logical	1. Provides facts
	2. Provides reasons
	3. Recognizes opposing arguments

Suppose you are writing a persuasive argument on the topic of school uniforms. The first decision to make when writing a persuasive argument is what position you will take. Once you have chosen your position, you can start to researching existing arguments and other information. Suppose your position is that school uniforms help to protect students and promote learning.

Provide your audience with statistics and researched information:

Research has shown that schools requiring students to wear uniforms have better attendance rates, higher academic achievement, and less fighting.

Appeal to your reader's emotions or ethical beliefs:

Teachers have been frustrated in the past because their classes are regularly disrupted by students looking at themselves in the mirror, painting their fingernails, combing their hair, or comparing designer labels. Parents who are on tight budgets often watch in dismay and helplessness as their children are bullied for wearing "uncool" clothes.

Relate a personal anecdote to bring your audience closer to your position. Rather than sharing statistics or numbers, a personal story can make an audience feel the emotional impact your issue can have:

When I went to school, we had to wear uniforms. I remember a time when a student misbehaved on the bus going home. A passenger (who recognized the uniform as belonging to our school) reported the incident to our principal. The principal was very quick to reprimand the culprit, who was identified by his bright red hair and freckled face!

Give examples of cases where your argument can be supported:

> An individual does not lose his personality when wearing a uniform. Uniforms are commonplace to people in many walks of life, such as flight attendants, bus or train drivers, postal workers, restaurant employees, military personnel, members of school sports teams, and choirs or bands. These people are able to wear uniforms without any loss of personality or personal freedoms.

CLARIFYING AND DEFENDING YOUR POSITION

Being clear in defending your position means making sure your reader knows what you are trying to say. Get a classmate or friend to read over an opinion-based text you have written. Do they understand what you are trying to say after reading it through only one time? If they do, that is a good sign that your ideas and opinions are clear. To clarify and defend your position, use precise and relevant evidence including facts, expert opinions, quotations, expressions of commonly accepted beliefs, and logical reasoning.

As you prepare your arguments, ask people their views and record them. Additionally, you could research the findings of someone like Dr. David Brunsma, from the University of Alabama, who has written numerous books and articles on the subject of school uniforms. You could use the Internet to look up court cases and appeals involving school boards that have a school uniform policy. WHEN (World Home Education Network) also has statements on its website regarding school uniforms. The more facts you can find to support your argument, the more persuasive your argument will be.

ADDRESSING YOUR AUDIENCE

As you prepare your composition, you must be prepared to address concerns from both sides of your argument. While remembering that your position is that the use of school uniforms is a way to protect students and promote learning, you can argue that:

- The safety of Canadian students is fundamentally more important than any loss of freedom of expression that might occur by introducing school uniforms.

- It is an infringement on citizens' clearly established constitutional rights to tell students what to wear to school.

- School uniforms are not nearly as important as a good school atmosphere, clear rules and expectations, and parental involvement in student learning.

Thinking of a variety of arguments will help you pick out which ones you think are most effective for your particular audience. You might choose different arguments when you are writing for your class than when you are writing a letter to the teachers in your school.

CREATIVE METHODS OF RELATING INFORMATION

Many teachers will allow you freedom of creative choice when it comes to selecting a writing form. If you are studying Greek mythology, for instance, instead of researching and preparing a list of Greek mythological figures, you could look in books or perform an Internet search to find information.

Greek Mythological Figures

Achilles was the half-mortal son of the sea-goddess, Thetis. Because Thetis held her infant son by the heel when she dipped him in the river of immortality, he was immune to mortal attacks, except through his un-dipped heel. Hence, one's fatal flaw or weakness is sometimes known as one's "Achilles' heel."

Atlas was a Titan of immense physical strength who carried the sky upon his shoulders. The Titans were an ancient race of giants.

Medusa was a terrifying Gorgon sister, whose hairdo was a squirming, writhing mass of hissing snakes.

Narcissus was a boy who fell in love with his own reflection in a stream, gazing at it so long that he grew roots and grew into a flower on the bank.

To make your information more distinctive, you could use it to create a set of trading cards of mythological figures. Drawing pictures of the figures on the cards to accompany the text information would not only be more enjoyable for you as a student, but it would also make the information easier to remember. Always try to choose the best form to serve your purpose and engage your audience, even if your audience is only yourself!

ON 9R2.3   *Identify several different elements of style in texts and explain how they help communicate meaning and enhance the effectiveness of the text*

ELEMENTS OF STYLE

Different elements of style in text communicate meaning and enhance effectiveness. For the purposes of this section, *style* refers to a particular or characteristic manner of writing to achieve deliberate effects in a text or responses in the readers.

Figurative Language

Figurative language creates imagery. Imagery is created when a writer paints a picture in a reader's mind by appealing to his or her senses of smell, taste, touch, sight, and hearing. For example, the sentence "The tops of the trees were swaying in the howling wind as all around flew dried-up leaves of brown and yellow" should paint a picture in your mind.

A **simile** occurs when a writer compares two or more things or ideas using *like* or *as*.

When I shook his hand, it was as cold as ice.

She left the campfire like a whisper, disappearing softly into the trees.

A **metaphor** occurs when a writer compares two or more things or ideas directly, without using the words *like* or *as*. A metaphor can occur within a sentence, a paragraph, or throughout an entire piece of writing.

For example, in the sentence "The stars were diamonds in the sky," the stars are being compared to diamonds.

> The silver grin on the Man in the Moon held secrets we could only guess.

Personification is a literary device that gives human characteristics to an animal or an inanimate object.

> soared smoothly above the stadium
>
> bellowed brokenly
>
> tarnished the twinkling timelessness

Alliteration occurs when initial consonant sounds are repeated in adjacent or nearby words.

> soared smoothly above the stadium
>
> bellowed brokenly
>
> tarnished the twinkling timelessness

Onomatopoeia occurs when a word actually seems to sound like the thing it represents.

> Swishing
>
> Hushing
>
> Sizzle
>
> Thump

SYMBOLISM

Symbolism is used to enhance a theme, suggest a mood, or create an effect. Symbolism occurs when a writer uses an object, a situation, or an action to suggest another meaning. A writer might use a tiger to symbolize strength or fierceness. Another writer might use a lamb to suggest peace and gentleness. Symbols usually occur throughout a story. Generally, if an image or word is used three times or more in a story, there is a good chance that it is being used as a symbol.

"The Most Dangerous Game" is a well-known short story by Richard Connell. The story is about the blood sport of trophy hunting, which has deteriorated into full-blown brutality. In the story, the reader is drawn into a sinister plot where the hunter who proposed the contest is actually pursuing his rival as prey. The following analysis shows how the symbol of smoking can reveal to the reader enhanced levels of meaning in a text.

The symbolism associated with smoking in the story allows you to analyse the story more closely. Smoking seems to be a symbol of power. At the beginning of the story, the protagonist, Rainsford, is a confident and powerful man who speaks as a successful hunter while smoking his pipe. The following quotation explains his actions after he is thrown from the boat: "He leaped upon the rail and balanced himself there, to get greater elevation; his pipe, striking a rope, was knocked from his mouth. He lunged for it; a short, hoarse cry came from his lips as he realized he had reached too far and had lost his balance." Rainsford losing his pipe symbolizes his loss of power: he is no longer the hunter.

Once on the island, Zaroff, who wants to hunt and kill Rainsford, has all the power over his prey. He smokes "black cigarettes," and his smoking symbolizes his authority as the dominant hunter. The following quotation describes Zaroff's behaviour when he is close to finding Rainsford's hiding spot in the jungle: "… he straightened up and took from his case one of his black cigarettes; its pungent incenselike smoke floated up to Rainsford's nostrils." Zaroff's smoking indicates that he is in control and is dominant over Rainsford at this point in the story.

In "The Most Dangerous Game," Rainsford begins as an accomplished hunter and ends up as the prey of another hunter. Smoking symbolizes the power and authority of hunting. Rainsford possesses this power at the beginning of the story, and Zaroff possesses the power throughout the hunt, although Rainsford ultimately triumphs over Zaroff. Smoking is symbolic of dominance and power. The hunter dominates, and this dominant position is symbolized through smoking.

Symbolism can be complicated or simple. There is a certain amount of creativity in trying to figure out if something is a symbol or not. After reading through a story, try to think of the images and ideas that stood out to you. This can be a good start to discovering symbols in a text.

Irony

Irony, or dramatic irony, as it is sometimes called, occurs when the reader or audience has information that the characters do not possess.

In Shakespeare's *Romeo and Juliet*, Romeo discovers Juliet lying motionless and still in a tomb. He assumes that she is dead and, acting upon his incorrect assumption, he commits suicide. The audience knows that Juliet has swallowed a sleeping potion and is not dead, but merely unconscious. The result is dramatic irony.

DIALECTS IN LITERATURE

Dialect refers to a variety of language within a language that has its own pronunciations and can even use different words and phrases. Many people in Quebec, for example, speak a dialect of French that is different from the French spoken in France. A dialect is usually a product of the speaker's cultural or regional background.

Cockney, for example, is a dialect used by people native to south London. The musical *My Fair Lady*, based on the play *Pygmalion* by George Bernard Shaw, provides a wealth of examples of Cockney dialect from its main character, Eliza Doolittle. In an opening scene of the musical, Professor Higgins, a linguistics professor, is hiding behind a nearby pillar, copying every word she says. He is intrigued by how different Eliza's dialect is from formal English. Eliza is heard to remark, "I say, capt'n' n'baw ya flahr orf a pore gel," which Higgins translates into formal English as "I say, captain, now buy yourself a flower off a poor girl."

Writers employ dialect to make their characters more believable according to the setting in which the story takes place. Sometimes writers will even spell words according to how they sound in a certain dialect.

FORMAL AND INFORMAL LANGUAGE

The choice of words in writing determines whether the writing is formal or informal. It is important to decide before you begin writing whether you want to use formal or informal language. Usually, you will make this decision after taking into consideration your intended audience.

Formal writing uses words and expressions that are chosen carefully to avoid slang and contractions. In general, formal writing should follow the rules of grammar. Formal writing shows that you have spent time thinking about and polishing your work. Formal writing uses proper English and should be used in schoolwork. Formal writing is also necessary in job applications and resumes, thank-you letters for scholarships and awards, and any other situation in which you want to show that you have applied time and intelligence to your work.

Informal writing allows the use of contractions and is more relaxed in terms of word choice and grammatical rules. Informal writing, especially in journals or friendly letters, allows the use of colloquial expressions or slang. In an informal narrative that includes dialogue, the characters speak to each other informally as well. For example, the sentence "My buddies bought the coolest clothes on the weekend" contains colloquial or slang words and has a casual tone.

Leetspeak is an example of very informal language. It is a form of symbolic writing made up of Internet slang terms developed by early users of online bulletin boards. *Leetspeak* makes messages easier and quicker to write and, in the case of text messaging on cellphones, also makes messages less expensive to send by limiting the number of words that are used. For example, a shorter way to say "What's up? Are you coming over tonight?" would be "wuz up r u comin ovr 2nite."

Unless you are writing creatively, *leetspeak* should never be used in schoolwork or for other formal documents such as resumes or scholarship applications. It may save time, but it is incorrect English and will most likely be regarded as lazy and unprofessional.

When you read a text, you can determine whether the language is formal or informal in the same way that you would recognize it in your own writing. Most textbooks are written in formal style because they are addressed to a general audience that includes educators, parents, and students.

WORD CHOICE AND PERSONAL STYLE

Writing style refers to how writers use words and sentences to present ideas. Writing is clearer, livelier, and more enjoyable to read when writers choose their words carefully so that their sentences are precise and varied in length and structure.

General Word	More Specific or Descriptive Words
Fear (n)	terror, trepidation, panic, nervousness, horror, cowardice
Tidy (adj)	orderly, fastidious, clean, neat, smart, well-groomed
Ask (v)	inquire, request, probe, interrogate, challenge, question, query

Notice the vivid and descriptive words in the following excerpt from Edgar Allan Poe's short story "The Tell-Tale Heart." Phrases containing particularly vivid word choices have been underlined.

FROM THE TELL-TALE HEART

It is impossible to say how first the idea entered my brain; but once conceived, it haunted me day and night. Object there was none. Passion there was none. I loved the old man. He had never wronged me. He had never given me insult. For his gold I had no desire. I think it was his eye! Yes, it was this! One of his eyes resembled that of a vulture—a pale blue eye, with a film over it. Whenever it fell upon me, my blood ran cold; and so by degrees—very gradually—I made up my mind to take the life of the old man, and thus rid myself of the eye forever.

Now this is the point. You fancy me mad. Madmen know nothing. But you should have seen *me*. You should have seen how wisely I proceeded—with what caution—with what foresight—with what dissimulation I went to work! I was never kinder to the old man than during the whole week before I killed him.

–by Edgar Allan Poe

SENTENCE VARIETY

Successful writers use a variety of sentence types: questions, commands, exclamations, and statements. They also vary sentence beginnings and sentence lengths because this helps create interesting rhythms and a more enjoyable reading experience.

Look at how Edgar Allan Poe has constructed his sentences at the beginning of "The Tell-Tale Heart."

True!—Nervous—very, very dreadfully nervous I had been and am; but why will you say that I am mad? The disease has sharpened my senses—not destroyed—not dulled them. Above all was the sense of hearing acute. I heard all things in the heaven and in the earth. I heard many things in hell. How, then, am I mad? Hearken! And observe how healthily—how calmly I can tell you the whole story.

By using the word "true" as an exclamation, he alerts the reader to the fact that he is about to claim something. Then, through the question "why will you say that I am mad?" the narrator addresses the reader, which draws the reader into thinking more actively about the story.

USE OF STYLE TO CREATE TONE AND MOOD

A writer's style and tone help to create the mood of a piece of writing. As you read more, you will be able to recognize how style, tone, and mood all work together in a text.

Tone

A writer's tone is the overall attitude that he or she has toward what is written. Tone is established by the writer's word choice, or diction. The tone conveys the writer's attitude toward the story or characters. It sets the mood of the writing, and it must always be appropriate for the writer's purpose and audience. The tone of a story can be, for example, serious, light-hearted, sad, emotional, formal, or informal. Because writers create tone through their choice and arrangement of words, punctuation, sentence length, and so on.

In the same excerpt from Poe's "The Tell-Tale Heart," the writer's tone allows the reader to have insight into the narrator's mental state. The more and more the narrator talks about his decision to murder the old man, the better the reader can understand that he is not in his right mind.

> True!—Nervous—very, very dreadfully nervous I had been and am; but why will you say that I am mad? The disease has sharpened my senses—not destroyed—not dulled them. Above all was the sense of hearing acute. I heard all things in the heaven and in the earth. I heard many things in hell. How, then, am I mad? Hearken! And observe how healthily—how calmly I can tell you the whole story. It is impossible to say how first the idea entered my brain; but once conceived, it haunted me day and night. Object there was none. Passion there was none. I loved the old man. He had never wronged me. He had never given me insult. For his gold I had no desire. I think it was his eye! Yes, it was this! One of his eyes resembled that of a vulture—a pale blue eye, with a film over it. Whenever it fell upon me, my blood ran cold; and so by degrees—very gradually—
> I made up my mind to take the life of the old man, and thus rid myself of the eye forever.

Poe's tone can be seen in his attitude toward the narrator in the story. The narrator uses eccentric, strange, and defensive language, which reveals that the writer perceives the character to have those traits.

Mood

While tone describes a writer's attitude toward his or her story, mood is the feeling a text creates within the reader. Writers choose their words, phrases, and images carefully in order to lead their readers to feel certain emotions. In the following passage, a mood of anger and frustration is created by the writer's word choice, punctuation, and use of repetition and sarcasm.

> ### GARBAGE
>
> Garbage! Garbage! Garbage! Why is there so much garbage and waste? Do people think it will disappear on its own? I work hard to recycle and reuse, yet garbage heaps up on us all the time! There is no end to it!

The mood of a story can be angry, sad, frightening, suspenseful, enthusiastic, scary, and so on. You can use a variety of words to create mood. For example, in the following paragraph from *Island of the Blue Dolphins*, Scott O'Dell creates a mood of eeriness, suspense, and loneliness. As a reader, you wonder what is going to happen, and you can feel the narrator's loneliness and sadness.

> It was a morning of thick fog and the sound of far off waves breaking on the shore. I had never noticed before how silent the village was. Fog crept in and out of the empty huts. It made shapes as it drifted and it reminded me of all the people who were dead and those who were gone. The noise of the surf seemed to be their voices speaking.

In this passage, it is the writer's style of writing—the short, simple sentences and the tone that is established through the choice of words such as "thick fog," "waves breaking," and "fog crept in and out… it made shapes"—that creates the mood you experience as you read.

In summary, tone and mood are closely related but separate aspects of style. Tone is the writer's apparent attitude toward his or her subject, characters, or readers. The writer's tone, depending on such aspects as subject matter, use of formal or informal language, and characterization, may come across to you, the reader, as serious, light, cynical, sympathetic, indifferent, or passionate. Mood, on the other hand, describes the emotions the reader feels while reading a text.

AN AUTHOR'S UNIQUE STYLE

Some well-known authors have imprinted their writing with personal style preferences. These style choices are usually consistent within an author's body of work but are different from the style choices of other authors. If you become familiar with these style choices, often you can determine the author of a work just by examining the writing style.

For example, Charles Dickens, author of *A Christmas Carol*, *Oliver Twist*, *A Tale of Two Cities*, and many other books, is well known for long, descriptive sentences and passages. Dickens often describes his characters in meticulous detail, in both appearance and manner.

Guy de Maupassant, credited with the earliest examples of the short story genre, liked to present human nature in stories such as "The Piece of String" and "The Diamond Necklace." In these stories, the plot seemed to play second fiddle to well-drawn character studies. The characters portrayed by this author, like Maitre Hauchecorne and Madam Loisel, are memorable mainly because of the character flaws that lead to great misfortune in their lives.

EVOCATIVE LANGUAGE AND MOOD

Now that you have reviewed a number of elements of style that enhance or clarify texts, you can consider examples from literature. The following examples show elements of style as they relate to actual texts.

The first paragraph of Charles Dickens' novel, *A Tale of Two Cities*, is a good example of the use of evocative language. The side-by-side phrases, known as juxtaposition, are crafted by the writer to create a mood of tension between two countries (England and France), two approaches to change, and two contrasting characters.

FROM A TALE OF TWO CITIES

It was the best of times, it was the worst of times, it was the age of wisdom, it was the age of foolishness, it was the epoch of belief, it was the epoch of incredulity, it was the season of Light, it was the season of Darkness, it was the spring of hope, it was the winter of despair, we had everything before us, we had nothing before us, we were all going direct to Heaven, we were all going direct the other way—in short, the period was so far like the present period, that some of its noisiest authorities insisted on its being received, for good or for evil, in the superlative degree of comparison only.

There were a king with a large jaw and a queen with a plain face, on the throne of England; there were a king with a large jaw and a queen with a fair face, on the throne of France. In both countries it was clearer than crystal to the lords of the State preserves of loaves and fishes, that things in general were settled for ever.

—by Charles Dickens

The persistent use of comparison and contrast serves to describe the emotional moods of the two countries of Britain and France. The "king with a large jaw" and "queen with a plain face" were King George III and his queen, Charlotte Sophia; the other pair were King Louise XVI and Marie Antoinette of France. The French royals, as it turned out, were destined to lose their heads to the guillotine during the French Revolution. During the same period in England, the British royals kept their heads, both literally and figuratively, and most of the dissent was resolved, not in the streets, but in the House of Parliament. The language used by the author is memorable, evocative, and crafted to create one of the most well-known opening passages in literature.

INCONGRUITY

Incongruity in a text refers to a writer using words or ideas that are out of place or inconsistent. Stephen Leacock, a Canadian humorist, uses incongruous language for the purpose of entertainment in a piece entitled "Soaked in Seaweed." The story was created to poke fun at swashbuckling pirate adventure stories such as Treasure Island. Here is an excerpt illustrating humorous use of incongruous language.

---

from Soaked in Seaweed

Captain Bilge, with a megaphone to his lips, kept calling out to the men in his rough sailor fashion:

"Now, then, don't over-exert yourselves, gentlemen. Remember, please, that we have plenty of time. Keep out of the sun as much as you can. Step carefully in the rigging there, Jones; I fear it's just a little high for you. Tut, tut, Williams, don't get yourself so dirty with that tar: you won't look fit to be seen."

–by Stephen Leacock

The language in the above excerpt is incongruous because it is far too polite and formal for the situation. A real captain would be more likely to yell commands at his sailors, and he would not concern himself with the sailors' appearances or be mindful of their feelings.

REPETITION IN SONG LYRICS

Music and lyrics have an important relationship. They influence each other and add to the emotional effect created by a song. The repetition of words and phrases is an example of deliberate word choice, usually for dramatic effect, emphasis, or to make a phrase more memorable. Consider, for example, repeated choruses and refrains in songs: you may not remember all the words of a song, but you can usually join in on the chorus. In many popular songs, the focus is on the beat and musical texture of the song, so there may only be a few lines of lyrics.

Repetition anchors an idea and makes it memorable. You can see the effectiveness of repetition in the lyrics of the following song by Hank Williams.

I'M SO LONESOME, I COULD CRY

Hear that lonesome whipporrwill
He sounds too blue to fly
The midnight train is whining low
I'm so lonesome I could cry
I've never seen a night so long,
When time goes crawling by;
The moon just went behind a cloud;
I'm so lonesome I could cry.
Did you ever see a robin weep
When leaves began to die
That means he's lost the will to live
I'm so lonesome I could cry
The silence of a falling star
Lights up a purple sky
And as I wonder where you are
I'm so lonesome I could cry
I'm so lonesome I could cry

–by Hank Williams

The line "I'm so lonesome I could cry" not only illustrates the song's theme, but its repetition solidifies the theme in the mind of the listener. Repeated phrases in songs often give the listener clues about the theme of the song. It is likely that the theme of the song can be found among the words or phrases that are repeated the most often.

It is worth noting that sometimes repeated words or phrases can make lyrics annoying to music fans, who may criticize a song for being superficial. While some people listen to music for a catchy beat or melody, others value songs for having well-crafted lyrics. When lyrics in songs are too repetitive or lack meaning, many listeners will criticize or simply choose not to listen to those songs.

WORD MEANING IN POETRY

The application of a couple of style elements can be seen in the following short poem by Robert Frost.

NOTHING GOLD CAN STAY

Nature's first green is gold,
Her hardest hue to hold.
Her early leaf's a flower;
But only so an hour.
Then leaf subsides to leaf.
So Eden sank to grief,
So dawn goes down to day.
Nothing gold can stay.

–by Robert Frost

The word "gold" is used three times in this poem: in the title, in the first line, and in the last line. A word mentioned so many times in such a short work serves as a signal that the word is probably an important key to understanding the poem.

In this poem, the poet is referring to how the "first green" of nature is gold but also "hardest to hold." Gold is a precious metal, which means that it is highly valued and many people desire it. Gold often indicates the top level of something, such as the gold medal at a sporting event. The poet is saying that possessions and achievements may be golden, and people may strive to have them, but they will fade in time. The "first green" of youth may be something people long for for the rest of their lives.

STYLE OVERVIEW

Read the following essay by the late actor and author Chief Dan George. As you read the prose, ask yourself the following questions: What is the effect or mood created by this passage? What is the tone or attitude of the writer? Would the effect be enhanced or diminished if different words were used? Think about how you will answer these questions as you read the passage. These questions will help you examine elements of style.

HOW LONG HAVE I KNOWN YOU, OH CANADA?

How long have I known you, Oh Canada? A hundred years? Yes, a hundred years. And many many *seelanum*[1] more. And today, when you celebrate your hundred years, oh Canada, I am sad for all the Indian people throughout the land.

For I have known you when your forests were mine; when they gave me my meat and clothing. I have known you in your streams and rivers where your fish flashed and danced in the sun, where the waters said to come, come and eat of my abundance. I have known you in the freedom of your winds, and my spirit like the winds, once roamed your good lands.

But in the long hundred years since the white man came, I have seen my freedom disappear like the salmon going mysteriously out to sea. The white man's strange customs which I could not understand, pressed down upon me until I could no longer breathe.

When I fought to protect my land and my home, I was called a savage. When I neither understood nor welcomed this way of life, I was called lazy. When I tried to rule my people, I was stripped of my authority.

My nation was ignored in your history textbooks—they were little more important in the history of Canada than the buffalo that ranged the plains. I was ridiculed in your plays and motion pictures, and when I drank your fire-water, I got drunk—very, very drunk. And I forgot.

Oh Canada, how can I celebrate with you this Centenary, this hundred years? Shall I thank you for the reserves that are left me of my beautiful forests? For the canned fish of my rivers? For the loss of my pride and authority, even among my own people? For the lack of my will to fight back? No! I must forget what's past and gone.

Oh God in Heaven! Give me back the courage of the olden Chiefs. Let me wrestle with my surroundings. Let me again, as in the days of old, dominate my environment. Let me humbly accept this new culture and through it rise up and go on.

Oh God! Like the Thunderbird[2] of old I shall rise again out of the sea; I shall grab the instruments of the white man's success—his education, his skills, and with these new tools I shall build my race into the proudest segment of your society. Before I follow the great Chiefs who have gone before us, oh Canada, I shall see these things come to pass.

I shall see our young braves and our chiefs sitting in the houses of law and government, ruling and being ruled by the knowledge and freedoms of our great land. So shall we shatter the barriers of our isolation. So shall the next hundred years be the greatest in the proud history of our tribes and nations.

—by Chief Dan George

What words would you use to describe Dan George's writing style? How would you describe the tone and mood of this text? What do details like footnotes tell you about the form of the text? Try to write a description of how the writing style of this text. This type of analysis will make aspects of form and style more obvious to you.

---

[1] *seelanum*: A Squamish Indian word meaning "lunar months".

[2] *Thunderbird*: a mythical bird which, according to an Indian legend, created thunder in a struggle with a whale. The thunderbird is commonly seen on totem poles of Pacific Coast Indians.

*ON 9W2.2   Students will establish an identifiable voice in their writing, modifying language and tone
to suit the form, audience, and purpose for writing*

A WRITER'S VOICE

What is a writer's voice? Generally, a writer's voice can be described as how the writing sounds, or its overall effect on the writer's audience. The writer's voice is a unique blend of careful word choices that express what the writer means, as well as the writer's attitude toward their topic. Voice becomes an important part of the writer's writing style, combining word choices, phrasing, and word arrangement in distinctive sentence patterns. Even punctuation plays a part. As you discover your own writer's voice in different writing assignments, remember that the use of big words is not nearly as important as the way those words are put together. Voice should be deliberate, appropriate, and consistently adapted to your form, audience, and purpose for writing.

VOICE AND FORM

Your voice will vary according to the form of your writing. In a book report, for example, your form should include some sort of evaluation of the book's merits, supported by evidence. An interview would probably use a voice that imitates the speaking style of at least one character. A letter to a teacher or other adult would have a polite and formal voice.

VOICE AND AUDIENCE

You should adjust the level of formality in your writing to your audience. Your readers could be adults, peers, or children. Another aspect of voice that would change according to your audience is the use of technical language. You will want to use technical language that suits the level of expertise of the audience. For example, a research report may require a voice that explains difficult words or technical terms. You would probably have to assume that your audience is uninformed and lacks background information. A sports article for the school newspaper, on the other hand, might be in a more familiar voice, with contractions, exaggerations, possibly some slang, or jokes you know your readers will understand.

Voice and Purpose

To an extent, your purpose for writing will determine the voice of your writing. If you are sharing or relating a personal experience, your voice will probably be written in first person, and your writing will include specific details along with personal thoughts, feelings, and reactions. If your purpose is to inform, your voice will most likely be written in third-person objective, a more detached, unemotional voice. Adding humour might seem out of place or might detract from the information you are presenting.

If your purpose is to entertain or inform, your voice might vary. If you were writing an article for a school newspaper section, for example, your voice might change according to the type of article you are writing. On the front page, your voice would be precise, clear, and objective, while the sports section could depict a writer's voice that included lively, age-appropriate description, exaggeration, humour, and even slang.

VOICE CONSISTENCY

As a writer, try to keep a consistent voice throughout your writing piece. Consistency makes your writing clear. Different people use different language. Depending on what kind of assignment you are writing, you may want to experiment with using different voices. Trying to write using someone else's voice can be challenging but rewarding. For example, if you decide to write from the point of view of a young child, listen to the younger children you interact with. What words do they use? How do they express emotions? When you begin to write, try to imitate their voices.

As you read the following examples, notice how voice changes depending on the person who is writing. In this example, a 16-year-old boy has just received word that he has won an achievement award in the "20 Under 20" contest sponsored nationwide by the CBC for a homelessness awareness program he initiated in his Toronto high school. As a result of this young man's leadership, hundreds of blankets, jackets, toques, gloves, and scarves have been provided to inner-city shelters. Additionally, the boy has arranged for non-perishable foods and coffee from the community's independent grocery store to be distributed to the needy. Among many congratulatory messages, he received the following two emails.

Email from Dad, who is in Vancouver on business

When my Blackberry started to flash in the middle of my meeting, I knew it was Mom with the news. I am so proud to be your Dad. I wanted to interrupt the meeting and shout to the chandeliers, but the company president, who was presenting our quarterly sales figures at the time, might not have appreciated my enthusiasm. Mom and I have always tried to remind you that not everyone is as fortunate as you and your sister. Son, I can't give you any advice for the future, except to keep growing in all the right directions. I am so glad that our country recognizes youthful role models. The people of Canada can definitely learn much from the young. I will be home for the presentation ceremony on Friday. Save me a good spot!

Love,

Dad

Email from best friend

So, dude! You made the Big Leagues! Whazzup for the next run—youngest Prime Minister? I knew when you were nominated you would make the top 50, but top 20? You cool with all that attention? Don't forget your friends when you move into the fast lane of fame and fortune. I'm always here for ya, bud.

See you soon,

Randy

Contrast between voice and tone is observable in the two messages. The father's voice is informal and loving, but adult in vocabulary and tone. As you would expect, the friend is even more informal, admiring, but reluctant to be overly complimentary. The language choices are loose and peppered with slang.

ON 9W2.3   *Students will use appropriate descriptive and evocative words, phrases and expressions to make their writing clear and vivid for their intended audience*

WORD CHOICE

Diction, perhaps the most basic element of writing style, is the term for a writer's distinctive choices in vocabulary. It is important that your ideas are expressed simply and accurately so that your reader can easily understand them. The denotation of a word is the dictionary definition. Using words that mean what you want then to mean helps you express your ideas clearly. The connotation of a word refers to all the associations the word takes on through everyday speech and culture.

When you are speaking, your tone is easily attained from your body language, facial expressions, and intonation. When you are writing, however, your choice of words indicates your tone or attitude. The following chart provides some examples of words you could use to change the tone of your writing. As you look at the different words, think of how each word might change the meaning of your writing slightly.

Example

Word	Possible Alternatives
Sarcastic	cynical, derisive, jeering, mocking, sardonic, taunting
Threatening	bullying, menacing, hostile, intimidating, terrorizing, warning
Light-hearted	animated, bright, cheerful, joyful, spirited, sunny
Optimistic	confident, buoyant, encouraged, expectant, hopeful, positive

Take, for example, the word *sarcastic*. The words *derisive* and *jeering* are more spiteful in connotation than the words *cynical* and *sardonic*. Although using a different word might change the meaning only , slightly, all of the small changes you make to your diction will add up to create your tone.

As you can see from the information in this section, form and style have many different elements. Understanding the different aspects of form and style allows you to look at writing from a more analytical perspective. When you understand form and style in the texts you read, you can apply that understanding to your own writing. In time, you will be able to develop your personal writing style and come to know your preferred forms of writing. Maybe you will find that you prefer expressing yourself through poetry or short stories, or maybe you will discover that you like writing research papers and formal essays. Perhaps your favourite writing style is humorous, dramatic, or analytical. The variety of texts you read will help you determine what kind of texts you like to write.

PRACTICE QUESTIONS

Read the following passage to answer questions 1 and 2.

THE COMING OF MUTT

During my lifetime we had owned, or had been owned by, a steady succession of dogs. As a newborn baby I had been guarded by a Border collie named Sapper, who was one day doused with boiling water by a vicious neighbour, and who went insane as a result. But there had always been other dogs during my first eight years, until we moved to the west and became, for the moment, dogless. The prairies could be only half real to a boy without a dog.

I began agitating for one almost as soon as we arrived and I found a willing ally in my father—though his motives were not mine.

For many years he had been exposed to the colourful tales of my Great-uncle Frank, who homesteaded in Alberta in 1900. Frank was a hunter born, and most of his stories dealt with the superlative shooting to be had on the western plains. Before we were properly settled in Saskatoon my father determined to test those tales. He bought a fine English shotgun, a shooting coat, cases of ammunition, a copy of the Saskatchewan Game Laws, and a handbook on shotgun shooting. There remained only one indispensable item—a hunting dog.

One evening he arrived home from the library with such a beast in tow behind him. Its name was Crown Prince Challenge Indefatigable. It stood about as high as the dining-room table and, as far as Mother and I could judge, consisted mainly of feet and tongue. Father was annoyed at our levity and haughtily informed us that the Crown Prince was an Irish Setter, kennel bred and field trained, and a dog to delight the heart of any expert. We remained unimpressed. Purebred he may have been, and the possessor of innumerable cups and ribbons, but to my eyes he seemed a singularly useless sort of beast with but one redeeming feature: I greatly admired the way he drooled. I have never known a dog who could drool as the Crown Prince could. He never stopped, except to flop his way to the kitchen sink and tank up on water. He left a wet and sticky trail wherever he went. He had little else to recommend him, for he was moronic.

Mother might have overlooked his obvious defects, had it not been for his price. She could not overlook that, for the owner was asking two hundred dollars, and we could no more afford such a sum than we could have afforded a Cadillac. Crown Prince left the next morning, but Father was not discouraged, and it was clear that he would try again.

My parents had been married long enough to achieve that delicate balance of power which enables a married couple to endure each other. They were both adept in the evasive tactics of marital politics—but Mother was a little more adept.

She realized that a dog was now inevitable, and when chance brought the duck boy—as we afterwards referred to him—to our door on that dusty August day, Mother showed her mettle by snatching the initiative right out of my father's hands.

By buying the duck boy's pup, she not only placed herself in a position to forestall the purchase of an expensive dog of my father's choice, but she was also able to save six cents in cash. She was never one to despise a bargain.

When I came home from school the bargain was installed in a soap carton in the kitchen. He looked to be a somewhat dubious buy at any price. Small, emaciated, and caked liberally with cow manure, he peered up at me in a near-sighted sort of way. But when I knelt beside him and extended an exploratory hand he roused himself and sank his puppy teeth into my thumb with such satisfactory gusto that my doubts dissolved. I knew that he and I would get along.

–by Farley Mowat

1. The name of the Irish Setter, "Crown Prince Challenge Indefatigable," is ironic because
   A. he is a purebred animal
   B. the Irish Setter is expected to be a hunting dog
   C. the most impressive thing the dog can do is drool
   D. he is the possessor of innumerable cups and ribbon

2. The writer's tone in the passage can best be described as
   A. subtly resentful
   B. coolly detached
   C. humorously satirical
   D. thoughtfully reminiscent

Read the following passage to answer questions 3 to 9.

THE GHOST TOWN

Margaret picked up the old yellowed photograph that was lying on top of the pile. It was in black and white. It was better that way, aged, like her memories. Color photographs capture the image, but black and whites capture its soul; it was the soul of this picture that captured her attention now.

It was a simple picture of children playing. A woman, her mother, was standing at the bottom of the slide, her arms outstretched, ready to catch a little girl with pigtails and laughing eyes, her sister. An older boy and a girl of about eight were climbing on the teeter-totter. In the background, she could see the jungle gym filled with walkways and monkey bars. She remembered the squeak and groan of the teeter-totter as it crashed up and down. Oh how she loved teeter-tottering!

She reached for another picture, this one taken only a few weeks ago. Her brother had taken it on his last visit to Fireside. It was a black and white of the playground, overgrown and forgotten. Weeds grew up around the base of the equipment. The bar from the teeter-totter was lost in long grasses and climbing flowers. The sand was blown smooth with nary a footprint left in the sand. If she looked hard enough at the picture, she could almost see the ghosts of the children who used to play there. She could almost hear their laughter echoing off the old jungle gym with its rusting bars and rotting wooden posts.

The next picture, this one in color, was of the old hotel with its windows boarded up, locking the world out and the memories in. Like the playground, green tangles of weeds and grasses grew unchecked along the walls, the green contrasting sharply with the faded red paint. The glass-framed phone booth was tucked away near the side door. She didn't remember a glass phone booth. They changed that after she left. The phone itself still worked; she knew because her brother had used it two weeks ago when he phoned. She was sure the lights still worked too. One flip of the switch would illuminate the layers of dust and cobwebs of the dining room and the stage where the dance hall girls used to perform.

She closed her eyes, remembering. She was eight. Her sister was a little older. They were sneaking up to the windows to peer inside. They stretched up on tiptoes, pressing their faces tight against the glass. They could see the girls in their sparkling dresses dancing while the miners sat in groups around the tables drinking and playing cards. The girls were so beautiful.

They never got to watch for long. As soon as Mr. Uchanko saw them, he shooed them away. "Not for the eyes of little girls," he told them as they scurried away.

She unfolded the letter. Her brother's messy handwriting was scrawled across the crisp white surface. Dear Margaret, he wrote, I hope this letter finds you well. The next few words were scratched out as if he was trying to say something, but the words weren't coming out right. She knew what was coming. She forced herself to read on:

I know you have heard about the new interstate highway. It will run straight through the middle of Fireside. All the buildings will be torn down and moved. The playground and the school will be paved, the hotel dismantled. You know what is beneath those floorboards. You know what is inside that hotel. Margaret, I need your help. We can't let them destroy Fireside. John.

She re-read the note three times before folding it up and tucking it back in the shoebox full of pictures. She wasn't ready to open up the past, not now, not ever. There were too many demons lurking in those shadows.

She pulled her old shawl tight around her shoulders. Why couldn't the secrets have stayed lost for just a few more years? Why couldn't it have waited until she was dead and no one was left to remember? Why—the word hung in the evening air like a herald of doom.

3. Which of the following words best describes the old woman's recollection of her childhood?
   A. Sad
   B. Happy
   C. Haunted
   D. Carefree

4. The phrase "echoing off the old jungle gym with its rusting bars and rotting wooden posts" uses descriptive language to convey the
   A. passing of time
   B. appeal of old playgrounds
   C. condition of the playground
   D. fact that the playground needs upkeep

5. When did the events Margaret is recalling most likely take place? Provide evidence from the story in your answer.

The events Margaret is recalling most likely to a time when she was a toddler. "Oh how she loved teeter-tottering!" implies that she loved to play at the park when she was preferably younger.

6. Which of the following words best describes Margaret's mood?

A. Nervous

B. Annoyed

C. Frustrated

D. Apprehensive

7. This passage can best be categorized as belonging to the genre of

A. fantasy

B. mystery

C. suspense

D. adventure

8. The quotation "Why—the word hung in the evening air like a herald of doom" is an example of which form of figurative language?

The quotation is an example of foreshadowing. It gives the sense that something bad is about to happen.

9. The phrase "Why—the word hung in the air like a herald of doom" contains an example of which of the following literary devices?

A. Idiom

B. Simile

C. Analogy

D. Metaphor

Read the following passage to answer questions 10 to 12.

AN ENCOUNTER UNDER THE LAMPPOST

The lamppost stood tall and straight in the evening shadows. There was a little rust around its base, and its light had dimmed with age, but it was still the same beautiful lamppost it had been all those years ago when oil lamps first lined the city streets. Those were the days before kerosene when whale oil was still popular and the whales were not extinct. The lamp had been converted to burn kerosene, but even that was becoming rare as the wasteful age of fossil-fuel energy was finally stalling out.

Preserved by city decree, the lamp stood as a testimonial to forgotten years when men wore tall hats and women wore elegant dresses and exchanged smiles of goodwill and gestures of kindness. Those were the days when a handshake still sealed a deal and men honored their word. All that had changed now. Smiles were tightlipped mockeries of the original thing. People hid behind deceptions, insinuations, lies, and half-truths, shaking hands as a leftover formality from bygone years.

Zachariah felt like the lamppost. He did not fit in with the bustle and hustle of the modern world. He did not understand computer games and car racing games. Instead, he learned to whittle wood. Sometimes he thought he had inherited more than just his great grandfather's name. Sometimes he thought his great grandfather was in him, a part of him, guiding his hands as he cut and carved until the soul of the wood was set free in beautiful ornate carvings.

It was late evening. The harsh light of day had been replaced by the soft glow of the city lamps. Zachariah sat with his back pressed against the lamppost eyeing his latest carving. It was a bear. The proportions looked all right, although it was hard to tell for sure. He used pictures to guide his carving. Somewhere behind him, he heard the sound of footsteps cracking on the old, cobblestone courtyard. Time to go, he supposed, tucking his whittle knife in his pocket.

"Where do you think he got to?" a harsh, guttural voice whispered. Zachariah froze.

"He'll be here," a second voice said.

"But he's late."

"Shhh," the second voice hissed. "People will hear you."

"There's no one here," the first voice complained.

"Shhh," the second voice hissed again. "Your impatience will be your downfall. Remember, you are here to observe only."

"I know, I know," the first voice whined, "I stay hidden in the shadows. I don't say a word. You do all the transactions."

"Good. Now get back. I hear someone coming."

There was a shuffling of feet as the hoarse-voiced man shifted back a few paces. Just as Zachariah was contemplating whether to run or stay, the thick crunching steps of a third person came out of the shadows.

"Have you got the item?" a sinister voice asked. There was a rustling sound of an object exchanging hands. "The scroll?" the voice asked.

"Yes."

"Good. You know what to do next?"

"Yes." The scuffling feet moved off back down the alley. "What do we do next?" the rough young voice asked, staring after the departing shadow.

"We kill the king," the older voice said with a sigh.

"What? That wasn't part of the deal. You never said anything about killing anyone."

"Do you want to save your sister?"

"Of course but—"

"Then you must accept the consequences of the deal."

"But ..."

"Either you are a man and you will go through with this or you are still a sniffling boy from the back alleys of Tyr. Which is it? Decide now." There was a hard edge in the second voice, an edge that showed neither weakness nor sympathy. Zachariah found himself drawn to the voice. Bit by bit, he eased his body around until his chest was pressed against the lamppost. He poked his head out just far enough to see two burly shapes dressed in black.

"Ho, who are you? Who's that?" the smaller figure said, pointing.

10. The phrase "The lamppost stood tall and straight" contains an example of which of the following literary devices?

   A. Idiom

   B. Analogy

   C. Hyperbole

   D. Personification

11. This passage is an example of writing in the genre of

   A. mystery

   B. adventure

   C. science fiction

   D. historical fiction

12. Which of the following words best describes Zachariah's perception of his great-grandfather?

   A. Skilled

   B. Elderly

   C. Deceased

   D. Reincarnated

Read the following passage to answer questions 13 and 14.

SAFE WORK PROCEDURES

Working Alone

There may be times when you have to work alone. Here are some procedures to help you deal with this situation.

Have someone contact you periodically to ensure that you are okay. The checking procedure must require you to take some predetermined action to confirm that you are all right and do not need help.

Contact may be in person, by telephone, or by any other effective means. This may include reciprocal agreements with other company locations, adjacent merchants, or security firms. These agreements can include:

telephone contact at predetermined intervals

visual contact or signal to workers in adjacent premises or to security patrols

Use personal alarms or monitored video surveillance systems, provided that:

they are properly maintained

the response to signs of distress is made immediately by qualified personnel

Make arrangements with adjacent employers to have employees watch each other's premises.

Prominently display notices indicating:

that the premises are monitored

the emergency numbers to call for assistance

If possible, do not open back doors or leave them open and unattended.

If possible, do not empty the garbage at night, especially if the dumpster is in a secluded spot or back alley.

Assault Prevention Tips

If attacked, scream—as loudly and long as possible—and run to a neighboring store or the nearest well-lit area. Continue calling for help.

If someone grabs your purse, deposit bag, or other personal property, do not resist, and do not chase the thief.

Call the police immediately after any incident, and record the appearance and mannerisms of the offender.

---

13. The writer's main purpose in writing this passage was to

   A. inform employees how they can stay secure when working alone

   B. provide alternative methods for contacting other companies

   C. explain how to deal with thieves and burglars

   D. help employers keep staffing costs down

14. Which of the following types of businesses would be most likely to find this document useful?

   A. Retail store

   B. Convenience store

   C. Manufacturing business

   D. Multiplex movie theatre

Read the following passage to answer questions 15 to 21.

This cartogram shows how the world would probably look if the number of international visitors to a country determined its size.

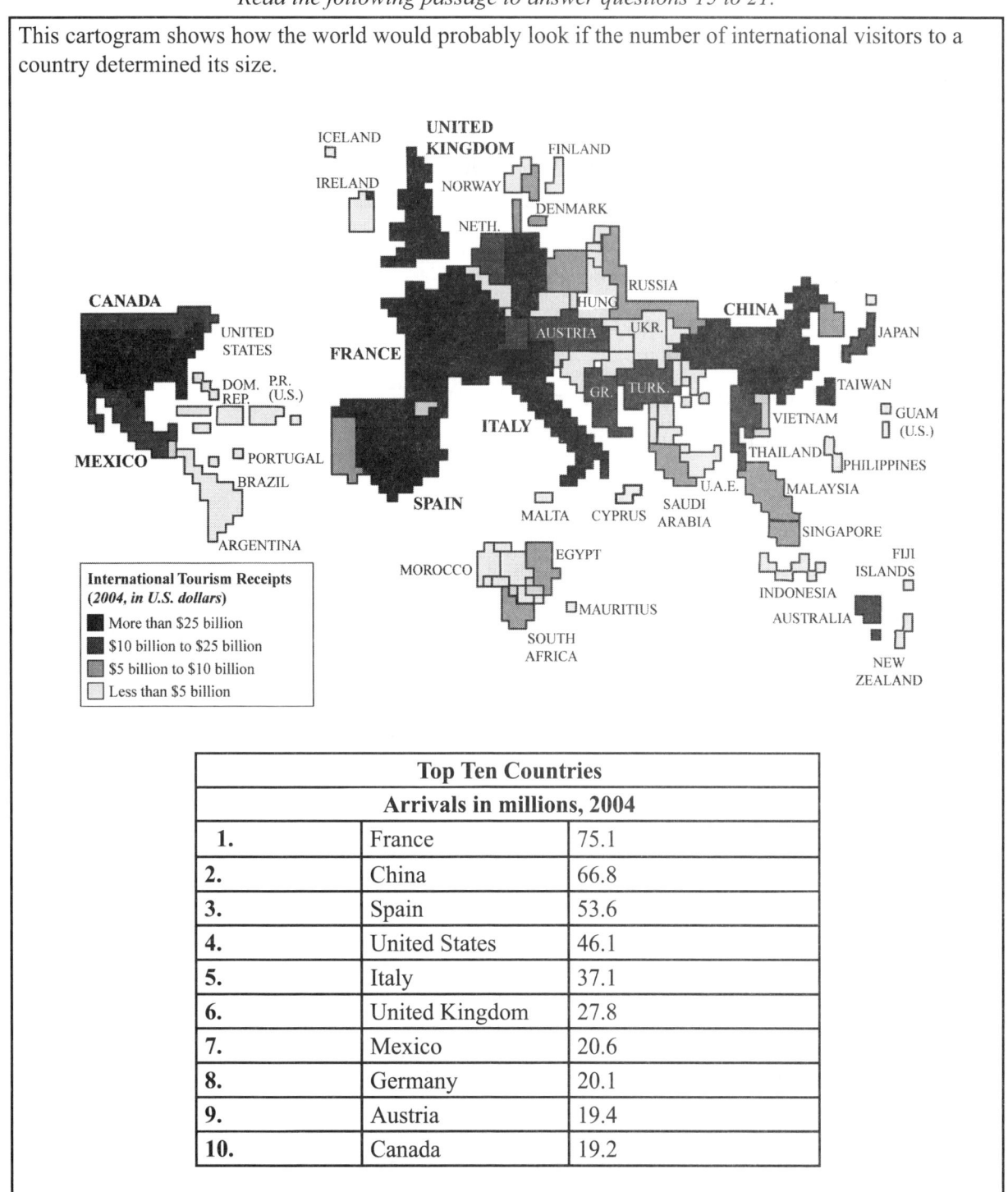

Top Ten Countries		
Arrivals in millions, 2004		
1.	France	75.1
2.	China	66.8
3.	Spain	53.6
4.	United States	46.1
5.	Italy	37.1
6.	United Kingdom	27.8
7.	Mexico	20.6
8.	Germany	20.1
9.	Austria	19.4
10.	Canada	19.2

Fact: Germans spent the most on travel in 2004: 71 billion dollars. Most European countries provide at least 20 days of vacation per year, but Germans receive 24.

Fact: The continent of Africa received 41 million visitors in 2004, 20 million of whom went to sub-Saharan Africa. The conflicts in Sudan kept tourists away.

Fact: Although Asia has faced several disasters: SARS in 2003, the tsunami on December 26, 2004, and the avian flu, its tourism industry is still thriving.

People are travelling more than ever before in history. International tourist arrivals increased from about 540 million in 1995 to 763 million in 2004. Last year, international arrivals worldwide topped 808 million. Tourism decreased briefly due to the devastating 2004 hurricane season in the Caribbean, rioting in France, terrorist attacks in Turkey and the Middle East, and the horrifying Indian Ocean tsunami. Even with all the fear of natural disasters, the desire to travel still wins. Crossings between countries by car, bus, and train have also increased. Low-cost airline flights are also feeding the trend. One carrier recently offered a round-trip ticket from London to Brest, in France, for less than two dollars.

15. This diagram is best described as a cartogram because it
 A. uses satellite imagery
 B. provides statistical information
 C. makes use of computer-generated images
 D. is an accurate geographical map of the world

16. The design coding on the map is used to indicate
 A. total international visitors
 B. international tourism arrivals
 C. international tourism receipts
 D. total United States dollars spent in the country

17. Some countries on the map are labelled in larger print in order to indicate that they are
 A. wealthy
 B. politically stable
 C. frequently visited
 D. developed nations

18. Subtitles are used in this article primarily to

    A. highlight key points

    B. reinforce important facts

    C. provide supplemental information

    D. cover points not discussed elsewhere

19. In the context of the phrases "devastating hurricane season" and "horrifying Indian Ocean tsunami," the descriptive words "devastating" and "horrifying" are most likely used to

    A. create fear and discourage travel

    B. emphasize the threats from natural disasters

    C. advise caution when travelling to certain countries

    D. remind the reader how catastrophic these events were

20. The writer's main purpose in writing this article was to

    A. list the most popular holiday destinations

    B. communicate international tourism patterns

    C. explain why tourism has increased over the last few years

    D. make clear which countries have the best tourism industries

21. Which of the following sources was not used as a tool to support the theme of this article?

    A. Maps

    B. Tables

    C. Subtext

    D. Interviews

Read the following passage to answer questions 22 to 24.

MULGA BILL'S BICYCLE

'Twas Mulga Bill, from Eaglehawk, that caught the cycling craze;
He turned away the good old horse that served him many days;
He dressed himself in cycling clothes, resplendent to be seen;
He hurried off to town and bought a shining new machine;
And as he wheeled it through the door, with air of lordly pride,
The grinning shop assistant said, "Excuse me, can you ride?"
"See here, young man," said Mulga Bill, "from Walgett to the sea,
From Conroy's Gap to Castlereagh, there's none can ride like me.
I'm good all round at everything as everybody knows,
Although I'm not the one to talk—I hate a man that blows.
But riding is my special gift, my chiefest, sole delight;
Just ask a wild duck can it swim, a wildcat can it fight.
There's nothing clothed in hair or hide, or built of flesh or steel,
There's nothing walks or jumps, or runs, on axle, hoof, or wheel,
But what I'll sit, while hide will hold and girths and straps are tight:
I'll ride this here two-wheeled concern right straight away at sight."
'Twas Mulga Bill, from Eaglehawk, that sought his own abode,
That perched above Dead Man's Creek, beside the mountain road.
He turned the cycle down the hill and mounted for the fray,
But 'ere he'd gone a dozen yards it bolted clean away.
It left the track, and through the trees, just like a silver streak,
It whistled down the awful slope toward the Dead Man's Creek.
It shaved a stump by half an inch, it dodged a big white-box:
The very wallaroos in fright went scrambling up the rocks,
The wombats hiding in their caves dug deeper underground,
As Mulga Bill, as white as chalk, sat tight to every bound.
It struck a stone and gave a spring that cleared a fallen tree,
It raced beside a precipice as close as close could be;
And then as Mulga Bill let out one last despairing shriek
It made a leap of twenty feet into the Dead Man's Creek.
'Twas Mulga Bill, from Eaglehawk, that slowly swam ashore:
He said, "I've had some narrer shaves and lively rides before;
I've rode a wild bull round a yard to win a five-pound bet,
But this was the most awful ride that I've encountered yet.
I'll give that two-wheeled outlaw best; it's shaken all my nerve
To feel it whistle through the air and plunge and buck and swerve.
It's safe at rest in Dead Man's Creek, we'll leave it lying still;
A horse's back is good enough henceforth for Mulga Bill."

—by A.B. "Banjo" Paterson

22. In your own words, describe the poet's use of sentences in this poem.

_____

_____

_____

_____

_____

23. Which of the following lines contains an example of a sound effect that enhances the reader's understanding of the action in this poem?

A. "'Although I'm not the one to talk—I hate a man that blows.'"

B. "'Just ask a wild duck can it swim, a wildcat can it fight.'"

C. "It whistled down the awful slope toward the Dead Man's Creek."

D. "'I'll give that two-wheeled outlaw best; it's shaken all my nerve'"

24. The poet develops the character of Mulga Bill most effectively through

A. descriptions of the setting

B. dialogue and visual imagery

C. conversations with other characters

D. explanations of the responses of the animals

ANSWERS AND SOLUTIONS—PRACTICE QUESTIONS

1. C	7. C	13. A	19. D
2. C	8. WR	14. B	20. B
3. D	9. B	15. B	21. D
4. A	10. D	16. D	22. WR
5. WR	11. C	17. C	23. C
6. D	12. D	18. C	24. B

1. C

The fact that he is a purebred Irish Setter does not make the dog's name ironi**C.** Crown Prince's hunting abilities are not discussed by the narrator, although his cups and ribbons suggest he has skill. Regardless, this ability is not very important to the narrator, and it is not clear how well the dog hunts.

One would expect a dog with a name that speaks of royalty and strength to display superior physical and intellectual abilities; the opposite is true in the case of Crown Prince. The narrator says that the dog "left a wet and sticky trail wherever he went" and also calls him "moronic." Irony involves a discrepancy between what is perceived or expected and what is true. Irony is usually conveyed through contradictions between appearance and reality. The dog's name is ironic because when it is first heard, an expectation is developed that the dog will be regal and superior. In actuality, the dog is not very smart or special at all.

2. C

The writer is not resentful. He does not feel bitter about the events that occurred; in fact, the story seems to be a very humorous recollection. He is obviously amused by Crown Prince and his parents' negotiations.

Instead of being coolly detached, the writer expresses several emotions. These include a sense of longing for a dog, amusement at the irony, and thankfulness at finding Mutt.

The writer's tone is humorously critical, or satirical. He gently and humorously pokes fun at those who insist money and breeding define superiority. The description of "Crown Prince Challenge Indefatigable" is humorous and ironic because he turns out to be a rather slow-witted, funny-looking beast that drools.

3. D

The old woman remembers playing on the teeter-totter and spying on the dance hall girls, activities that suggest a carefree childhoo**D.** The letter from her brother and her desire to have the past stay buried do suggest that something else happened that the reader is not aware of yet, but these facts do not diminish the somewhat peaceful childhood memories the woman is recollecting.

4. A

The descriptive language in this phrase serves to create a feeling of time passing. The more decay, rot, and rust that appear, the more time has elapsed and the older the playground is.

5. WRITTEN RESPONSE

Margaret describes seeing dance hall girls in sparkling dresses performing on the stage in the hotel, which suggests that the events she is recalling took place sometime around the turn of the 20th century. Pay phones were introduced in 1905, but glass phone booths were not introduced until the 1950s. Margaret remembers the pay phone but does not remember the glass phone booth, which suggests that the story took place during the 1930s after phone booths became popular but before the wooden booths were replaced by plastic ones.

6. D

The word apprehensive means fearful about something that might happen in the future. Margaret is apprehensive because she is scared and fearful about what might happen if someone discovers what is hidden beneath the hotel floorboards.

7. C

This passage creates a mood of tension and the feeling that something bad is about to happen, characteristics that are typically associated with the suspense genre. Fantasy stories usually involve mythical characters who use magic or the supernatural; mystery stories revolve around a puzzle that must be solved; and adventure stories usually follow a hero or heroine on a quest in an exotic location.

8. WRITTEN RESPONSE

Although the phrase could be described as a simile, its use here is best described as an example of foreshadowing because it suggests something bad is about to happen.

9. B

A simile is a comparison between two unlike things using like or as. In this case, the word "why" is compared to a herald of doom to create a sense of foreboding.

10. D

Personification attributes human characteristics, emotions, or actions to animals or inanimate objects. Standing tall and straight is a human action that is being attributed to the lamppost.

11. C

Science fiction stories are usually set in the future and are based on scientific knowledge. Several details suggest this story is set in the future: whales are extinct, bears are also probably extinct, and fossil fuels are scarce. In addition, the selection's opening paragraphs focus on contrasting the past and present of the story. These facts make it most likely that this passage is from the science fiction genre.

12. D

Zachariah believes his great-grandfather has been reincarnated because he thinks his grandfather lives inside him, guiding his hands as he carves.

13. A

The passage provides basic procedures for employees to follow to stay secure while working alone.

14. B

A convenience store is the most likely of the four businesses listed to have employees working alone. Security concerns would also be more relevant for a convenience store because these businesses are often at a greater risk for robberies.

15. B

A cartogram presents statistical information and data on geographic maps. The correct representations of the area of the countries on the map are not important, as the map is used for other purposes than to judge distances. This map uses the number of international visits to each country to create a relative world map based on popularity as a tourist destination.

16. D

The colour coding is used to identify the amount of money in United States dollars that was spent in each country in 2004. This information is based on total international tourism receipts.

17. C

The countries labelled in larger print on the map are the most frequently visited countries. This corresponds with the list of the top-10 countries visited in 2004.

18. C

The subtitles are used to provide supplemental information that reinforces key points and facts presented on the map and in the supporting text.

19. D

The adjectives are used to create imagery that reminds the reader how severe these natural events were. This emphasizes the point that international travel has increased despite the threat of natural disasters, whose destructive potential is still fresh in the minds of many people.

20. B

The writer uses information such as the total number of international visits to a country to illustrate international travel patterns. The writer notes in the article that tourism has increased despite the occurrence of some major natural disasters.

21. D

The article uses a scaled cartogram to present international tourism statistics. Subtitles and tables are used to provide additional information to support the graph. The article finishes with a brief discussion but does not include any interviews.

22. WRITTEN RESPONSE

The writer uses a variety of long and short sentences. The sentences are most often complex or compound and are very descriptive.

23. C

The poet uses the word "whistle" to give the reader an understanding of the speed of the bicycle as it travels down the slope.

24. B

The reader learns about Mulga Bill's character mainly through the visual images created by descriptions of his actions and through the dialogue spoken by Mulga Bill himself. The setting does not really help characterization, and there is no formal introduction in this poem. Although some of Mulga Bill's character is shown in his conversation with the shop assistant, his character is also shown through the use of visual imagery.

UNIT TEST

Read the following passage to answer questions 1 to 4.

IN SEARCH OF SANTA

For centuries the world's most heroic scientists have challenged the mystery of Kris Kringle, but none have succeeded in uncovering the location of his secret polar fortress. That's why I considered it a unique privilege to be invited to join a new expedition to uncover the truth at last, captained by none other than scientific giant Sir Davis Thighton – the world's most accomplished corpulent explorer.

Sir Davis is of an ilk rare among today's namby-pamby researchers. He alone has the courage to turn every prevailing theory about Father Christmas on its head. "The North Pole is indeed Kringle's hiding place," Sir Davis told me when I met him in his Sydney office. "However the North Pole is not, in fact, boreal."

His loyal lieutenant Sarabjit placed a compass on the desk between us. "In the business of magnetism," explained Sir Davis, one eye narrowing behind his monocle, "like repels like." Since the north end of a compass needle invariably indicates the Arctic, he reasoned the pole there must be magnetically southern. And, in a leap of intuition that distinguishes geniuses like Sir Davis from the riff-raff of the Hawkings and Newtons of this world, he concluded that the secret compound of Father Christmas must therefore be somewhere in the Antarctic.

"Google Maps has revealed nothing unusual on the surface" reported Sir Davis, indicating his pink iBook, "which is why we now believe our quarry lies beneath the glaciers. Thus, we will descend through a crevasse to the continent itself."

He introduced the platoon of Nepalese sherpas in yak-hair jackets milling by the mantel. It was Sir Davis's theory that the sherpas' renowned mountaineering expertise could be turned to our advantage during our icy descent by inverting their faculties. To demonstrate, Sarabjit affixed devices behind the sherpas' ears designed to rotate the sense of balance by one hundred eighty degrees.

The sherpas fell down, and one of them threw up.

"How does it feel to be part of the noble pursuit of scientific truth?" I asked them, but received nothing printable in reply.

Although reluctant, I was obliged by the trained sense of integrity deep inside my journalistic giblets to remind Sir Davis that not all of his previous expeditions had come off well, including his ultimately unsuccessful attempt to find Aztec gold in a Melbourne shopping mall. "We were close," Sir Davis assured me. "Besides, this is no mere trinket hunt. This time we seek to penetrate the ultimate Christmas enigma!"

No expense had been spared to equip us. Sarabjit gave me a parka that was edible in case of crisis, and a pair of heated mittens that could be powered by my own urine. We were also outfitted with helmets and radios but, due to satellite interference, our test transmissions were overlaid by Swedish pop music. There was some confusion while the sherpas asked why Sir Davis kept threatening to break their hearts.

The crowd went wild. They went stark raving mad with joy, seemed ready to tear down the rink in their enthusiasm. They were still in a frenzy of rejoicing when the game ended a few moments later. A mob of fans carried O'Hara off the ice. And scores of them crowded around Ben Borstall, pounding him on the back.

Then, in gesture worthy of Scott, the great man nodded, and the palpable aura of his tenacious spirit wafted over me in an inspiring funk. "Our icebreaker awaits!"

I asked how we would travel to the harbour.

"We're jumping on a bus, actually," admitted Sir Davis with a cough. "Rather blew the budget with these radio helmets, don't you know."

And so we stand now assembled at the bus stop outside of Sir Davis's office, tapping our toes to Swedish pop, and ready to face the worst that Antarctica can muster in defence of Santa's secret hiding place. Sarabjit struggles to keep the packhorses calm despite the constant flow of traffic a few metres away, which has already claimed two dizzy sherpas. As the expedition's departure looms, I cannot help but find Sir Davis's optimism contagious. Father Christmas: watch out!

–by Matthew Frederick Davis Hemming

1. Which of the following words best describes the content of this short story?
   A. Irony
   B. Satire
   C. Mystery
   D. Adventure

2. What is the writer's main purpose in writing this story?

_____

_____

_____

_____

_____

3. Phrases such as "devices … designed to rotate the sense of balance," "The sherpas fell down, and one of them threw up," "a parka that was edible in case of crisis," and "'We're jumping on a bus'" enhance which of the following aspects of the story?
   A. Vocabulary
   B. Humour
   C. Fiction
   D. Mood

4. The writer develops his ideas primarily by
   A. giving anecdotes
   B. providing extra details
   C. comparing expeditions
   D. showing cause and effect

Read the following passage to answer questions 5 to 7.

THEY DIDN'T KNOW HOCKEY

Dan Hawley snagged the goalie's pass-out just inside the blue line and whirled away with the puck. Judge, the opposing centre, swooped in and tried to check him, but Dan hurdled Judge's stick, shot the rubber ahead and snapped it up again a moment later as he raced down the middle lane with Judge hard at his heels.

There was less than a minute to play and the score was tied with the teams nearing the limit of their overtime. The visiting Owls would be well satisfied with a tie, but Dan Hawley knew as well as anyone in the rink that anything but a win on home ice would be almost fatal to the Panthers' chances of grabbing the league title.

He streaked toward the Owl goal with the crowd whooping in a frenzy. There was an imploring, hysterical note in the roar of the mob. The Panther fans were begging for that goal; the one goal that would squeeze out a win; the goal that seemed impossible to get and that must be scored within the next fifty seconds, if it was to be scored at all.

Dan was tired, for it had been a long, grim game, and bush-league amateurs are expected to go the distance. He could hear the click and chop of Judge's skates as the Owl centre tried to overhaul him, but Dan knew he could out-foot Judge. He wasn't worrying about that.

But this next scoring play. It had to click. It had to be perfect. There mustn't be a slip-up. If it missed, there wouldn't be time for another. And both of his wings were covered.

The Owls had a hard-hitting defence. And their goalie was smart. Dan streaked in and fired from the outside.

It was a hard, low, wicked shot, but the high-pitched roar of the crowd changed to a long, deep groan. You couldn't beat the Owl goalie on long shots. Everyone knew that. And this shot, moreover, was wide of the net.

The puck spanked against the rear boards with a thud that could be heard the length of the rink.

The left defenceman swung around. And the Owl left winger, covering his check along the boards, began hotfooting it into the corner to pick up the rebound.

But Dan Hawley was already sifting through for that same rebound. He had shot purposely wide; he knew the exact angle at which the puck would ricochet from the boards; he knew exactly where he could pick it up.

It was perfectly timed. He was in like a streak. He got his stick on the puck as it skimmed across the ice on its rebound from the boards. And in the same motion, he pivoted and laid down a swift pass to his uncovered right winger, Ben Borstall.

The play had pulled all the Owls out of position. Borstall swooped in, went right to the net, saw that Steve O'Hara, the left winger, was uncovered and backing him up. Borstall faked a shot that pulled the goalie over, then banged the puck over to O'Hara.

And O'Hara socked the rubber into the upper corner for the perfect goal.

"Ben deserves credit too, don't forget!" bellowed one of the fans. "O'Hara scored that goal all right, but Ben gave him the pass."

A lot of people had nice things to say to Dan Hawley, too. "Nice game, Dan" "You were sure flyin' out there tonight, Dan." But for that matter every member of the team came in for his share of hero worship.

O'Hara, however, occupied the limelight. Wasn't he the league's leading scorer? And hadn't he banged home the winning goal?

"We won't be able to keep him here very long," said someone. "Some of the pro teams will be after him before we know it. A goal-getter like O'Hara would make good anywhere."

Dan Hawley, getting out of his uniform in the dressing room, grinned cynically. After all, what did the average fan know about hockey strategy? So far as Dan was concerned, he didn't care who got the credit, as long as the Panthers won the game.

–by Leslie McFarlane

5. The main reason the writer uses short sentences in this passage is to
   A. match the pace of the passage with the pace of a hockey game
   B. explain how players move around on the ice
   C. give examples of how the puck is shot
   D. make the passage easier to understand

6. The statement "There was an imploring, hysterical note in the roar of the mob" most likely implies that the crowd was
   A. eager to win
   B. unruly and wild
   C. supporting the players
   D. excited about the game

7. This passage is an example of writing in the genre of
   A. adventure
   B. biography
   C. realistic fiction
   D. historical fiction

Read the following passage to answer questions 8 to 10.

SPORT

A fisherman steps
to the banks of a river
a comfortable rainbow
lies still in the water
and slides to the surface
to dine on the hatches
the quick eye that follows
makes perfect the target
while seeking—mouth open
finds steel for its dinner
the stillness is broken
by ripples exploding
implacable bamboo
arcs out to the victim
but short is the battle
for scales are uneven
and mesh that is anxious
awaits gleaming silver
soon two pounds of muscle
lies dead in a basket
and fishermen heart-beats
are proud and disdainful
the womb of the mother
is spilled by the angler
and ten thousand children
lie dead in the sand.

–by Kirk Wirsig

---

8. The "ripples exploding" are caused by the
   A. distress of the captured fish
   B. fisherman's rush into the water
   C. slapping of the fishing rod on the water
   D. school of fish breaking the water's surface to escape

9. The quotation "mesh that is anxious" refers to
   A. a fishing net
   B. a wire basket
   C. the fisherman's hands
   D. the fish out of the water

10. How does the poet's choice of words like "victim" and "children" encourage the reader to feel?

The poet wants the reader to feel like a "victim" that has been hurt for almost no purpose. The damage to its eggs, who are the "children", causes an imbalance in that ecosystem. The words encourage the reader to feel sorrow about the loss of a life.

Read the following passage to answer questions 11 to 14.

NEVER LOOK A BABOON IN THE EYE

It was a critical moment—the time to move from planning and discussion to action. For months I had been working with my colleagues at CBC's Science Unit planning the development of ideas and plans for A Planet for the Taking, a special, eight-part series on nature, specifically our human place in nature. We had discussed and proposed, read and argued about the best way to present our proposition that humans are just one of many species on this planet, that nature is giving us increasingly strong signals that it will not be continued by us. Now it was time to go out and film.

The series' three producers had already made the plunge. They had left Toronto a month earlier. One was filming in Oman and the other two in southern India. I was writing the elements of my script that needed to be filmed in those locations. I was also waiting for my daughter, Sarika, to be born. My schedule had been carefully organized. Sarika would be born, I would have five days to share her introduction to the world with my wife, Tara, and then I would embark on a whirlwind rendezvous with the three film crews sprinkled across two continents.

But Sarika was late …

All of our plans were waylaid by good old Mother Nature. It was a small, but important, reminder of just how real A Planet for the Taking's message is. Natural events like birth and death are part of an independent network of life, a net worth with much more at stake than our self-serving timetables …

A similar reminder came in Kenya while I was filming a troop of baboons. We had been introduced to the baboons by Dr. Shirley Strum, an anthropologist who has been observing this same troop of baboons for years. Shirley is well acquainted with each individual baboon in the troop. She knows each baboon's age and place on the family tree. One by one, she introduced members of the film crew to the baboons. Because we, like most humans, have had little acquaintance with other animals in anything but dominating and controlling relationships, Shirley had to remind us of some basic inter-species etiquette. We were told not to look the baboons directly in the eye. That's an aggressive statement, arrogant and challenging.

Properly introduced and graciously accepted, we were ready to start filming. One of the things Shirley has discovered in her studies is that baboons are creatures of habit. Their days follow a strict routine of wandering, feeding, socializing and resting. Considerately we planned our day to fit the troop's schedule. We would rise before dawn to join them in their sunrise walk to a feeding spot. There, we would film the first of several items about how our observations of baboon behaviour—and anything else—are determined by what we expect to see.

Our sunrise rendezvous never happened. For some reason, the troop had decided on a different starting location that day. When we finally caught up with them there was a great sense of relief. According to our schedule of their schedule, the troop was due for a one or two hour stop.

They found a sunny spot and seemed to settle down. Hastily the crew unloaded cameras and tape recorders. I reviewed my lines, hoping they would still be there in my memory when the cameras were rolling. In less than a quarter of an hour we were ready. So, too, were the baboons. With a fleeting glance at our set-up, they ambled off.

Five or six times that day this same scenario unfolded itself. When the sun finally set we had covered several miles and had not shot even a single foot of film. We still don't know what happened to the baboons' ironclad schedule that day. Perhaps it was their equivalent of a human weekend, or perhaps it was a gentle reminder from their culture to ours that even well-intentioned, passive observers such as ourselves have an effect on whatever they are observing.

—by David Suzuki

11. The phrase "sprinkled across two continents" contains an example of

   A. simile

   B. imagery

   C. metaphor

   D. symbolism

12. The figure of speech contained in the phrase "All of our plans were waylaid by good old Mother Nature" is an example of

   A. simile

   B. metaphor

   C. alliteration

   D. personification

13. The type of writing used in this passage is best referred to as

   A. narrative writing   *tells a story*

   B. scientific writing

   C. expository writing   *gives information*

   D. biographical writing

14. The writer's main purpose in writing this passage is to examine the idea that

   A. natural events control all things

   B. Mother Nature waylays the plans of humans

   C. baboons do not like to be interrupted in their daily lives

   D. humans need to become acquainted with their surroundings

ANSWERS AND SOLUTIONS—UNIT TEST

1. B	5. A	9. A	13. C
2. WR	6. A	10. WR	14. B
3. B	7. C	11. B	
4. A	8. A	12. D	

1. B

Satire is a form of writing that criticizes something in a witty or humorous way. In this short story, the writer is humorously criticizing explorers and expeditions through his depiction of the character Sir Davis Thighton.

2. WRITTEN RESPONSE

The writer's purpose in writing this story is to entertain the reader with a satirical story about an expedition to find Santa's home. There is little serious information the story, although the writer does give factual information about sherpas and their mountaineering skills.

3. B

This story is not to be taken seriously, and the writer uses many phrases and expressions to ensure that it is not. The idea of setting out on an expedition to find Santa in Antarctica is humorous by itself, and the writer includes further humorous details in his work. The writer's descriptions of the explorers' gadgets and his characterization of Sir Davis serve to add humour to the story. This writing is a piece of fiction and has good vocabulary, but the phrases support the humour in the writing.

4. A

The writer develops his ideas primarily through anecdotes. He provides various to explain Sir Davis' eccentric behaviour. Some examples of anecdotal information can also be found in the descriptions of the sherpas' radio helmets and clothing and in the information about magnetism.

5. A

The writer uses short, simple sentences to emphasize the speed and excitement of a hockey game. During a hockey game, there is a great deal of action and little time for long periods of inactivity. The use of short sentences enhances the reader's sense of the fast pace of the game.

6. A

The crowd was yelling with excitement as Dan Hawley "streaked toward the Owl goal" because they were eager for their team to score a goal and win the game.

7. C

This passage is an example of writing in the genre of realistic fiction.

8. A

After the fish swallows the bait, "the stillness is broken / by ripples exploding." The fish is fighting its capture by flailing and slapping the water; hence the "exploding" of the water. These lines mark a significant change in the mood of the poem. The fishing rod "arcs" to support the weight of the fish as the fisherman pulls it onto the shore. It is not stated whether the fisherman enters the water.

The slapping of the fishing rod would be too minor to be described as "ripples exploding." Besides the fish, the only other marine life referred to in the poem is the hatches, or recently hatched fish.

9. A

Mesh is a material made up of a network of wire or thread. The fisherman is anxious to get the fish into the fishing net in order to secure the catch. The fish is stored in a basket after its death is assured. Mesh would be much more effective in securing the fish than the fisherman's hands. The fish is not mesh-like.

10. WRITTEN RESPONSE

The poet wants the reader to see the fish as a "victim" that has been destroyed for very little purpose. The destruction of its eggs, or "children," disturbs the natural balance of life in the area. These words are chosen to make the reader feel sorrow about the loss of life.

11. B

The phrase "three film crews sprinkled across two continents" contains an example of imagery. The writer is providing an image of the film crews dispersed over two continents. The use of imagery does not have any specific symbolic meaning.

12. D

Giving human attributes to inanimate objects is called personification. When the writer refers to nature as a female and a mother, he is personifying nature.

13. C

An expository piece of writing provides information about a certain topic. In this article, the writer is giving information about his attempts to make two separate films and how he was thwarted on each occasion by nature. This article is not a biography of the writer nor is it a scientific piece of writing. It is not a narrative, although there are narrative anecdotes in the article.

14. B

The main message in this article is that nature is in control and humans are not. The birth of a baby and the unexpected behaviour of a troop of baboons are the examples put forth in the passage to support this point of view.

NOTES

Developing and Organizing Content

DEVELOPING AND ORGANIZING CONTENT

Imagine you are going on a road trip. How would you prepare for it? Without a map and a planned route to your destination, your trip would probably not be very enjoyable. Preparation and organization are important in all areas of life, and writing is no exception. Planning before you write is very important. Developing your purpose for writing, your topic, and how you will organize your content will ensure that your writing is clear. It will also make the writing process much easier.

No matter what type of composition you are writing, being organized is key to clear communication. It is important to identify your key or main ideas and distinguish them from supporting details. There are different methods of grouping ideas, both during the planning stage and the drafting stage of your writing. Effective visual organizers and advice on how best to organize are included in this section of your KEY. Organizing your information throughout the writing process will save you time and will improve the quality of your writing.

9W1.4 Identify, sort, and order main ideas and supporting details for writing tasks, using several different strategies and organizational patterns suited to content and purpose for writing

ORGANIZING IDEAS DURING THE PLANNING STAGE

When you write according to an organized plan, your writing tends to flow more logically and coherently. Organizing your writing before you begin also saves you time. Use the planning strategy that works best for the topic and purpose of your writing piece.

GRAPHIC ORGANIZERS

Graphic organizers are pictorial representations of how ideas can be connected and organized. They help you organize and visualize important ideas. You can use graphic organizers to understand main ideas, how those ideas might be related, and how important details support main ideas.

Here are seven examples of graphic organizers:

- chronological sequence
- comparison/contrast
- concept pattern
- description
- episode
- generalization/principle
- process/cause and effect

Chronological Sequence

In a chronological sequence organizer, events are organized in the order in which they occur.

Example

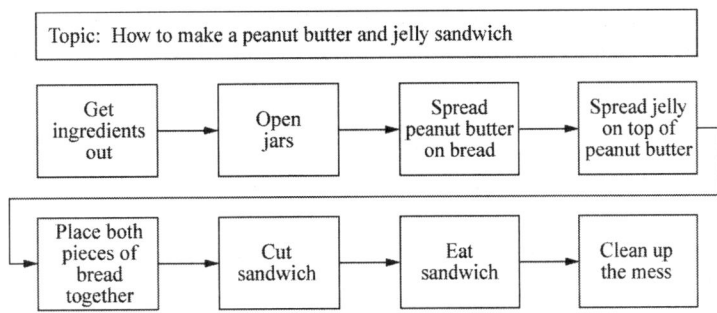

Comparison and Contrast

In a comparison and contrast organizer, information is organized according to the similarities and differences of two or more topics.

Venn Diagrams

Venn diagrams show similarities and differences between two ideas or things using overlapping circles. The section where the circles overlap contains similarities; the sections of the circles that do not overlap contain differences.

Concept Pattern

In a concept pattern, general information about people, places, things, and events is organized.

Attribute Webs

An attribute web lists all the potential characteristics of a concept or topic.

Description Organizers

Description organizers arrange facts about specific people, places, things, and events.

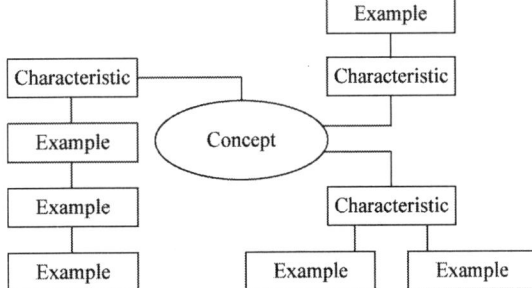

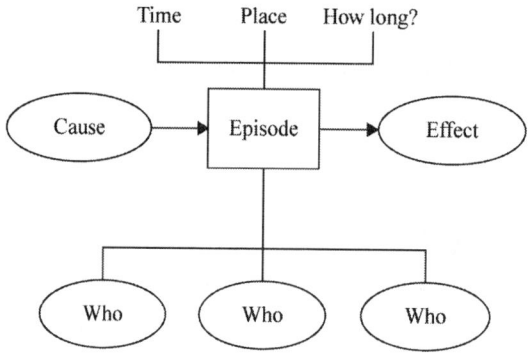

Episode Organizers

Episode organizers arrange information about specific events.

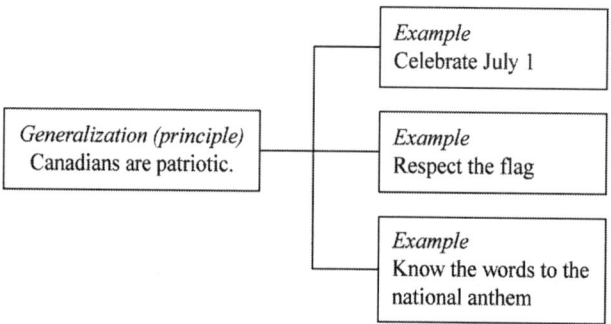

Generalization/Principle

Generalization or principle organizers arrange information into general statements.

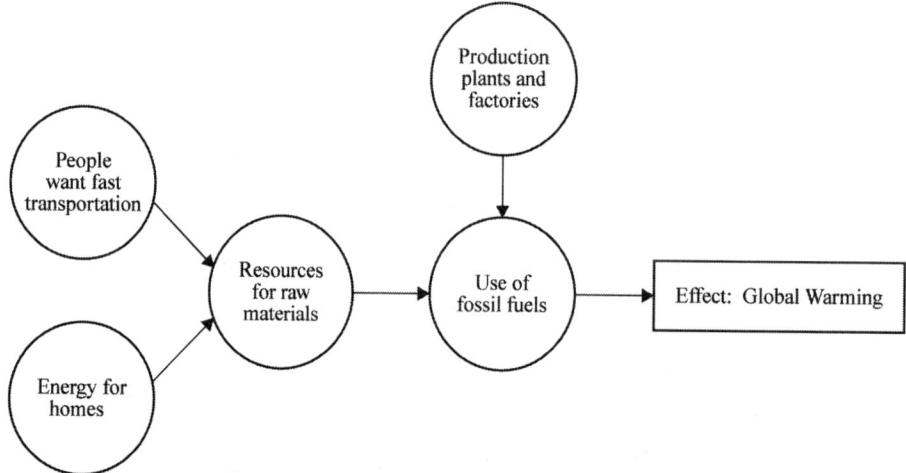

Process/Cause and Effect

Process or cause and effect organizers break down information into a series of steps that lead to a specific idea or outcome.

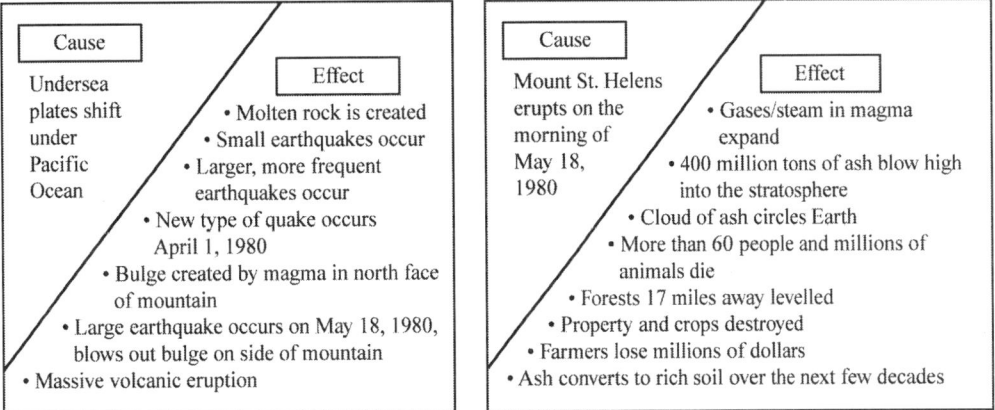

Cause	Effect
Undersea plates shift under Pacific Ocean	• Molten rock is created • Small earthquakes occur • Larger, more frequent earthquakes occur • New type of quake occurs April 1, 1980 • Bulge created by magma in north face of mountain • Large earthquake occurs on May 18, 1980, blows out bulge on side of mountain • Massive volcanic eruption

Cause	Effect
Mount St. Helens erupts on the morning of May 18, 1980	• Gases/steam in magma expand • 400 million tons of ash blow high into the stratosphere • Cloud of ash circles Earth • More than 60 people and millions of animals die • Forests 17 miles away levelled • Property and crops destroyed • Farmers lose millions of dollars • Ash converts to rich soil over the next few decades

Rather than an outcome-based cause-and-effect chart, the following chart is more of an analysis or a reflection of a historical event.

Example

Natural Disaster: Eruption of Mount St. Helens

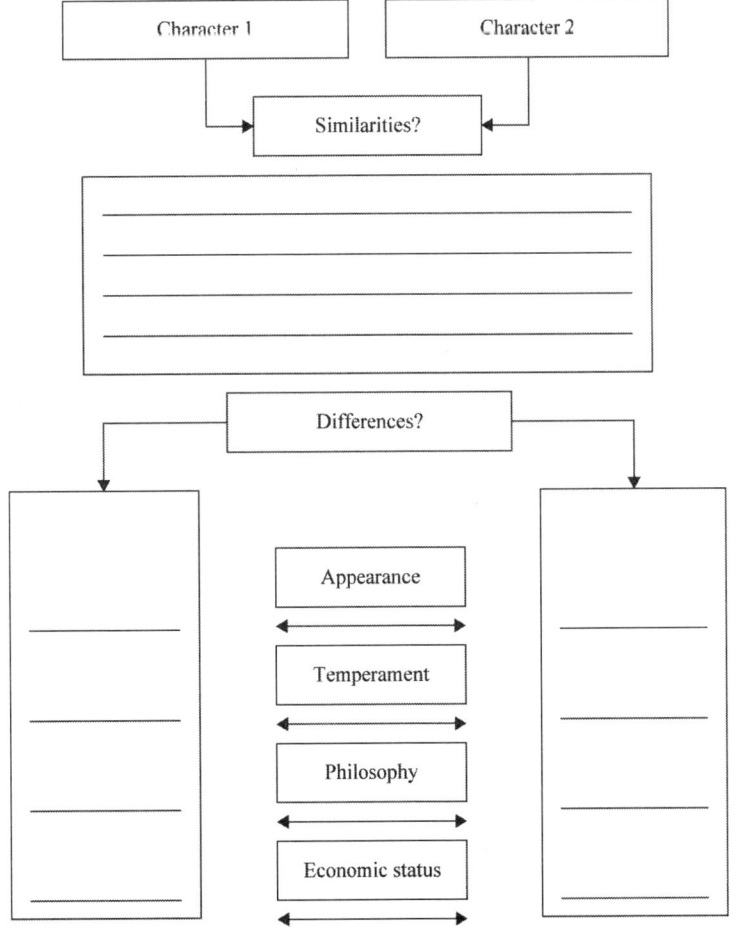

Sequential Order/Timeline

The information about Mount St. Helens can also be arranged in chronological or sequential order, which would be like a timeline of the events in the order in which they occurred. Your timeline might look something like this:

Timeline of Mount St. Helens Events

Ongoing   Juan de Fuca plate is shifting under North American plate, creating molten rock called magma

1480–1980   Mount St. Helens erupts several times

April 1, 1980   New type of earthquake appears on instruments

Sounds of creeping magma recorded

Small eruptions of ash and steam occur

Bulge pushes against north face of mountain as magma builds

May 18, 1980   Earthquake cracks bulge open

Huge blast of gases and steam emitted from mountain

Entire forests levelled as far as 17 miles away

Cloud created around the globe by 400 million tons of ash

More than 60 people die

Millions of animals and trees destroyed

Property and crops flattened or buried under ash

1980–present   Ash transformed into some of the best agricultural land in the world

Comparison Charts

Comparison charts can be very useful for getting ideas flowing about texts you have read. You might be asked to compare two characters from a short story, for example, Rainsford and General Zaroff in "The Most Dangerous Game" by Richard Connell. Because comparing involves analysing both similarities and differences, the following comparison chart is useful for organizing your thoughts before writing a comparison paragraph or essay.

Concept Pattern

A concept pattern organizer is best used to organize general information about people, places, things, and events.

Outlines

An outline is usually the best way to organize your research data before writing your paper or report. By developing a point-form outline, you will ensure that you have distinguished between the main ideas and the supporting details. Outlines also help you make sure that you are on topic and that your work will follow a logical order.

The following outline describes important events surrounding the eruption of Mount St. Helens:

Example

I.   Background

   A. Main cause

      1.   Undersea Juan de Fuca plate sliding under North American plate

   B. Clues and foreshadowing

      1.   Small earthquakes occurring under the volcano moving closer to surface

      2.   New type of quake occurs on April 1, 1980

         a)   Sound of creeping magma

         b)   Mini-eruptions of ash and steam

      3.   Biggest clue to eruption is a bulge growing on the north face of the mountain

II. Doomsday: eruption

   A. Time of day

      1.   May 18, 1980

      2.   Morning

   B. Main events

      1.   Large earthquake knocks bulge off north face of mountain

      2.   Escaping gas and steam cause huge blast

         a)   Forests up to 17 miles away levelled

         b)   Tons of ash hurl into stratosphere

         c)   Cloud circles Earth

         d)   More than 60 people die

         e)   Animals, forests, property, and crops destroyed

III. Afterward

   A. Agricultural effect

      1.   Fruit farmers lose millions in 1980

      2.   Over the next two decades, some of richest farming land in world develops because of volcanic ash in area

Storyboards

A storyboard layout is used to plan film or video versions of stories. This is a special graphic organizer that separates the audio and video components of the story presentation. The graphic box is like a slide that portrays a picture of what will be happening on the screen. Below the visual is a text box, either containing actual dialogue or else describing the audio effects that accompany the picture, such as music. When you scroll through the chapters on a DVD menu to select the point at which you wish to start your movie, you are looking at a modified storyboard format.

Example

Storyboard introduction for student film adaptation.

"Gift of the Magi"   Storyboard Introduction

by O. Henry   for student film adaptation

Della looks distraught at her table.
Della: One dollar and eighty-seven cents.
That was all. And sixty cents of it is in pennies.

Della is now on the couch crying.
Della: Oh Jim, my dear Jim, what am I to do?
It's Christmas Eve, Jim. One dollar and eighty-seven cents!

Cut to figure of Della walking slowly down Main St.,
stopping to stare into store windows.
Music: Ukrainian Bell Carol

Della stops by a store window to admire a watch.
She looks longingly at the watch and her hands slowly
touch her face as the camera zooms in on her.

CHAPTER ORGANIZERS

Often, chapters in textbooks are organized logically to help you locate information. For example, each chapter of a science text might contain elements such as

- a topic-related picture on the first page

- a list of chapter subtopics on the first page

- objectives and key terms beginning each subtopic

- hands-on activities

- student activities under headings such as:

    Checking Concepts

    Thinking Critically

    Interpreting Visuals

    Building Science Skills

    Designing an Experiment

- lab activities

- a chapter summary

    Key Term Challenges

    Content Challenges

    Concept Challenges

Chapter organizers are arranged according to the order of the content. Organizing and presenting material using many different styles can help you learn difficult material. These features also help you navigate through a chapter. This is especially useful if you want to read only certain kinds of material from each chapter as you study for an exam.

ON 9W1.1   *Students will identify the topic, purpose, and audience for several different types of writing tasks*

WRITING WITH PURPOSE

By Grade 9, you are becoming a more experienced writer. You have already accomplished a wide variety of writing tasks. Every writing task, from a short paragraph to a research report, shares the same first steps:

- determining a reason or purpose for writing
- choosing a topic
- considering the prospective audience for your finished product

The process of successful writing is like preparing for and going on a journey. If you plan and follow the steps in the writing process, you will reach your destination. Before starting to write, then, it is wise to sit back and think about your topic, purpose, and audience.

Choosing a Topic

Choosing a topic can be difficult if you are not sure where to begin or if you are having trouble choosing between topics you are interested in. Assigned topics and topics you choose yourself may present different challenges when you start organizing your work.

Assigned Topics: Often, a topic or a list of acceptable topics will be provided by your teacher. You may be asked to write a research paper, a story, a poem, a movie or book review, a business letter, or other creative text.

Self-Chosen Topics: If you decide to choose your own topic, some of the following guidelines may help you arrive at a decision:

- Think of issue-related topics. These are topics that generate a range of opinions, such as when teenagers should be eligible to drive, what world leaders should do about global warming, and so on.
- Think about topics of personal interest to you. When you are passionate about Canadian hockey, the harmful effects of cyberbullying, or future trends in transportation, you are more motivated to research and explore the topic thoroughly.
- Brainstorm and eliminate. Quickly think of and list six topics. Do a quick Internet search to see how much information is available online: this usually means information about those topics will likely be available at the library as well. Some topics may immediately lead you to a brick wall because resources on the topic do not seem to be available. Cross these topics off your list. You probably do not have time to spend hours hunting for related information.
- Think of topics that would be of interest to your target audience. Since your audience often consists of your peers, you can probably think of topics that would interest your classmates. These topics are more likely to motivate you, too, because you probably share many of the same interests as your classmates.
- Break down a broad topic to a manageable size. If your topic is too broad, you will need to sort through too much information. Narrowing your topic before you begin will make your writing task less frustrating and easier to handle.

Deciding on Your Purpose for Writing

Good writers usually have a specific purpose for writing a given text. Clarifying your purpose in writing an assignment before beginning to write can help you focus and stay on topic. Generally, there are five purposes for writing:

* *To inform* (to interpret in detail, to make clear): This form of writing is concerned with the "what" of a situation. Announcements, news broadcasts, catalogues, labels, and documentaries are all examples of communication that informs.

* *To explain* (to interpret, to make clear): This form of writing is concerned with the "why" or "how" of a situation. It is also known as explanatory writing because readers are given explanations and not just informed about an event. Charts, recipes, brochures, invitations, and textbooks are examples of communication that explains.

* *To entertain:* This form of writing is meant to be engaging and entertaining. Action, science fiction, and romance novels are examples of communication that entertains.

* *To impress* (to affect deeply): This form of writing aims to make readers feel strongly about a topic. Editorials, complaint letters, and self-help books are examples of communication that impresses.

* *To convince* (to persuade by argument): This form of writing aims to change the reader's beliefs; the writer will state a belief and then appeal to the reader's feelings. Advertisements, editorials, and debates are examples of communication that convinces.

Choosing an Audience

Another factor that affects a writer's purpose is his or her audience. Before writing a composition, writers must decide who their audience is and how they want their audience to react. For example, if you are writing an assignment for your teacher, you should write the report in a formal manner, keeping in mind that your audience is your teacher and that correct grammar, spelling, and punctuation are usually required. If you are writing a friendly letter to a friend, your manner can be less formal, and conventional rules are less important.

The following list is not exhaustive, but it includes a range of potential audiences for your writing:

* peers/classmates
* teacher
* prospective employer
* general public
* children
* parents
* pen pal
* politician
* celebrity
* role model

ON 9W1.2   Students will generate and focus idea for potential writing tasks, using several different strategies and print, electronic, and other resources, as appropriate

GENERATING AND DEVELOPING IDEAS

There are many different ideas to write about. Some can be borrowed from your personal experience, while others can come from your imagination or knowledge. Here are some examples of techniques writers use to generate ideas:

Brainstorming: Write down all ideas you have, no matter how trivial or silly they seem. Then choose the idea that is most compatible with your purpose and that you find the most interesting. Brainstorming is often most productive when you are in a group situation, because a variety of ideas are brought up.

Webbing: Also known as mapping or clustering, this technique involves using a diagram to sort out ideas. Place the general topic in a circle in the middle of a page. As you think of more specific details about the topic, place them on the page around the general topic. This technique allows you to create and expand upon specific details.

Free writing: Many interesting ideas can come from simply spending some time writing without planning what you want to write about. With this technique, rules about spelling, capitalization, punctuation, and grammar are not very important. The focus of free writing is to stimulate thinking in order to generate ideas.

Lists: Choose the general topic of your writing and brainstorm ideas about it. For each idea, create further ideas. Once you have a lot of ideas, you can arrange the list in order from the least important to the most important detail.

KWL Chart: This chart allows you to list what you already know about a topic, what you want to find out, and what you have learned during your research. A KWL chart provides focus for your inquiries and research. You could also expand the chart to meet your requirements as shown here:

What I already know	What I want to find out	Possible resources for research	What I learned from my research

Small Group Discussion: This type of discussion can produce ideas for an opinion piece. Group discussions allow for a variety of opinions.

QUESTIONS TO GUIDE YOUR INQUIRY

Once you have chosen a topic, try to think of some questions that will help you to focus or direct your inquiry. For instance, if you chose the topic "The Element of Surprise at Pearl Harbor," you might ask the following questions:

- How exactly did the Japanese launch a surprise attack on Pearl Harbor?
- Where in Pearl Harbor did they attack?
- How did the Americans respond to the attack?
- What did the Americans learn from this event?
- Did the Japanese successfully complete any other surprise attacks during the Second World War? If so, where?
- How did the Americans use the element of surprise to turn the tables on the Japanese?

To keep your research focused and effective, you need to evaluate your questions. You may choose to eliminate some questions that are not relevant enough to your topic, such as the last two questions on the list above.

You may wish to arrange the questions in a logical order to help you to organize the information for your paper. Often, key questions can be used as subtopics for your paper. For example, if the main topic for your paper is "Where in Pearl Harbor did the Japanese attack?" a subheading for your paper could be: "Attack Targets."

IDENTIFYING KEY WORDS AND PHRASES

The topic and inquiry questions you have generated can provide a great starting point for your research. As you begin to find books and Internet articles on your topic, watch for key words and phrases you can use to find more in-depth information. Some key words and phrases that would help you with Pearl Harbor research, for example, might include:

- Hickam Air Force Base
- Bellows Air Force Station
- Wheeler Army Airfield
- Casualties at Pearl Harbor
- United States Intelligence, Pearl Harbor
- Surprise attack on Pearl Harbor
- Aftermath of Pearl Harbor
- Warnings before the attack on Pearl Harbor

Keeping key terms and phrases organized will ensure that you do not forget any part of your assignment that you want to include. There are many different methods to help you get started in developing the content of your work; try a variety of methods to see which works best for you.

Organizing information helps you at several stages in the writing process. Staying organized while you are forming ideas at the developing stage of a writing assignment helps you understand what you want to write about. It also gives you ideas about the information you can use in your assignment. You can keep tabs on what information you want to use and what you might eventually like to leave out.

Once your ideas are developed, organizing your information helps your reader understand your ideas more precisely. Being organized in your writing helps you get your ideas across to your reader. Use the methods that work best for you. Time spent organizing before you sit down to write will save you a lot of time in the long run and will ensure that you create the best writing possible.

NOTES

Publishing Your Work

PUBLISHING YOUR WORK

ON 9W3.6   *Student will use several different presentation features, including print and script, fonts, graphics, and layout, to improve the clarity and coherence of their written work and to engage their audience*

How your work looks is important. The final stage of writing usually involves printing out your assignment, but publishing your work involves several stages of planning during your work process. Some of the key expectations this year include adequate development and organization of your information and ideas, appropriate use of form and style, and proper use of conventions. The following section of your KEY addresses formats for publishing your work and offers methods of publishing and formatting your assignments.

ON 9W3.7   *Students will produce pieces of published work to meet criteria identified by the teacher, based on the curriculum expectations*

ORGANIZATION OF IDEAS

In Grade 9, you will use your writing and creative skills to produce assignments that meet criteria set by your teacher. Since teachers usually give assignments to help you meet the expectations of the curriculum, it is important that you try to follow teacher guidelines consistently. If you are asked to write a business letter, for instance, follow the business letter guidelines provided in the classroom.

If the teacher has assigned an essay, the guidelines will probably involve some of the following criteria:

ESSAY STRUCTURE

- **Introduction:** This is the first paragraph or two of an essay. It is the point where the reader is made aware of the writer's intentions for the piece of writing. The introduction provides information on the topic and helps the reader determine what kind of essay it is.
- **Body:** This is the bulk of the essay, where most of the information is provided.
- **Conclusion:** This is the end of the essay, usually one or two paragraphs in length, where the writer wraps up the argument or otherwise ties together the content of the essay for the reader.
- **Thesis:** This is the main idea of the essay, which ties the whole piece together. It is like the theme in a short story.
- **Transitions:** These are words that help the reader move smoothly from one idea or paragraph to the next.

If the essay is persuasive, the teacher may require an outline to show that your points of argument are organized effectively. Effective organization includes a clear introduction, well-supported arguments, and a conclusion that meaningfully restates your main idea.

SHAPING YOUR IDEAS

Once you have collected ideas and information about your topic, organized these ideas in groups, and written your thesis statement, it is time to focus more specifically on the structure of your essay. A good method of structuring your essay is to shape your ideas into hierarchies. Establishing a hierarchy means deciding which ideas are more general and which are more specific. The following example shows you how an outline for an essay can be structured.

Example

Thesis Statement

I. First argument

    A. First section of the first argument

        1. First example or illustration

            a. First fact or detail

            b. Second fact or detail

        2. Second example or illustration

    B. Second section of the first argument

II. Second argument

You may have been asked to provide at least three arguments to support your thesis, so you would proceed to complete your outline following the pattern shown.

Creating an outline before you begin writing gives you the advantage of mapping out the terrain you plan to cover. With an outline, you are more likely to stay on topic. You should allow yourself some flexibility to change the outline as you write. While writing, you may discover that one section of the argument proceeds differently than what is mapped out in your outline. Shifting parts of the essay around is a common practice, especially when revising the first draft. As you are writing, try to stay flexible enough to alter the course of your argument if necessary. Use your outline as a guide, not a fixed format.

ADEQUATE DEVELOPMENT OF INFORMATION AND IDEAS

Development refers to improving and shaping your ideas while you work on an assignment. Development includes such things as examples, illustrations, definitions, descriptions, facts, statistics, anecdotes, and quotes. The following elements of writing will help you develop you ideas and decide what kind of information you want to include in your writing.

Narration and Description

Narration involves relating an event or sequence of events; description involves using words to create a picture of a person, place, or thing. Both narration and description should be used sparingly, since they do not advance arguments on their own. Instead, these techniques can be used in moderation to support the case you are making. You may be tempted to use narration and description too much, especially if your assignment calls for a word count and you are not sure you have enough to say. It is better to extend one of the arguments you are making instead. When used carefully, narration and description make an essay more engaging for a reader because they offer concrete examples to support abstract arguments.

Facts and Statistics

Facts are objective pieces of information; statistics are collections of facts organized into numerical data. When quoting facts or statistics in your essay, remember the importance of the source from which you draw your quote. A conversation overheard in the streets is not an authoritative source of information you could use in an assignment. If you are quoting statistics, you need to use credible, unbiased sources. Statistics from a university researcher regarding the link between cigarette smoking and lung cancer would be more credible that those provided by a cigarette manufacturer.

Definitions

Defining a key term is an excellent way to begin an essay or to solidify an argument in the middle of one. Definitions do not have to come from a dictionary, although this is a very good source. Other reliable books, such as textbooks, manuals, and encyclopedias offer definitions that could be useful in supporting your argument.

Unless your argument requires a definition, it should not take up too much room in the body of your paper. If you intend to use a definition, make sure that you are defining the word correctly. You will need to cite the source of your definition, whether it is from a dictionary, a textbook, or a website. Providing a definition shows the way in which you plan to use the term for your argument, although there may be several other ways it is used in everyday speech.

Be sure to develop your ideas and information, but always keep your writing relevant to your topic or subtopic. Teachers can tell when a student is padding their paper. Padding means adding non-essential or unrelated information to make your assignment appear longer. Longer is not necessarily better!

APPROPRIATE USE OF FORM AND STYLE

Your teacher will provide you with specific expectations regarding the following aspects of writing:

Form: short stories, sonnets, business letters, news stories, and editorials follow fairly specific form guidelines. For example, short stories generally follow a plot graph that includes the setting, conflict, rising action, turning point, and outcome; and sonnets are 14-line poems with specific rhyme schemes and rhythm patterns.

Style: formal writing style is expected in business letters and editorials. You might be allowed to write a short story using informal language.

Manuscript Requirements

When you are ready to write your final copy of an essay, report, or research paper, you need to find out from your teacher the correct format and any other specific instructions. There are many different formats for presenting your work, and your teacher may have certain requirements. The following example illustrates one format you could use to present your work:

Title Page

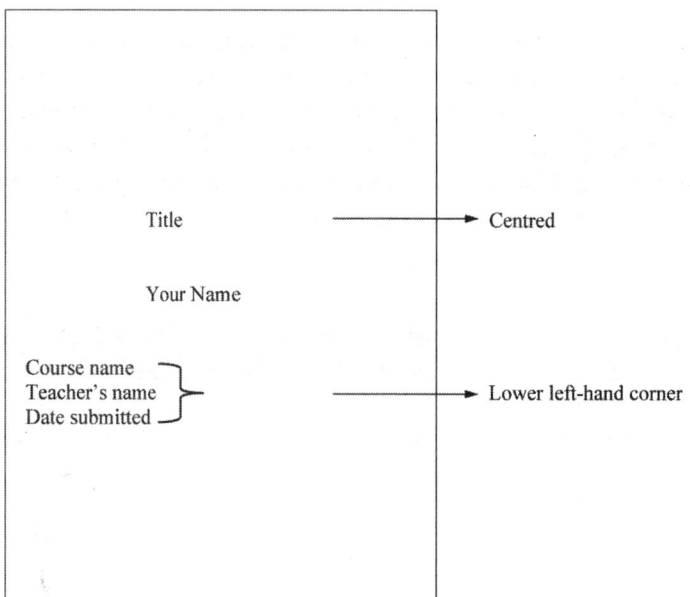

Pagination refers to the numbering of your pages. Your title page should not be numbered, so begin with your first page of text. Be consistent with where you place your page numbers: top right-hand corner or bottom centre.

Spacing and Margins: your work should be double-spaced and have margins set at one inch from the top, bottom, and sides of your text. Either indent five spaces for each new paragraph or leave an extra line above the new paragraph.

Integration of Source and Support Material

When you include short quotations, work them into your writing with as little disruption in the flow of your writing as possible.

Example

- Walt Disney was one of film's most imaginative creators, who built his empire on a "little mouse named Mickey."

Longer quotations should be indented an extra inch, and page numbers (for fiction or essays) or line numbers (for poetry) should be given.

Example

In an essay discussing Shakespeare's use of light images in *Romeo and Juliet*, you might write:

Light images seem to collect whenever Juliet's name is mentioned.

But, soft! What light through yonder window breaks?

It is the east, and Juliet is the sun.

Arise, fair sun, and kill the envious moon,

Who sis already sick and pale with grief,

That thou her maid art far move fair than she.

Romeo's well-known speech upon seeing Juliet at her window uses the extended metaphor of light and dark.

Whenever you use quotations, charts, diagrams, maps, or ideas that are not your own, you must use citations or footnotes. You may want to use reference books to decide how to document your sources, as there are many different formats. For example, the University of Chicago's style for documenting sources is one of the most versatile and comprehensive styles available. It covers how to document every type of publication from books, public documents, interviews, and reference materials to the Internet and unpublished materials.

At the end of your work, remember to create a bibliography on a separate sheet of paper in which you list all of the sources you have used, arranged in alphabetical order according to the writer's surname. The following example displays the proper format for a bibliography.

Example

Bibliography

"Arctic Lemmings," *The American Encyclopedia* 3rd ed. 2007. (Encyclopedia article)

Chartrand, Emily, 2001. *Myths About Lemmings*, New York: Avenue Publishers, 2001. (Book)

Doherty, Paul and, Phillips, John, and Rollester, David, eds. *Lemmings in the Wild.* Chicago: University of Chicago Press, 2002. (Book by more than one author.)

Gallager, Stuart, *Lemmings in the Arctic*, Special report prepared at the request of the Alaskan Department of Conservation, August 15, 1998. (Department document)

Hart, Susan. 2001. "Lemmings Unlimited," http://www.lemmingsunlimited.org/2001.html (accessed March 7, 2008). (Website)

APPROPRIATE USE OF CONVENTIONS

During the revision and editing stages of the writing process, teachers expect you to make your writing as correct as possible with respect to sentences, punctuation, capitalization, grammar, and spelling. Different writing forms have format rules or conventions. For example, consider the envelope for a business letter.

How to Address an Envelope

The return address includes the name and address of the person mailing the letter. If for some reason the post office is unable to deliver the letter, it can be returned to the person who sent it.

You should always write your name and address on the top left corner of the envelope. The return address consists of your name, street address, city, province, and postal code.

Example

Jennifer Ross
56 Ferret Lane
Windsor ON X1A 1J8
Mailing Address

The mailing address consists of the name and address of the individual to whom you are mailing the letter. This address should be placed in the centre of the envelope and should be identical to the inside address on the letter.

Example

Mr. Sam Smith
General Director
Widgets International
1101 Yonge Street
Toronto ON M1B 2B2

The following details are based on standards set by Canada Post. Keep these details in mind when you are addressing envelopes for your business letters.

• Addresses should be typed or written in uppercase or block letters.

• Format all lines of the address with a uniform left margin.

• Do not use punctuation marks unless they are part of a place name (St. John's).

• The postal code should always appear on the same line as the municipality and province name and should be separated from the province by two spaces.

• The two-letter symbol for the province name should be used wherever possible (see preceding examples).

The return address should be formatted in the same way as the main address.

PUBLISHING WITH A COMPUTER

If you use Microsoft Word, there are a number of program features that enable writers to improve the clarity and coherence of their written work. Become familiar with all of the features of Word or whatever word processor you use. Be curious and play around with some of the different features. The better you are at navigating Word, the quicker and easier it will be to publish clear and attractive assignments.

PRESENTATION FEATURES

1. Print and Script refers to your font. It can provide a more effective presentation for a note or memo inserted into a story or if your writing assignment is a friendly letter.

2. Fonts should be selected for the effect you wish to present. Make sure to check with your teacher about fonts. Sometimes your teacher may prefer a particular font for an assignment. Think about the type of font you want to use and experiment with different fonts, italics, and boldface type. The following are some examples of different fonts:

   • **Arial Black** and **Britannic Bold** are clear and easy to read.

   • Castellar is an open font you could use for titles.

   • Bernard Mt Condensed is a narrow font you could use to create newspaper headlines.

You can achieve emphatic effect simply by altering the size of the font you are using. You may want headings or titles to have a larger font size than the rest of your text. Check with your teacher to see if he or she has any preferences as to font size. Italic font is useful for typing the titles of published works in your text. Novels and films are examples of works that should be italicized in a writing assignment.

3. Graphics are an effective method of clarifying information in your document. By hand or with a computer, you can create flow charts, pie charts, diagrams, graphs, or use pictures from clip art or from your own illustrations to enhance an assignment. Remember to clarify the graphics using labels, captions, and titles as needed.

4. Layout refers to the overall appearance of your written document and inclusions like graphics. The following presentation features can be used to make your published work look appealing and professional:

• **Alignment:** You can choose left, centre, right, or justified alignment for any document.

Left aligned
Centre aligned
Right aligned

• **Justification:** Justifying your text makes your lines line up along a straight edge on the left and right margins. ("Ragged" means you align only the left margin.)

• **Bullets:** Use the bullet feature to clarify points or lists.

- **Emphasis Features:** You can make information stand out from the text using features like bolding, colour, font size, text boxes, and text pull-outs created with colour and size features. Text pull-outs are catchy quotes pulled from your magazine or newspaper article, enlarged, and printed below the article title, perhaps in a contrasting colour.

- **Paragraphs:** You have a choice to indent one tab space or to use block form, which requires no indentation. In block form, leave one space between paragraphs.

- **Columns:** Use the Microsoft Word column feature to create professional-looking layouts for newspaper and magazine articles.

- **Headers and Footers** are special lines at the top and bottom of pages. This feature is useful for numbering pages or for providing footnotes for quotes.

Colour for graphics or backgrounds is a presentation feature that requires some advance planning. Coloured text should be used with restraint. You could use colours on the title page or to label something on a chart or picture. For most assignments, however, you will want to stick with black text.

Having a balance of white space, text, and graphics means that you do not crowd the pictures on your title page but arrange them so that your finished product looks clean, organized, and attractive.

Before working on a school assignment, try playing around with Word using some text you can afford to make mistakes with. You can try out different fonts, insert graphics, and manipulate the text in as many different ways as you can find. This will acquaint you with all of the different features available to you in Word.

ON 9W1.3   *Students will locate and select information to support ideas for writing, using several different strategies and print, electronic, and other resources as appropriate*

RESEARCH

After you decide on a topic, you are ready to find ideas and information related to it. These ideas and information will be basic to the substance, or main body, of your writing. Following through with some or all of the steps and strategies below will help you keep your research manageable, find reliable resources, and acknowledge the experts and authors who provided you with your information.

CREATE A RESEARCH PLAN

A checklist-style plan can help you stay focused and on track, as shown in the following example:

Example

1. Topic chosen: _____

2. Assignment expectations: _____

3. KWL chart created

4. Webbing for preliminary ideas

5. Topic restated as a question

6. Preview of available information in the form of a quick list of readily available resources, such as books, journals, websites, and people you could interview.

7. Preliminary research conclusion: does my topic need to be adjusted so that it fits available resources?

8. Further questions related to the topic _____

9. Data collected and point-form notes completed

10. Source information recorded for bibliography

11. Information organized and outline drafted

12. Rough draft of paper completed

13. Good copy of paper completed

14. Bibliography added

15. Title page and table of contents added

Sticking to these steps will ensure that your writing will be the best it can be on the day the assignment is due.

BIBLIOGRAPHIES

In order to create a complete a correct bibliography, you will need to record a variety of information for all sources used in your research, including author, title, publisher data, website information, place of publication, and volume number.

Always follow the guidelines for creating a bibliography laid out by your teacher. The following formats provide examples of how you could record source information for references used in your research.

Book

Author. *Title*. City: Publisher, year.

Example

McCrae, Andrew. Teens and Their Culture.

Boston: Boston University Press, 2006.

Periodical (magazine, newspaper)

Author. "Title of Article." *Publication Name*, Date.

Example
Brolin, Megan. "Online Predators." *Teen by Teen News*,
May 7, 2007.

Encyclopedia

"Name of article." *Title of book*, edition number.
Publisher, Date.

Example
"Technology." *Encyclopaedia Britannica*, 15th ed.
Encyclopaedia Britannica, Inc., 2007.

Electronic Sources

Author (if known). "Document Title." Website or Database Title. Date of electronic publication. Name of Sponsoring Institution. Date information was accessed. <URL>
"Internet Safety Network for Teens." Parent Share. July 2006. Ontario Association of Children's Aid Societies. Nov 2007.
<http://www.occas.org/childwelfare/links.htm>

INFORMATION SOURCES

Online library catalogues are resources that can be found by typing the name of your local library into an Internet search (for example, Toronto Public Library, Burlington Public Library, Thunder Bay Public Library, and so on). When you perform this search, you will find links to:

- library catalogues
- databases by subject or title
- frequently asked questions such as "How do I use the library catalogue?"

Searching

You can search your library to find materials related to your topic by typing in any piece of information from the list below:

- title
- keyword
- author
- subject
- call number
- series title
- ISBN/ISSN: This is a cataloguing number found at the bottom of the credits page, and it looks like this: 0-03-052664-7 5-048 04 03 02
  (These numbers represent a text entitled *Elements of Language: A Second Course*)

Your catalogue search could produce titles and call numbers for several books on your topic, and you can take that information with you to your local library.

At the Library

When you go to a library, the librarian can help you find the information you are looking for. Most libraries are divided into sections to help people easily locate materials. Some sections the librarian might show you include:

- reference materials (dictionaries, encyclopedias, and atlases). Usually, these books can only be used in the library and cannot be checked out
- audio/visual (movies, music, and games)
- periodicals (newspapers, magazines, and journals)
- non-fiction books

All library books are classified or grouped according to one of two systems: the Dewey Decimal System or the Library of Congress Classification (LCC). Most Canadian and American libraries use the Dewey Decimal System. Usually, only very large libraries use the Library of Congress Classification. The following tables show how these two systems organize non-fiction books by number or letter.

Dewey Decimal System	
000	General works
100	Philosophy
200	Religion
300	Social sciences
400	Language
500	Science
600	Technology
700	Fine arts
800	Literature
900	History and geography

Library of Congress Classification	
A	General works
B	Philosophy, psychology, religion
C	History and related sciences
D	History: general and Old World
E–F	History: the Americas
G	Geography, anthropology, recreation
H	Social sciences
J	Political science
K	Law
L	Education
M	Music
N	Fine arts
P	Language and literature
Q	Science
R	Medicine
S	Agriculture
T	Technology
U	Military science
V	Naval science
Z	Bibliography and library science

The following chart explains the Dewey Decimal System classification for a book called *The Biology of the Honey Bee*, by Mark L. Winston.

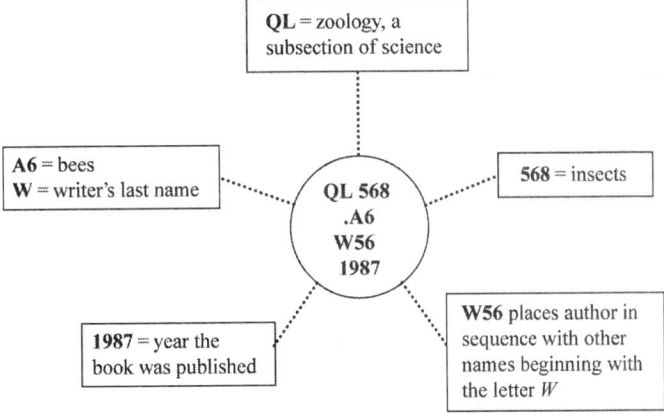

To find this book in the library, look in numerical order among the QL section for 568. Then, look in alphabetical order among the books under QL568 for A6. Finally, look among the books under QL568. A6 for W56.

Online Searches

Online searches involve using key words and phrases related to your topic. Be as specific as possible when searching. For example, using the keywords "provincial election in Ontario" will yield more specific results than using only the keywords "provincial election." Sometimes you have to try a few different keywords or phrases before you find sites that match what you are looking for. When you find an article related to your topic, watch for hyperlinks to other related articles or websites.

The sites listed first in an online search are determined in different ways, depending on which search engine you are using. Some search engines index sites by number of hits or number of links. Sometimes, the owners of websites will pay to have their websites placed on the first page of a search. Usually, the websites listed on the first page of your search results will be the most relevant, but this is not always the case. Play around with key words and phrases. Often, the sites you see more than once are the sites most likely to be relevant.

Information from the Internet is like any other kind of published information, and you must be sure to cite the source in your bibliography.

Dictionaries and Encyclopedias

Dictionaries and encylopedias are among the most useful reference materials in the library. Both dictionaries and encyclopedias can be particularly useful when you are starting a research project and want basic information.

Dictionaries are a good place to start when you are looking for the meaning of a word. Look for the meaning of the word associated with the specific subject or content area. For instance, the word revolution, shown in the sample dictionary definition below, is used in both science and social studies, but the word has two totally different meanings.

---

rev•o•lu•tion (rev′ l ′shn), n. 1. the overthrow and replacement of an established government or political system by the people governed. 2. a sudden, complete, or radical change. 3. rotation on or as if on an axis. 4. the orbiting of one heavenly body around another. 5. a single cycle in a rotation or orbit. **–rev′o•lu′•tion•ary′y**, adj., n., pl –ies. – **rev′o•lu′• tion•ist**, n.

Encyclopedias are reliable sources of basic information about a large variety of subjects. Most libraries do not allow you to take encyclopedias out of the library, so you will have to do your research in the library. Remember that libraries also have electronic encyclopedias on CD-ROMs. The advantage of electronic encyclopedias is that the information is regularly updated as needed. If you want to cite a CD-ROM for a research paper, the following example shows a citation of a CD-ROM as it would appear in a bibliography.

"Technology." Encyclopaedia Britannica. CD-ROM. Encyclopaedia Britannica, Inc., 2008

CD-ROMs on many subjects and topics are available through your library. You can reference them in the same way as a CD-ROM encyclopedia. You can also access all major encyclopedias, such as *Encyclopedia Britannia Online,* from your computer. This is much less expensive than purchasing a printed set of encyclopedias.

Interviews with experts or community members can also yield excellent information. Interviews are especially useful if you are reporting on something that is very current. Chances are there will not be much published information on a very new topic or event going on in your area. In this situation, an interview might be the best resource for getting up-to-date information.

RECORD INFORMATION

As long as you record your information and research, any method you use is fine. One possible method you could use to record your information about your research is to organize it in point form. You could use index cards to record your information, with perhaps one source per index card. Keeping your information organized by source helps you to:

- organize the information later

- ensure that you never plagiarize

- keep quotes and sources of quotes separate from your other information

Make simple headings on index cards to organize your information, using practical topic headings such as "Quotes" or "References." As long as you have a written record of your information, notebooks, index cards, or files on your computer are all fine places to keep track of your sources.

CHECKING RELIABILITY

How do you decide whether or not to believe what you read? Can you tell fact from opinion? How do you decide whether or not you can trust the writer?

Factual statements are clear, accurate, and verifiable. Much of what you read has not been tested, but you usually accept it because it appears to be true, or others whom you trust say that it is true. Magazines, books, newspapers, websites, bulletin boards, and blogs, for example, should not be trusted until the writers' knowledge and experience on the subject has been verified. Faulty conclusions are often made because the evidence relied upon is based either on incorrect observations or on observations that are prejudiced, wishful, or imaginative.

In order to determine how credible a piece of writing is, try examining it from the following angles:

Writer's viewpoint: Who is the writer? What does he or she stand to gain or lose? An article about politics may be very biased if it is written, for example, by the leader of a political party.

Text structure: Is the information presented well? Are the arguments easy to understand, logical, and supported by reasonable evidence? Sloppy work may indicate that the work is not credible.

Writer's word choice: Do the writer's words express ideas and convey facts, or are they meant to inflame readers' emotions? Does the writer's tone seem balanced or angry?

Primary and secondary sources can sometimes determine the degree of accuracy and reliability of the information. A research article with a variety of sources can usually be taken more seriously than a research article that does not use many sources.

More on Primary and Secondary Sources

Primary and secondary sources are both important elements of research. The following chart shows examples of both kinds of sources.

Example

Primary Source	Secondary Source
Autobiography	Biography
Interview with a Titanic survivor	News story written after the Titanic sank
Original manuscript of a book	Translated or revised edition of a book, like a children's version of *Treasure Island*

Interviews can be either primary or secondary sources of information. For example, if you were doing a research paper on the Quebec ice storm, a primary source interview would be with a person who lived through the disaster. A secondary source interview would be with a professor who studies the impact of disasters on regions in Canada. Both primary and secondary source interviews are excellent sources for gathering information you might not find in a book.

Final Tips on Reliability and Accuracy

- Compare facts using various resources and watch for differences or contradictions
- Consider the publishing date: is the information current?
- Consider the expertise and reputation of the source
- Watch for biases. Is the information objective or does it favour or criticize a particular group?
- Double-check Internet sources: is there proof of the writer's expertise? Is the site reliable overall? How recent is the information on the website? Is the website educational or commercial in nature?
- Double-checking accuracy is an important part of publishing your work. Make sure your information is valid before doing a final print of your assignment.

This section of your *KEY* illustrates how different aspects of reading and writing contribute to publishing your work. How your final product looks is important to your reader being able to understand your writing easily. A clean, organized, accurate, and attractive final product will make it as easy as possible for your reader to interpret your writing and find it appealing. Publishing your work usually occurs near the end of the writing process, so it also gives you an opportunity to think about what you have written and how you want your writing to look once it is on the page.

Metacognition

METACOGNITION

The word metacognition refers to thinking about how you think; this process also includes thinking about how you learn. As you discover and think about the strategies that work best with your individual learning style, you will become a more confident and productive learner. It is important to ask yourself questions to determine how you learn best. Do you work better in groups or on your own? Do you memorize things visually? What kind of reading do you like to do best? The more time you spend analysing how you think and learn, the better able you will be to pinpoint areas you excel at and areas you have trouble with.

The following section of your KEY gives you many examples and guidelines on metacognition. The examples are designed to show how an individual student can perform metacognition activities. Keep in mind that the way you think and learn is unique, so different methods may appeal to you more than others. Learning what appeals to you is also a part of metacognition.

ON 9R4.1   Describe several different strategies they used before, during, and after reading, explaining which ones they found most helpful, and identifying specific steps they can take to improve as readers

READING METACOGNITION CHECKLIST

The following examples are of questions that use metacognition to examine your learning:

• What is the best way to approach this learning task?

• At this point, how well do I understand the information, concepts, characters, etc.?

• How can I maintain my motivation to complete what I have started?

• Am I using the best tools for this learning task?

The checklist below shows different strategies you can use to get the most out of your reading. More importantly, it helps you think about how you approach various reading tasks. You could use this checklist several times during the school year to help you understand or change your approach.

USING THE CHECKLIST

Put checkmarks in the "Most Effective for Me" column next to the five strategies in the checklist that work best for you.

• Write a number beside each checkmark showing how effective the strategy is for you (1 is most effective, and 5 is least effective).

• Think of logical reasons for the order you have chosen.

• Discuss and compare your top five most effective strategies with a peer.

• Collaborate to identify the top five strategies from both of you and describe the best uses for each strategy.

• List five ways you and your peer can become better readers.

READING METACOGNITION CHECKLIST

Thinking About My Reading Strategies	Most Effective for Me	Use Most Often	Use Sometimes	Should Try
Before Reading				
I preview (look over exams, texts, stories, articles, and assignments) to determine: What is involved in this text? What is my purpose for reading? How should I approach this? How should I read (speed, etc.)?				
I think about my prior knowledge: what I already know that is relevant to the topic or task in front of me.				
I visualize or try to picture the characters, setting, what I hope to find out, and so on.				
While Reading				
I check back to verify things like definitions and information about characters and settings.				
I use vocabulary strategies like context clues, root words, prefixes, and suffixes to understand unfamiliar words and phrases.				
I make point-form notes or graphic organizers when I need to remember plots and key ideas.				
I pause while reading and predict what I think will happen next in the story.				
I tag text with sticky notes or mark parts I find confusing so I can ask about them later.				
I use a highlighter—when I am allowed—to mark the text for key phrases and important ideas.				
I write notes, questions, and comments in margins if I am allowed. Sometimes, I use these later on to clarify information.				
I ask questions such as the following to monitor my understanding of what I read: Does this make sense to me? What exactly is the writer saying? What is the narrator's point of view? Do I agree? Why or why not?				

When the text does not state something directly, I make inferences and draw conclusions from my reading.				
I deliberately use skimming and scanning skills when appropriate, such as to locate a specific answer or idea in the text.				
I adjust my reading rate as needed, slowing down for detailed information.				
I pay attention to diagrams, pictures, charts, and graphs: anything that may help me make more sense of the text.				
After Reading				
I summarize, using notes or a graphic organizer.				
I write my thoughts, questions, and reactions in a personal response journal.				
I share with a peer in the following ways: • In written form, like a double response journal, in which we write back and forth • by discussing informally within a share-pair or small group • by explaining a newly-learned concept • I try to support my own opinions and show respect for the opinions of others.				
I write critical responses to text when invited to do so. I try to include comments on the form, purpose, writer's viewpoint, historical context, mood, imagery, and so on. When possible, I point out comparisons to other texts or draw from my personal experiences to deepen my response.				

SAMPLE APPLICATIONS OF METACOGNITION

The following section shows you some strategies that involve metacognition. Journals, visual charts, and book clubs are all great methods of making yourself more aware of how you read. Some of these may be more useful to you than others. Figuring out which methods work best for you will give you insight into your learning style.

PERSONAL RESPONSE JOURNAL

A personal response journal can be a great record of what you read. A journal can also be a good starting point to get ideas for homework assignments. A journal entry should include the date, title, and name of the work you are describing. The entry should express your connections with the text. How does the work connect to your experiences? How does it relate to your opinions?

> **DRAGON NIGHT**
>
> Little flame mouths,
>
> Cool your tongues.
>
> Dreamtime starts,
>
> My furnace-lungs.
>
> Rest your wings now,
>
> Little flappers,
>
> Cave mouth calls
>
> To dragon nappers.
>
> Night is coming,
>
> Bank your fire.
>
> Time for dragons
>
> To retire.
>
> Hiss.
>
> Hush.
>
> Sleep.
>
> *—by Jane Yolen*

The following example shows a poem and one student's personal response journal entry regarding that poem. The personal response describes the student's individual experience with the poem. To practise metacognition, try writing your own response to this poem.

> **Personal Response Journal Entry: "Dragon Night" by Jane Yolen February 27, 2008**
>
> Although this poem seems to be written as a lullaby for baby dragons, it means something different and very personal to me. Of all the poems we studied in our September poetry unit, this is my absolute favourite. It brought back lots of memories of the summer, sitting with my family on the deck of our cottage at Muskoka Lake, relaxing and looking at the lake. As I read the poem, I thought of tiny flashes of light down by the lakeshore: fireflies flicking their mini-lanterns on and off.
> The poem has lots of summer/evening imagery. I felt quiet and relaxed by the end of the poem.

The great thing about journal entries is that you do not have to worry that you are being too casual with your language. Even though the entry may be casual and talk about your own life experiences, the information about your opinions can be used to write something more formal later on. Keeping a journal about what you read is a great tool for keeping track of your learning.

VENN DIAGRAMS AND OTHER VISUALS

A Venn diagram is a useful tool for comparing and contrasting two different types of text. It can also help you compare and contrast the strategies you use to read them. Look at the following comparison of a poem and an advertisement and think about the ways you would approach each of them as a reader.

Example

Venn Diagram: Poems versus Advertisements

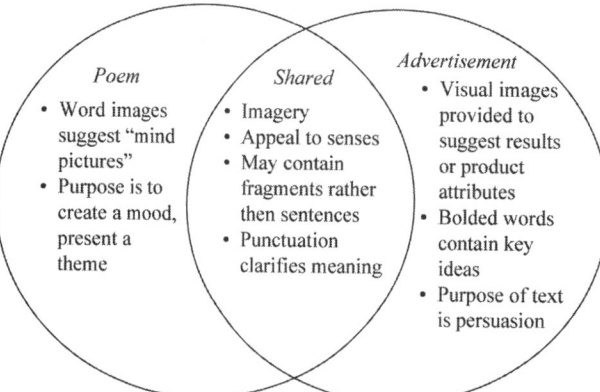

One purpose of a poem is to create mind pictures. Slowing down to think about the meaning of the images a poem creates is important. An advertisement, on the other hand, is meant to grab your attention and get its message across right away. It would be a disadvantage if an advertisement compelled you to slow down and think about its meaning. Advertisements tend to be as simple as possible in order to grab your attention.

LITERATURE CIRCLES AND BOOK CLUBS

A literature circle or a book club may help you better understand a novel. It can also be a fun way to talk with classmates about literature in a more casual way than in the classroom. Everyone interprets literary works a little differently. By talking to others freely about your impressions of a text, you can learn about different ways of looking at it. You also gain a better understanding of your own opinions by having to express them to others.

ON 9R4.2   Identify several of their skills in listening, speaking, writing, viewing, and representing and explain how the skills helped them read more effectively

SKILLS THAT AID READING

Now that you are in Grade 9, you have developed a variety of communication skills that both help you as a reader and improve as you read more. As your reading improves, for example, your ability to state your opinions aloud also improves. Honing your skills in presenting ideas in different media, such as plays or poster art, can improve your skills in summarizing or understanding concepts as you read.

Being able to communicate using one skill will boost your ability to communicate using another. The following examples show how you can increase your language skills by improving your communication skills in a variety of different ways.

LISTENING AND READING

When good readers read out loud, they use several tools to make their reading effective: clear articulation, appropriate tone and expression, pacing, rate of reading, and pauses. As you acquire these skills through listening, you can use them when you read out loud.

- As you listen to peers in a small group setting, you can:
- clarify things you missed or misunderstood
- hear a description of an experience you may not have had or thought about
- discuss views and opinions arising from the same text and learn to use text to support your own viewpoint
- consider the viewpoint of a peer, which could be just as well supported in the text as your own opinion

Speaking and Reading

- As you share your insights and viewpoints from your reading, you will:
- improve your reading comprehension
- learn to support your viewpoint using text statements and inferences
- improve your oral reading skills as you read aloud

In a pair or a small group, comfortably express your ideas from your reading. In a peer group there is no pressure to use precise or formal language. You can feel free to explain your ideas in a more casual setting. Discussion is used to shape your ideas, so they do not have to be perfectly formed at this time.

Writing and Reading

When you write a response to your reading, you can craft a thoughtful response that uses carefully chosen words. Written responses are also an efficient way for you to answer questions from a text and to reread parts of it: both strategies used by effective readers.

Viewing and Reading

Viewing material can enrich your reading experience by adding a visual component. When characterization, costumes, and settings in a film are true to the descriptions in the book it is based on, the stories come to life in a new way. Viewing a film version of a book may help you associate better with the characters in the book. Sometimes, you will find that the film version is not how you imagined the story as you read it. Perhaps the actors do not look the way you imagined the characters to look or the setting is different than you pictured it. Sometimes, readers become resentful if a movie does not seem true to the novel from which it was adapted.

It is important to keep in mind that the film version of a novel is only the interpretation of the people who made the film. One of the best things about reading is that you, in a sense, have the power to create the same visuals in your mind that a director does when making a movie. You direct the movement and appearance of a story in the same way a director might. In order to understand your interpretation of a novel better, you could adapt portions of the story to a dramatic form. This will enhance your effectiveness as a reader as you review the story for accurate dialogue and consistent character portrayal.

PRESENTING IDEAS USING DIFFERENT MEDIA

When you present ideas from a text in a different medium, you understand the ideas better. After you read a book, taking ideas from it and addressing them in a play or on a poster can give you a better understanding of the book's focus and themes. Presenting a text in a new way can highlight aspects of the book's theme, mood, character qualities, or symbolism that you would not have thought about otherwise. For example, a poster or a collage could be used to show the dominant theme in a novel using nothing but pictures cut from magazines.

Applying Your Skills

The next section provides a few examples to demonstrate more specific learning situations in which interconnected skills are used to understand text more effectively. A single work is shown to be presented in different media. This example can give you ideas as to how you could do a similar project with texts you have read.

Presenting a Work Using Different Forms

After reading the legend "The Fork in the Graveyard," two students were asked to dramatize some of the dialogue from the story and use it to share with the class how this project helped them better understand Peter, the main character. Their project is reproduced for you here.

"The Fork in the Graveyard" is an exciting a story of the supernatural that is retold to this day by the people of Tracadie who puzzle over the truth of the episode. The story was originally written in the form of a short story.

THE FORK IN THE GRAVEYARD

The spirit, or ghost, of a dead man is said to have committed the dastardly deed of murdering Peter, a Scottish settler, who arrived in the area on the good ship Alexander in 1773.

The scene is set [with] men relaxing around the warmth of a stove, chatting of mysterious events. When Peter arrives, room is made for him in the warmth, and conversation continues until one Ben Peters mentions having seen a light in the old French burying place at Scotch Fort.
He describes a huge ball of fire dancing across the graves, lighting up the whole cemetery.

Peter, the newcomer, scoffs at the idea, boasting that such exaggerations will not keep him from walking through any churchyard, even the Scotch Fort one, on that very night.

There are, he claims, more devils to fear among his mortal companions than in the resting place of the dead.

His boasting, of course, is quickly taken up on, and the challenge thrown out to do more than brag by the comfort of the fire.

"It's all very well to put on a brave front when yer in the company of humans," pipes a fellow lounger. "But going to a graveyard that's haunted in the dead of night, and alone, is a horse of another colour. Why, man, you must be clear off your beam to even suggest such a thing let alone go through with it. That old cemetery may be full of dead men's bones, but it's also full of dead men's spirits."

Peter takes offence at the remarks, shrugging off superstitious talk as nonsense. The ire is up in his companions who are slighted by his attitude and quickly a bet is made that Peter should go to the old cemetery and plant a hay-fork in a grave to prove he has been there. Should he succeed, a pound of tobacco will be his.

Peter accepts the challenge, and with a jaunty air leaves the cabin, telling them to have his tobacco ready on the morn. "I don't expect to be detained by the dead," he says. "I've never known dead people to harm anyone."

As it is midnight, all file from the store. Peter, in a long black rain slicker, is given the hay-fork and bid on his way to Scotch Fort, while the others scuttle for the dry warmth of their own beds.

Come dawn, all are seeking Peter, who it seems has disappeared. His cabin is empty and cold, obviously vacant for some time. More ominous, his livestock is bleating with hunger. With the realization that Peter is not to be found comes fear, fear for the fate of a man brazen enough to risk defying the very spirits of the dead at the witching hour on a night that seems to portray the very depths of Hell itself.

The men arm themselves, justifying their actions by expressing a concern about bears in the vicinity, and set out to solve the mystery.

The cemetery is a small clearing in the heart of the forest, reached by means of a narrow footpath, permitting not more than two persons to walk abreast. Every now and then the search party stop to peer through the branches of the trees, their voices never above a whisper. Finally they are out of the woods and stare in amazement at the sight that meets their eyes.

The handle of a hay-fork shows plainly above a grave situated right in the centre of the graveyard. A large black object is curled up on the ground beside it.

Cautiously the party press forward, and, as they near the spot, the black object begins to take shape. A few more steps and they raise their voices in unison, "Peter! Can't you speak to us?"

There is no answer save the echo of their own voices. MacIntyre's body lies across the grave, his face turned toward them. It is a face frozen in agony, a haunted, fear-crazed face that makes the living tremble and wish they'd never seen it.

A hand reaches out and grabs the dead man's collar. The hand pulls hard on the collar but the body won't come loose.

A second hand reaches out and grasps the fork. It has been driven into the grave with a powerful thrust and right through the tail of Peter MacIntyre's long black coat.

—retold by Julie V. Watson

The following passage is a dramatization of the story you just read. As you read this rewritten dramatic dialogue, think about what has changed from the original form and what has stayed the same. Think about why certain changes are made when a different form of writing is used. Think about some of the works you have read that might make exciting plays or movies.

Rewriting as Dramatic Dialogue

Dramatic Dialogue Version of "The Fork in the Graveyard"

Characters

Ben Peters

John Smith

Mike Holland   Middle-aged men, dressed in casual shirts and pants

Dan Elliott

Peter MacIntyre   Younger than the others

Setting: A smallish cabin with a large stove in the middle of the room. The men are sitting around the stove warming themselves. The sounds of a wintry storm can be heard outside. Peter enters. He takes off his rain slicker and hangs it on a hook beside the door. The men greet Peter as they make room for him in the warmth.

Ben: I saw a light tonight at the old French burying place at Scotch Fort. The light looked like a huge ball of fire dancing around and over the graves, and it lit up the whole cemetery.

Peter: Must have been your imagination. There is nothing to light up that old cemetery. Cemeteries don't bother me by day or by night, and even your ball of fire wouldn't scare me away from Scotch Fort tonight or any other night. I fear mortal people more than any dead man.

John:	Oh, come on. You're boasting!
Mike:	It's alright to talk like that when you are sitting here keeping warm by the fire. Midnight in a cemetery is scary enough for me.
Dan:	It's all very well to put on a brave front when yer in the company of humans. But going to a graveyard that's haunted in the dead of night, and alone, is a horse of another colour. Why, man, you must be clear off your beam to even suggest such a thing, let alone go through with it. That old cemetery may be full of dead men's bones, but it's also full of dead men's spirits.
Peter:	Yer all just a bunch of superstitious old codgers. The very idea of dead men's spirits makes me laugh.
Ben:	You haven't seen the light. I have, and you don't know what yer talkin' about. It was scary.
John:	I bet you wouldn't go right now in this awful weather to the cemetery.
Peter:	Yes I would. Superstition doesn't scare me.
Mike:	Rising and fetching a hay-fork that was propped up by the door. Alright, then. You take this hay-fork and plant it in a grave in the middle of the cemetery. You come back to us and a pound of tobacco is yours.
Dan:	Great idea. The hay-fork will be the proof you have been to the cemetery.
Peter:	I could do with a pound of tobacco—get it ready, mates. I don't expect to be detained by the dead. I've never known dead people to harm anyone.
Mike:	Handing the hay-fork to Peter. Off you go, then. Visit the dead. We're off to our beds. (Exits)
Peter puts on his black rain slicker, takes the hay-fork, and exits.	
Dan:	Good night. See you in the morn.
Ben:	See you.
John:	Goodnight.
	All exit.

Following their brief dramatic presentation, the two students share their comments about how they adapted the story:

Student A: I didn't really like Peter when we first read the story. I thought he was kind of stupid and gullible to fall for such an obvious trick to scare him. Why didn't he just walk out of the cabin and leave the old guys to their stories? He probably came to the area to work, not to listen to stories. But when we turned the story into spoken words, my opinion changed. He was a newcomer, and probably terrified of failure. He had to make a good impression on the people who had lived in the area longer. He wanted to be accepted. I decided that his boasting was really just being brave because he wanted to look confident to the men.

Student B: We talked about Peter a lot while we were writing the play. We decided he was kind of a victim. Ben, John, and Mike were like students who go on a power trip to show off to a new guy who moves to the school. We saw them as bullies.
We are pretty sure Peter jabbed the fork by accident through his own cloak, which was dragging on the ground. When he thought a ghost was grabbing on to his cloak, he was literally scared to death. Those three men must have felt awful when they found him the next day. No one ever expects their pranks to go wrong, but sometimes they do. You may not agree with our interpretation, but that's how we saw it.

As you can see by the students' remarks, they developed empathy and understanding for the characters when they changed the text into another form. An important skill the students used in this assignment was drawing inferences that they could logically support. Working with and changing a text can help you understand the original work better than you did previously.

USING RESEARCH IN PROJECTS

Research is a vital part of writing formal papers. Metacognition can be applied to your research to help you see where you can improve your research techniques. In the following fictional account, two students are given a news article about a local issue and are asked to use research to clarify and extend their understanding of the article and the issues it presents. As you read about their assignment, think about how you would go about researching this issue if it were your own assignment. How would the techniques you would use be different from the ones used by the fictional students in this example?

Example

Two students are given two weeks to work on a current-events project. The students are asked to identify an issue raised in a news article, track the issue for two weeks, consider alternative perspectives and possible outcomes, and afterwards engage their classmates in a discussion about the issue.

The news article they chose dealt with airline safety concerns brought up following a recent crash landing at Pearson International Airport. According to the news item, an Air France jet carrying 309 passengers and crew landed halfway down the runway during a summer rainstorm. Overshooting the 90-metre buffer zone at the end of the runway, the plane careened over a bank and finally came to a stop. Fortunately, before the damaged aircraft burst into flames, everyone on board was safely evacuated and removed from danger. The crash was caused by human error, but the incident raised concerns about passenger safety and accident prevention.

After reading all the information, the students felt that the runway buffer zones at Pearson Airport should be extended to 300 metres, the required length at most major European airports. The students decide to use a tracking log to record what they did to clarify or extend their understanding of this story and the issues it raised. This is what they recorded during the two-week period in which they completed their assignment:

CLASS PROJECT: THE PEARSON AIRPORT CRASH

1. We collected stories on the topic from the newspaper, television, and Internet for about two weeks. We ended up with a total of 21 news items.

2. We recorded facts or messages common to all of the stories, such as:

- the Pearson runway has a 90-metre buffer zone
- the weather conditions were severe
- the pilot landed halfway down the runway
- incidents such as this happen more frequently than is commonly believed

3. We looked for public reactions on the newspaper and television websites and on the editorial page of the newspaper, and we recorded repeated responses, such as:

- safety is of major concern
- the expense of extending the runway is justifiable because it could possibly save lives
- Pearson airport should have the same standards as the rest of the world

4. We watched for different opinions on the issue and found opinion articles from:

- the Air Line Pilots' Association
- the Ontario Department of Tourism
- city and provincial governments

5. Based on all that we found, we tried to predict an outcome:

- the runway extension would be built over the next two years, funded by the province

6. We watched to see if the issue was resolved in two weeks. It was not, but the matter was under review by a transportation committee.

7. We summarized our findings and prepared our class presentation.

8. After our presentation, we will allow a brief time for discussion on our issue. We will then ask Miss Ferguson to review business-letter format and take us to the computer lab to write letters to the Transportation Safety Board of Canada, to be forwarded to the Honourable Lawrence Cannon, Minister of Transport, Ottawa. The purpose of the letters will be to request mandatory lengthened buffer zones for major Canadian Airport runways by 2010.

Our Concluding Comments:

Through reading, research, and discussion, we clarified and extended our understanding of an important and newsworthy safety issue. We came to have a strong personal interest in the outcome of this issue because, like most Canadians, we will use air travel throughout our lives. If a short-sighted decision is made, we ourselves could someday be victims.

Research is critical to writing non-fiction text. The more you learn about an issue, the better able you will be to form an opinion that is informed and balanced. Finding information that is accurate and that does not have a bias can be difficult. As you become a better researcher, understanding how to find good information will become easier.

Use metacognition the next time you are researching for a project. Think about areas of research you may have missed and how you could use the research you have found effectively.

ON 9W4.1   *Describe several different strategies they used before, during, and after writing; explain which ones they found most helpful; and identify several specific steps they can take to improve as writers*

EVALUATING YOUR PROCESS

Metacognition consists of two processes occurring at the same time: monitoring your progress as you learn, and changing and adapting your strategies as necessary. In writing, this involves identifying which strategies you found most helpful before, during, and after writing and which steps you can take to improve as a writer. After you have finished a writing project, think back to how you developed your ideas for writing, the research you did, and how you sorted and organized it. This will help you to identify the strategies you used. The next time you do similar writing, use the strategies that worked best for you and reconsider the others. For example, a Grade-9 student came up with the following list of strategies he had used during the first half of the year.

Example

My Writing Strategies

Before Writing:

- Went online to find information about topics when I could, like the natural disaster topic after we read the short story "The Worst Day Ever."
- Jotted down books, TV shows, and music titles related to the topic.
- Talked with mom about topic choice.
- Wrote down purpose, audience.
- Made a web plan or outline.

During Writing:

- Made outlines on the computer.
- Tried to follow outlines.
- Checked with assignment criteria.
- Tried to write correctly.
- Tried to use good transitions.
- Tried to include things the teacher was emphasizing, like different sentence openers, "said is dead" replacements, etc.

After Writing:

- Labelled my revisions to make sure I was intentionally including teacher suggestions.
- Read drafts aloud from computer screen while revising and editing.
- Paid attention to my peer partner so we could help each other improve.

Next, the student explained the strategy he found the most helpful. The strategy he chose was the idea of labelling revisions to require thinking specifically about what he was changing and why. Since the students were sharing their metacognition activities with the teacher, he submitted the following paragraph:

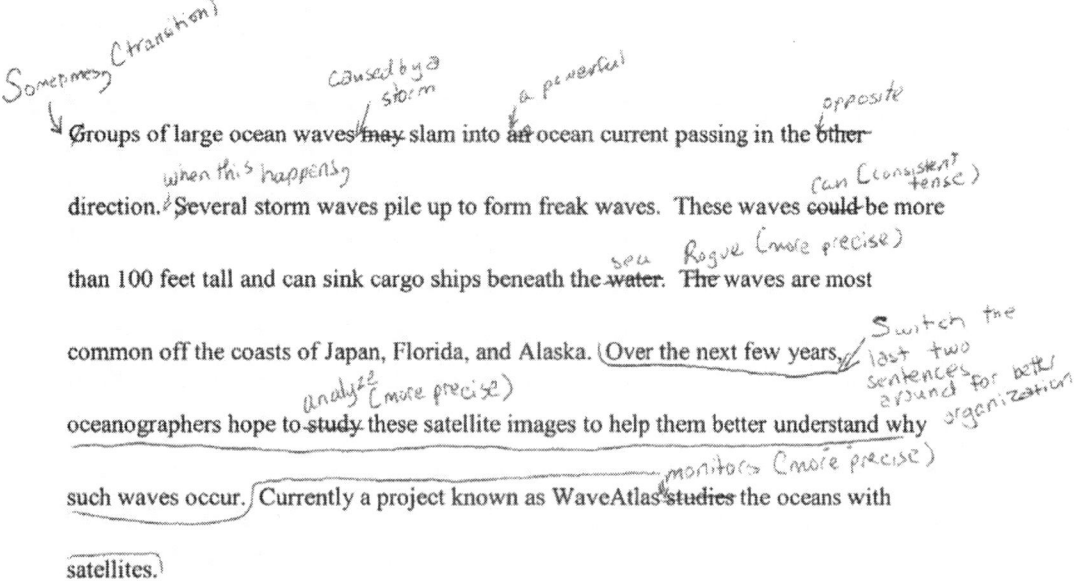

The handwritten annotations on the paragraph read:

Sometimes (transition)

caused by a storm

a powerful

opposite

Groups of large ocean waves may slam into an ocean current passing in the other

when this happens

direction. Several storm waves pile up to form freak waves. These waves could be more

can (consistent tense)

than 100 feet tall and can sink cargo ships beneath the water. The waves are most

sea   Rogue (more precise)

common off the coasts of Japan, Florida, and Alaska. Over the next few years,

Switch the last two sentences around for better organization

analyze (more precise)

oceanographers hope to study these satellite images to help them better understand why

monitors (more precise)

such waves occur. Currently a project known as WaveAtlas studies the oceans with

satellites.

In a note to the teacher under the paragraph, the student added the following note:

Ms. Harmon: Thanks for making us stop to think about our growth as writers. It is helping
me improve. I just wanted to add that there should not be many errors in the paragraph
because I really tried to be careful and to write correctly. That did make the
revision easier.

    Your Student,

    Lyle

P.S. I tried to use the points you listed on the board when I was revising, like improving
organization and using transitions; making ideas consistent and clear; and making details precise.

Finally, the student identified several steps he could take to improve as a writer. His list included the following ideas:

1. Keep a writing log with sections including Spelling Errors, Writing Errors, and Story Ideas.

2. Start a list of words I want to use in my writing.

3. Look online for sites where I can share some of my writing.

After collecting the class's reflections, Ms. Harmon gave the students two 4 x 6 cards to tape inside their writing logs. The cards contained reminders to help the students think about each piece of writing.

Example

This Piece

- What is best?

- What could I improve upon?

- Which stage was smoothest?

- What ideas could I use for new writing?

Learning from this piece

• Have I learned any new techniques?

• Did I try something new?

• Have I eliminated errors I have commonly made in the past, like sentence fragments?

WRITER'S REFLECTION

Reflecting on your writing is something you probably have to do in class. The following example shows you a fictional student's response to metacognition questions from his or her class. You may have to answer questions similar to these about your own writing and language skills. See if you can answer the following questions yourself.

Example

Before Grade 9, what did you know or understand to be your strengths as a writer? Has this changed?

I always thought that my greatest strength was writing humour. It was because I found it easy to remember the punch line of a good joke, and I could always seem to make my friends laugh, sometimes at the wrong time, like in the middle of your class on sentence fragments! In September, when you asked us to think hard about our strengths and to think of ways to branch out from those strengths, I realized that one reason I can describe things in a humorous way is that I am a people watcher. I am always watching what people do, how they react, and what they say in certain situations. I used that strength to branch out when I wrote my one-act play on peer pressure. With realistic sounding dialogue and characters based on what I had really seen around me, I think I was able to get some serious points across using humour. During your comments after my group presented my play, you said our dialogue was convincing and real.

What did you learn about yourself as a writer as a result of the group writing experience?

You mean the short story project. The truth is, I wasn't too happy at first. I actually like writing independent stories from my own head, so it was annoying to have to stop and pay attention to the other two guys in my group. One hated writing, period, and the other didn't want to write anything but fantasy, which I have never read. We wasted a bit of time in the beginning, but when you started posting deadlines on the board we had to think of something. We had just learned about parodies, so we decided to write a modernized parody of a well-known fairy tale. The partner who hated writing didn't mind working from a basic plot we all knew: "Little Red Riding Hood". He even started to contribute a few ideas. My other partner added some twists, I added some ideas for humour, and we all liked the result, because it turned out like a bit of a fantasy. What I learned about myself as a writer was that:

I am more creative than I realized.

Sometimes, other points of view can improve writing.

I can motivate a peer who thinks writing is an unpleasant chore.

How do you determine whether the peer feedback you receive is valid or not?

I pay the closest attention to revision ideas. I figure if my ideas are boring or confusing to any reader, especially a peer, I need to fix that. Sometimes it's just the organization that is confusing, so I make it more chronological, or use better transitions. When a peer suggests different spelling or punctuation, I look at it, but not as hard, unless the peer is a classmate I know to be a strong speller, or one who makes very few errors in his or her own writing. Even when I don't agree with the peer feedback, it does force me to take another look at my writing before publishing the final draft.

How you learn matters. Keeping track of what has affected your language skills is important. How easy was it to answer the three questions in the example? Could you think of any other questions that might be good to ask about your learning? Metacognition means thinking about your learning while you are learning. The more you ask yourself questions like the ones in the given example, the more aware you will become of your learning.

ON 9W4.2   Identify several different skills they have in listening, speaking, reading, viewing, and representing and explain how the skills help them write more effectively

INTERCONNECTED SKILLS

Learning to be a good writer does not happen in isolation. What you hear, speak, and see influences what you write. Many of the skills you practise every day help you develop as a writer. In fact, everything you do and experience can become part of your writing, if you take time to reflect on it. To start thinking about how language skills are connected, consider the following questions:

- What do you know about different media texts that might help when you are writing? (Media texts are found in newspapers and magazines as well as in advertising, posters, and leaflets.)
- In what ways do you think reading helps you as a writer? Can you give an example?
- What do you listen to that might help you as a writer (radio talk shows, conversations between adults sharing their opinions, etc.)?
- Have you ever seen a picture or a movie that made you think of a story? Or, have you ever written a story based on something you saw?

The following chart shows how different communication skills overlap and interconnect to help you write more effectively.

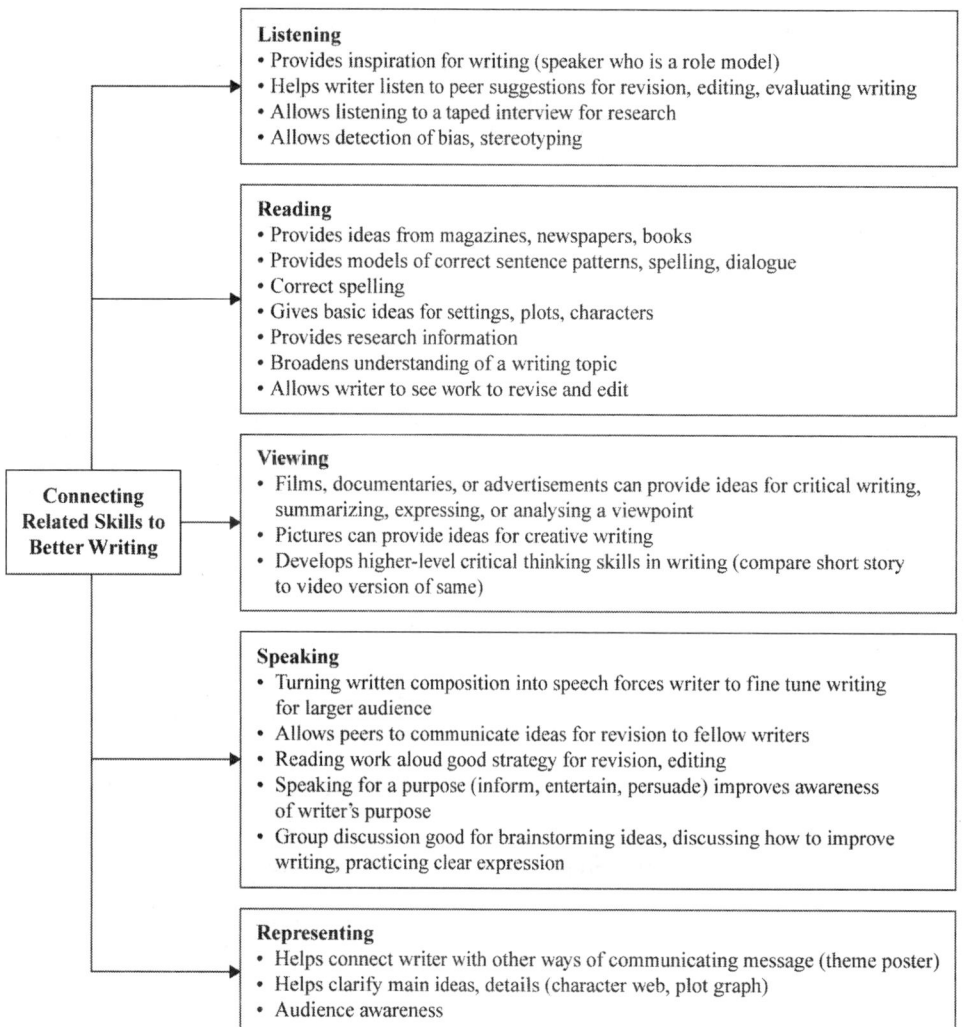

Connecting Related Skills to Better Writing

Listening
- Provides inspiration for writing (speaker who is a role model)
- Helps writer listen to peer suggestions for revision, editing, evaluating writing
- Allows listening to a taped interview for research
- Allows detection of bias, stereotyping

Reading
- Provides ideas from magazines, newspapers, books
- Provides models of correct sentence patterns, spelling, dialogue
- Correct spelling
- Gives basic ideas for settings, plots, characters
- Provides research information
- Broadens understanding of a writing topic
- Allows writer to see work to revise and edit

Viewing
- Films, documentaries, or advertisements can provide ideas for critical writing, summarizing, expressing, or analysing a viewpoint
- Pictures can provide ideas for creative writing
- Develops higher-level critical thinking skills in writing (compare short story to video version of same)

Speaking
- Turning written composition into speech forces writer to fine tune writing for larger audience
- Allows peers to communicate ideas for revision to fellow writers
- Reading work aloud good strategy for revision, editing
- Speaking for a purpose (inform, entertain, persuade) improves awareness of writer's purpose
- Group discussion good for brainstorming ideas, discussing how to improve writing, practicing clear expression

Representing
- Helps connect writer with other ways of communicating message (theme poster)
- Helps clarify main ideas, details (character web, plot graph)
- Audience awareness

Read the following fictional experience of Timothy, a Grade-9 student, which shows how using interconnected skills helped Timothy to write more effectively. Timothy uses *listening*, *reading* and *viewing*, *writing*, *speaking*, and *reflection* together to enhance his knowledge and understanding about a subject. As you read, think about how your own experiences in Language Arts can be improved upon by using a variety of skills.

EXAMPLE OF INTERCONNECTED SKILLS AND WRITING IMPROVEMENT

Listening

Timothy is sitting with his friends in a Grade-9 Assembly. He does not know what to expect as his English teacher, Mr. Kennedy, introduces the guest speaker:

"Ladies and gentlemen, our guest today was once a teacher like myself. Like me, he, too, wracked his brains on a daily basis, trying to think of ways to encourage his students to write, to get them excited about writing. He came up with the idea of writing a novel for them. The novel, Stand Your Ground, was set in the school where he worked. The setting was his community. Many of the characters had the same names as his students. That novel came out in 1993. It was a big hit, especially with the students who found their names in the book. Since 1993, our guest has given up his teaching career to become the full-time writer of at least 45 novels, with more on the way. He has won more than 30 awards, including the Ontario Library Association Silver Birch Award, which he has won three times. The selection panel was made up of over 750,000 young people like yourselves, country-wide, who voted for Mr. Eric Walters. It is my honour to present him to you today. Eric Walters is a man who loves a great story, and who knows how to turn young people into fans of his books."

As the author approaches the podium, Timothy starts to pay attention, especially when Mr. Walters launches into the dramatic reading of a chapter from his novel called Shattered. The chapter is about a 15-year-old boy, Ian, starting to work as a volunteer in a soup kitchen as part of a social studies project. After a near mugging, from which Ian was saved by a homeless man, Ian spots the man at the soup kitchen. It turns out that he is a retired member of the Canadian Armed Forces whose last tour involved peacekeeping duties in Rwanda.

Mr. Walters also reads a foreword from a novel composed by Canadian General Romeo Dallaire, Force Commander for the United Nations Mission to Rwanda.

The rest of the presentation is a blur. Mr. Walters calls up a couple of students who have prepared some interview questions. He is both entertaining and serious as he talks about writing and about researching historical events in Canada to get ideas for writing. All Timothy can think about is getting his hands on that first novel. Timothy is not from Rwanda, but his parents did come to Canada from Zaire before it was renamed Congo. He was too young to remember, but he wants to find out about why his parents ended up in a refugee camp for a year before they emigrated.

READING AND VIEWING

Timothy signs out the novel Shattered from the school library. The librarian suggests that he might also like to watch the movie Hotel Rwanda, which is about a courageous hotel manager who saved some people from being caught in a tribal massacre during the Rwandan crisis. Timothy rents the movie after he finishes the book.

Writing

The teacher, Mr. Kennedy, has encouraged his students to try writing some form of historical fiction, using suggestions from Eric Walters. Timothy decides to create five journal entries written by a fictional character, Akunda, who lives with his parents in a refugee camp in the Congo. Akunda and his family are hoping to emigrate from the Congo and start a new life in Canada.

Speaking

Timothy tapes his journal entries to play for his writing group. He uses his older brother to be the voice of Akunda, and he reads the part of the narrator. As a writer, Timothy is supposed to use the group's suggestions to help him revise his writing.

Reflection

Mr. Kennedy poses the following two questions to his student writers, which they are to attach to the final draft of their writing before handing it in. You can read Timothy's answers to both questions:

How did listening to the taped reading of your writing help you to revise it?

One of my peer listeners suggested that I write two more entries to show the contrast when Akunda started his new life in Canada. He said the journalended too abruptly. I thought that was a good idea, so I added those to my assignment. They also thought I could make the African entries a bit more realistic if I used actual places, so I looked up a map of the Congo on the Internet when I went home and changed a couple of location names.

What did you discover from reading young-adult fiction that you could apply to your own story?

After Mr. Walters spoke to us a month ago, I read his novel Shattered. I tried to make my character, Akunda, seem as real as Ian seemed to me when I read the book. I also did some research on the Congo and talked to my parents about their experiences to make the journal entries as authentic as I could. I went on Eric Walters' website for more ideas, but what I learned from that one novel was:

- use real places and events
- make your main character have the some worries and concerns as young people all over the world, with dreams of a better life, a successful future, and solid friendships

Timothy's experience shows how connected language skills are. The great thing about all your language skills being connected is that you can tailor your learning to how you learn best. If you learn better by talking to others or by speaking out loud about your ideas, do that. Your writing will improve if your ideas come to you more easily through verbal communication. Or maybe you need to write out what you think before you prepare a formal essay. Some people learn better by reading, and some learn better by listening to others speak or by watching others demonstrate something visually.

It is important to remember that related skills in listening, speaking, reading, viewing, and representing contribute to improving your proficiency as a writer. The more you are able to recognize these connections, the better your writing will become.

ON 9W4.3   *Select several examples of different types of writing that they think most clearly reflect their growth and competence as writers an explain the reasons for their choice*

PORTFOLIOS

A portfolio is a collection of your writing pieces, usually representing a time period of at least one school year. Keeping your writing together allows you to:

- see your growth as a writer
- review topics and writing forms you have tried
- evaluate your writing skills
- set goals for improving or refining your skills

A portfolio may also contain a writer's log or journal, personal spelling list, personal error record, or reflections about your writing. In this section, you will find some examples of ways you could use your portfolio as a resource to help you improve your writing skills.

In the following example, a student compares a first draft to a final draft, both of which she has found in her writing portfolio. Look at the first draft of a paragraph on rogue waves that appears earlier in this section. Next, read the revised final draft from the student's portfolio. By comparing the two drafts, the student was able not only to pinpoint the improvements she made, but also to explain what she learned from the redrafting process.

Example

Revised Final Draft of Rogue Waves Paragraph

Sometimes, groups of large ocean waves caused by a storm slam into a powerful ocean current passing in the opposite direction. When this happens, several storm waves pile up to form rogue waves. These waves can be more than 100 feet high and can bury cargo ships beneath the sea. Rogue waves are most common off the coasts of Japan, Florida, and Alaska. Currently, a project known as WaveAtlas monitors the oceans with satellites. Over the next few years, oceanographers hope to analyse these satellite images to help them better understand why freak waves, or "rogue waves," as they are known to scientists, occur, so that scientific warnings can prevent unnecessary tragedies at sea.

Improvements Made:

- used better transitions
- used more precise and consistent vocabulary
- used consistent verb tenses throughout paragraph
- created a more logical order in last section of paragraph
- added a safety reason for scientific studies to round out paragraph

What I Learned from the Redrafting Process:

- read out loud to make sure writing flows smoothly
- when you use consistent verb tenses throughout a piece of writing, the ideas are clearer to the reader
- your writing will sound better if you take the time to think about changes for improvement
- it is more satisfying to hand in redrafted work because you are sure that it is clear and says what you want it to

---

In the following example from a fictional student's writing portfolio, the student has been given point-form information from a local television news broadcast during a week of bitter cold in the city:

- only 826 of 1 200 available overnight Shelter Spots being used
- fears homeless people not using shelters
- hotline number to call 416-SHELTER
- citizens urged to co-operate to prevent homeless from freezing
- city spokesperson Ellen McCall

The assignment involved writing a poem and a news report based on the information the student was given. He was asked to include a reflection with his writing, comparing the processes used for each form and identifying the challenges he had to overcome.

Included here are the student's two writing pieces, followed by the reflection that accompanied the pieces in the portfolio.

BALLAD OF A COLD MAN

The winds they chill me to the bone,
A man who calls Toronto home,
My cardboard walls are way too thin
I wish I could go home again.

Chorus

Home again, yes home again,
I wish I could go home again,
To Mother's stew without the pain,
I wish I could go home again.
The streets they mock me with their ice,
The cops assume I act with vice,
My cardboard walls no shelter give,
Must move if I expect to live.

Chorus

How did I reach this point so low?
How did my dreams descend below?
The ice outside, that's not so bad,
It's ice within, that makes me sad.

And so if winter's got you down,
And risky drivers make you frown,
Just pause while at that traffic light,
And say a prayer for someone's plight.
I too was once a man like you,
The 401 my trial too,
But life can change and paths can turn,
So don't complain, be still, and learn.

> **Deep Freeze Increases Risk to Homeless**
>
> **Fears Grow for Unsheltered**
>
> By E. Meyer
> Toronto Sun City Desk
>
> Toronto – While most of us struggle with getting the car to start and risking a fender-bender on the way to work, the homeless of our city struggle with survival in the frigid temperatures that have gripped the region this past week.
>
> Ellen McCall, spokesperson for city shelter co-ordination, reports that 1 200 beds prepared for weather emergencies are being filled nightly.
>
> While no one is being turned away from shelter facilities, it is feared that some people needing shelter may not be finding it for a variety of reasons, including voluntary choices to spend the night in makeshift temporary shelters outside.
>
> Bus drivers and police have been cautioned to be on the alert for anyone needing assistance or shelter.
>
> Commuters and other citizens are asked to report possible shelter-related emergencies to the shelter hotline at 416-SHELTER (743-5837). All calls will be treated as urgent.
>
> So far, there have been no reported deaths due to freezing. However, each period of severe cold in the past has generated at least one fatality in the city. It is hoped that 2008 will remain fatality-free.

The student's reflection has allowed him to see which parts of the assignment gave him trouble and which parts he enjoyed or came easily to him.

METACOGNITION AND MAKING REVISIONS

In this third example from a fictional student's writing portfolio, the student was asked to revise a descriptive paragraph by creating a variety of sentence beginnings using different openers, such as adjectives,
prepositional phrases, and past participles to replace the overused pattern of "the" plus a noun (subject). The original draft and the revised paragraph are reproduced below. A student reflection follows the two paragraphs, in which the student comments on the effect of the revision on the writing. Both drafts and the reflection would be kept in the student's portfolio. Take a look at the revisions and make a note of what has changed and see if you prefer the revisions. What might you change about the original paragraph?

Example

First Draft of Descriptive Paragraph

The room where I feel most relaxed is my bedroom. Mother and I painted it in my favourite colour scheme, pale green and navy blue. The wide south window looks out over our sweeping back lawn with its massive weeping willow, where I once played as a child. I would play house, pretend it was a robbers' hideout, or even read a book under the umbrella of its cool shade on a hot July afternoon. The window is framed in white, with a softly draped sheer navy valance across its top. I like to sit by that window in my white wicker armchair during a thunderstorm, watching lightning stab the sky in jagged tears as angry raindrops pound against the glass. I feel cozy and secure. This is my own special place.

The following text is the revised version of the first descriptive paragraph. What changes have been made? Do you think they are improvements?

My Challenges for this Writing Assignment

The news story was not too difficult to write because of the notes we had from class on the inverted-pyramid format for news reporting. Most of the key facts were provided in the points listed on the board, so I tried to be as factual as possible. To create the byline and dateline correctly, I checked a newspaper at home and tried to make it look similar with my computer, using special fonts and the column feature. I sometimes make spelling mistakes on words like "frigid," so I used spellcheck and also had my older sister proofread my draft for spelling. I remembered that newspaper reporting should always be correct English, so I used sentence patterns I could use with confidence and did not try anything fancy.

I was able to be more creative with the poem. I chose the ballad form because of the repetitive rhyme scheme and chorus, which I thought I could imitate, and because I think the misfortunes of the homeless make a sad story that seems to have no end, just like a sad ballad that goes on and on. I struggled with the line in the chorus, "To Mother's stew without the pain," because I didn't really like the effect of that wording, but I could not seem to come up with a better line that would express the emotional pain against something comforting like a mother's cooking. My favourite line was the figurative language in "It's ice within, that makes me sad." Other than that, I think my biggest challenge was expressing the ideas I had according to the poetic form I had chosen.

Example

Paragraph with Revisions

Painted in my favourite colour scheme of pale green and navy blue, the room where I feel most relaxed is my bedroom. (Began sentence with a past participle) The wide south window looks out over our sweeping back lawn with its massive weeping willow, where I once played as a child. Under the umbrella of its cool shade, I would play house, pretend it was a robbers' hideout, or even read a book on a hot July afternoon. (Began sentence with two prepositional phrases) The window is framed in white, with a softly draped, sheer navy valance across its top. In my white wicker armchair, I like to sit by that window during a thunderstorm, watching lightning
stab the navy sky with jagged tears as angry raindrops pound against the glass. (Began sentence with a prepositional phrase) Cozy and secure, I burrow deeper into my chair. (Began sentence with two adjectives) This is my own special place.

Now take a look at the student's reflection on the revisions. How did the student approach the assignment? How did the student organize the reflection? Think about how you might use this example as a model for your own reflection.

Example

STUDENT REFLECTION ON REVISIONS

I thought my original draft was quite good, probably because I enjoy describing things, and my room is a special place that I was able to share through precise description. When you taught us about sentence beginnings, I could see right away from your examples that this was a good way of adding variety to writing. It is hard to believe that we fall into the habit of repeating the same sentence pattern, even while using lots of effective descriptive phrases. Here is how I thought the revisions improved my writing with this paragraph:

1. Placing the participle "Painted" at the beginning of the first sentence helped the reader to immediately see the colour scheme, which is probably the most striking feature of the room.

2. The prepositional phrases in this sentence ("Under the umbrella of its cool shade") provided a good transition and link with the "weeping willow" that I introduced in the preceding sentence.

3. This prepositional phrase ("In my white wicker armchair") provided a change from the more predictable beginning of the sentence just before it ("The window is …").

4. These two adjectives ("Cozy and secure") describe the atmosphere of my room, as well as how I felt there during the storm. By moving them to the beginning of the sentence, I was able to give the adjectives a more important status and stress the mood in the room.

I liked the freedom to move words and phrasing around to add variety to my paragraph without eliminating vocabulary I had carefully chosen for the description. I thought the overall effect was much improved!

The applications of metacognition in this section are only examples. You can apply the language skills you have learned in many different ways. Reading out loud, reading with others, discussion, writing, and reworking texts are all useful. As you try different methods, you will begin to see which ones are the most effective for your learning style. The more information you can process and understand, the better able you will be to interact with and interpret the world. Reflecting on how you read and write also helps you practise your reading and writing skills, since you can read, write, and revise the reflections like you would other written work.

Taking time to focus on metacognition will improve your skills in language arts. There is no one correct method for metacognition. It is best to use a variety of methods in order to determine how you learn best. Reflecting on how you learn should be an ongoing process. Metacognition is something you can use throughout your life: in school, work, and other areas. Examining how and why you do certain things gives you insight into how you can change and improve.

NOTES

254

Key Strategies for Success on Tests

KEY STRATEGIES FOR SUCCESS ON TESTS

THINGS TO CONSIDER WHEN TAKING A TEST

It is normal to feel anxious before you write a test. You can manage this anxiety by using the following strategies:

- Think positive thoughts. Imagine yourself doing well on the test.

- Make a conscious effort to relax by taking several slow, deep, controlled breaths. Concentrate on the air going in and out of your body.

- Before you begin the test, ask questions if you are unsure of anything.

- Jot down key words or phrases from any instructions your teacher gives you.

- Look over the entire test to find out the number and kinds of questions on the test.

- Read each question closely, and reread if necessary.

- Pay close attention to key vocabulary words. Sometimes, these words are **bolded** or *italicized*, and they are usually important words in the question.

- If you are putting your answers on an answer sheet, mark your answers carefully. Always print clearly. If you wish to change an answer, erase the mark completely, and ensure that your final answer is darker than the one you have erased.

- Use highlighting to note directions, key words, and vocabulary that you find confusing or that are important to answering the question.

- Double-check to make sure you have answered everything before handing in your test.

- When taking tests, students often overlook the easy words. Failure to pay close attention to these words can result in an incorrect answer. One way to avoid this is to be aware of these words and to underline, circle, or highlight them while you are taking the test.

- Even though some words are easy to understand, they can change the meaning of the entire question, so it is important that you pay attention to them. Here are some examples.

all	always	most likely	probably	best	not
difference	usually	except	most	unlikely	likely

Example

1. Which of the following expressions is **incorrect**?
   A. $3 + 2 \geq 5$
   B. $4 - 3 < 2$
   C. $5 \times 4 < 15$
   D. $6 \times 3 \geq 18$

TEST PREPARATION AND TEST-TAKING SKILLS

HELPFUL STRATEGIES FOR ANSWERING MULTIPLE-CHOICE QUESTIONS

A multiple-choice question gives you some information and then asks you to select an answer from four choices. Each question has one correct answer. The other choices are distractors, which are incorrect.

The following strategies can help you when answering multiple-choice questions:

- Quickly skim through the entire test. Find out how many questions there are, and plan your time accordingly.

- Read and reread questions carefully. Underline key words, and try to think of an answer before looking at the choices.

- If there is a graphic, look at the graphic, read the question, and go back to the graphic. Then, you may want to underline the important information from the question.

- Carefully read the choices. Read the question first and then each choice that goes with it.

- When choosing an answer, try to eliminate those choices that are clearly wrong or do not make sense.

- Some questions may ask you to select the best answer. These questions will always include words like *best*, *most appropriate*, or *most likely*. All of the choices will be correct to some degree, but one of the choices will be better than the others in some way. Carefully read all four choices before choosing the answer you think is the best.

- If you do not know the answer, or if the question does not make sense to you, it is better to guess than to leave it blank.

- Do not spend too much time on any one question. Make a mark (*) beside a difficult question, and come back to it later. If you are leaving a question to come back to later, make sure you also leave the space on the answer sheet, if you are using one.

- Remember to go back to the difficult questions at the end of the test; sometimes, clues are given throughout the test that will provide you with answers.

- Note any negative words like *no* or *not*, and be sure your answer fits the question.

- Before changing an answer, be sure you have a very good reason to do so.

- Do not look for patterns on your answer sheet, if you are using one.

HELPFUL STRATEGIES FOR ANSWERING WRITTEN-RESPONSE QUESTIONS

A written response requires you to respond to a question or directive indicated by words such as explain, predict, list, describe, show your work, solve, or calculate. The following strategies can help you when answering written-response questions:

- Read and reread the question carefully.

- Recognize and pay close attention to directing words such as *explain*, *show your work*, and *describe*.

- Underline key words and phrases that indicate what is required in your answer, such as *explain*, *estimate*, *answer*, *calculate*, or *show your work*.

- Write down rough, point-form notes regarding the information you want to include in your answer.

- Think about what you want to say, and organize information and ideas in a coherent and concise manner within the time limit you have for the question.

- Be sure to answer every part of the question that is asked.

- Include as much information as you can when you are asked to explain your thinking.

- Include a picture or diagram if it will help to explain your thinking.

- Try to put your final answer to a problem in a complete sentence to be sure it is reasonable.

- Reread your response to ensure you have answered the question.

- Ask yourself if your answer makes sense.

- Ask yourself if your answer sounds right.

- Use appropriate subject vocabulary and terms in your response.

TEST PREPARATION COUNTDOWN

If you develop a plan for studying and test preparation, you will perform well on tests.

Here is a general plan to follow seven days before you write a test.

COUNTDOWN: 7 DAYS BEFORE THE TEST

1. Use "Finding Out about the Test" to help you make your own personal test preparation plan.

2. Review the following information:

    – Areas to be included on the test

    – Types of test items

    – General and specific test tips

3. Start preparing for the test at least seven days before the test. Develop your test preparation plan, and set time aside to prepare and study.

COUNTDOWN: 6, 5, 4, 3, 2 DAYS BEFORE THE TEST

1. Review old homework assignments, quizzes, and tests.

2. Rework problems on quizzes and tests to make sure you still know how to solve them.

3. Correct any errors made on quizzes and tests.

4. Review key concepts, processes, formulas, and vocabulary.

5. Create practice test questions for yourself, and answer them. Work out many sample problems.

COUNTDOWN: THE NIGHT BEFORE THE TEST

1. Use the night before the test for final preparation, which includes reviewing and gathering materials needed for the test before going to bed.

2. Most importantly, get a good night's rest, and know you have done everything possible to do well on the test.

TEST DAY

1. Eat a healthy and nutritious breakfast.

2. Ensure you have all the necessary materials.

3. Think positive thoughts, such as "I can do this," "I am ready," and "I know I can do well."

4. Arrive at your school early, so you are not rushing, which can cause you anxiety and stress.

SUMMARY OF HOW TO BE SUCCESSFUL DURING A TEST

You may find some of the following strategies useful for writing a test:

- Take two or three deep breaths to help you relax.
- Read the directions carefully, and underline, circle, or highlight any important words.
- Look over the entire test to understand what you will need to do.
- Budget your time.
- Begin with an easy question or a question you know you can answer correctly rather than follow the numerical question order of the test.
- If you cannot remember how to answer a question, try repeating the deep breathing and physical relaxation activities. Then, move on to visualization and positive self-talk to get yourself going.
- When answering questions with graphics (pictures, diagrams, tables, or graphs), look at the question carefully, and use the following steps:
    1. Read the title of the graphic and any key words.
    2. Read the test question carefully to figure out what information you need to find in the graphic.
    3. Go back to the graphic to find the information you need.
- Write down anything you remember about the subject on the reverse side of your test paper. This activity sometimes helps to remind you that you do know something and are capable of writing the test.
- Look over your test when you have finished, and double-check your answers to be sure you did not forget anything.

Practice Tests

PRACTICE TEST 1

Read the following passage to answer questions 1 to 7.

CHALLENGES

If people are unable to adapt to the changing environment, they will not survive. I have been struggling to adapt to Canada for ten months with the result that I have lost seven pounds.

Changing from the Orient to the Occident was not as easy as I thought. The earth goes around the sun so that when the east is in the daytime, the west is in the night. In my very first month in Canada I watched TV, or sat up in bed crying when other people slept, and slept when others worked. Those were the desperate days I have conquered. There was no friend, nobody to chat with. This cold new world looked hostile to me. I didn't even know who my neighbours were. If there had been no TV, I would have died of loneliness. I remembered what my fourth elder brother had said: "You'll know much more about life when you get to Canada. You don't really know what life is yet. Here, everybody is with you and everything is done for you."

He was absolutely right. My life had started in Canada. For the first two months, I considered life miserable. I desperately needed my mother's company when it was impossible to get it. I missed my nieces and nephews, my brothers, sisters, and my friends. Only then did I realize how important friends were. In Burma, I had slept between my mother and sister. When I got here, my sister-in-law told me that all Canadians sleep alone from childhood; therefore, to Canadianize, I had to learn to sleep bravely in my own room, but I prayed a lot before I slept and never watched ghost stories.

My next barrier to overcome is to assimilate into Canadian culture. I disagree with Canadian girls having dates with their boyfriends frequently. It is so easy for them to accept a date, whereas in Burma, girls have to think it over very carefully, as if risking their lives. Especially in Chinese culture, a person is supposed to have only one man or woman in one's life; therefore, for a girl, caution is essential in choosing a boyfriend. If she dates him, she is engaged to him. Last summer when I was riding on a roller coaster, I saw a young couple kissing right in front of me. I blushed and couldn't find a place to hide my face.

When I attended school, I experienced a new system of teaching and a different relationship between teachers and students. In Burma, when the teacher asks a question, a student must get up and fold hands before answering. Teachers give notes and the students must memorize the notes. Term marks are not counted; the final examination is everything. The exams are quite easy if one memorizes the notes. In Canada, however, the education is a "sticky and tricky" business. I have many sleepless nights because of unfinished homework. I feel frustrated because of poor, poor term marks. I'm in despair to do the play presentation in English since I loathe speaking in public. Now, I know life is a challenge.

Anyway, I have accepted these challenges for my future. I must struggle as best I can.

—by Jodie Chen

1. The writer's main purpose in writing this passage was to
   A. persuade
   B. entertain
   C. explain
   D. inform

2. The narrator of this passage moved to Canada from
    A. Japan
    B. China
    C. Korea
    D. Burma

3. The term "the Occident" refers to
    A. the West
    B. a challenge
    C. an accident
    D. Western Europe

4. According to the information in the passage, in order to "Canadianize," the narrator had to
    A. make friends
    B. learn how to study for final exams
    C. adjust to sleeping alone in her own room
    D. get used to witnessing public displays of affection

5. Explain in your own words how the narrator describes education in Canada.

    The narrator describes education in canada as a "sticky
    and tricky" business. Unlike in Burma, all your marks
    count, not just the final examination. Also, all your
    learning isn't completely based off the notes your
    teacher gives you. There is increased homework as well

6. When she first arrived in Canada, the narrator avoided loneliness by
    A. watching television
    B. making new friends
    C. focusing on losing weight
    D. calling her family every day

7. The lesson learned by the narrator as a result of her experiences in Canada is best summarized by which of the following statements?
    A. Making friends helps one adapt.
    B. Confronting challenges allows for progress.
    C. Adapting to a hostile environment makes a person stronger.
    D. Learning English and assimilating into Canadian culture is necessary.

Read the following passage to answer questions 8 to 15.

THE GOBLINS

Meegosh sat on the edge of the cliff looking down. From her vantage point, she could see the valley floor for several miles in both directions. Anything that tried to pass through that valley would have to pass by her, and that was exactly what she wanted. She needed to know if her suspicions were right. She needed to know if Herconda's goblin army was using this trail to smuggle prisoners out of the city.

She didn't have to wait long. Just before noon, the hunched form of a goblin appeared lumbering down the trail. It was the most grotesque thing she had ever seen. One-half of its body trailed behind like a disfigured appendage. She knew that goblin. She had seen it before. He was one of the goblins that escaped the fight two weeks earlier, one of the ones they hadn't managed to kill.

Meegosh waited for the goblin to get further down the trail before she slipped out of her hiding place. She was careful to stay far enough behind so that he wouldn't notice her, but there was always a chance he might.

The goblin lumbered down the trail, and suddenly, he disappeared. Meegosh froze. There were no sounds ahead of her and nothing behind her. It was as if the goblin had vanished. Not good. Meegosh dropped behind some small brush, flattening herself in to the ground as much as she could.

"Gotcha!" A large hand grabbed her by her long, gray ponytail. The next thing she knew, she was being hauled unceremoniously into an inn. Someone had tied her up! She looked up to see a giant of a man half pushing, half dragging her along. "Enough, or I'll knock you out again," a threatening voice warned her. Meegosh went still. She was no match for the six-foot giant and she knew it.

"Bartender, I'll have the finest meal you've got," her captor said, dropping her in a heap on the floor. "I caught me a gnome."

"There are lots of gnomes in these parts," the bartender said, pushing a plate of food across the counter.

"This isn't just any gnome. This is Meegosh. There's a 2 000 gold piece reward on her head. Traitor to the king," he said through a mouthful of food. Back by the fireplace, a hooded figure sat, quietly watching.

"Picked the wrong pocket did you gnome?" a dwarf roared in laughter. TeliC. Meegosh groaned. The last thing she needed right now was to be heckled by the dwarf.

"She was skulking around the hills," Meegosh's captor informed him. "Up to no good I'm sure."

"Good riddance," Telic said, lifting his glass in a toast.

"Good riddance," the giant tipped his glass to the dwarf.

Of all people, it would be Telic who saw her tied up like this. He was never going to let her forget this one. Twisting in her bonds, she struggled to find a weak point in the knots.

"Stay still," a voice whispered beside her. She felt a sharp knife cut through her bonds. "Wait for my signal," Traya whispered. "He is cunning, that one; has magic on his side. Be careful, Meegosh." Traya melted back into the shadows as quietly as she had appeared.

The door crashed open. Ardayk burst into the room, yelling "Goblins! Goblins!" at the top of his lungs. That was her cue. Meegosh slipped off the stool into the crowd.

"Where's my gnome," her former captor roared, catching sight of the suddenly empty chair. "That reward is mine!" His voice was drowned out in the ensuing chaos as everyone scrambled for weapons—plates, cups, anything sharp enough to fend off a goblin. Meegosh slipped in behind the lumbering brute, reached up, and expertly lifted his money pouch. "That's for messing with the wrong gnome." She spun on her heel and disappeared up the stairs. Her companions would be along soon.

8. Which of the following words best describes Meegosh?
    A. Resilient
    B. Confident
    C. Competent
    D. Resourceful

9. In this passage, the goblins can best be described as
    A. protagonists
    B. antagonists
    C. villains
    D. pawns

10. Describe the relationship between Telic and Meegosh.

_____

_____

_____

_____

11. The dash in the clause "everyone scrambled for weapons—plates, cups, anything sharp enough to fend off a goblin" is used to
    A. provide an explanation of a word
    B. replace a coordinating conjunction
    C. serve as an abrupt end to a thought
    D. join an afterthought to the sentence

12. This passage can best be categorized as belonging to the genre of

    A. fantasy ✓

    B. fairy tale

    C. mythology

    D. science fiction

13. Which of the following statements about the city described in the passage is true?

    A. The city is at war with the goblins.

    B. The city is being invaded by goblins.

    C. The city is in a state of social upheaval.

    D. The city is under the control of Herconda.

14. Meegosh and her companions are most likely

    A. mercenaries

    B. protecting the city

    C. fighting Herconda

    D. fighting the goblins

15. Telic initiates a conversation with Meegosh's captor in order to

    A. mock Meegosh

    B. betray Meegosh

    C. create a diversion

    D. gather information

Read the following passage to answer questions 16 to 22.

LETTER

I am an elementary school bus driver and a university student. As I expected, the children were excited this morning. I've discovered that many of the older boys (on my bus that's ages ten to thirteen) who normally sit at the back of the bus sit in the front whenever anything important happens. Important at this age can be the Al Iafrate trade or the outbreak of war in the Persian Gulf. The pattern continues with them talking about the event much louder than they would normally discuss anything. I've learned that this is my signal to enter the conversation.

Today the boys were giddy with excitement. I understand how they felt; several times last night as I watched the CNN reporters in Baghdad, who were unquestionably heady with the events they watched out their hotel windows, I too caught myself overwhelmed with the alleged success of the program of strategic bombing. I let the boys go on a little longer than I normally do. It was when they started imitating the sounds of video games and suggesting that none of the allies were or would be killed that I interjected.

At this point I trudged out that old truism—that the first casualty of war is the truth. I then pointed out that, in war, people on both sides always get killed. I predicted that on the news they would undoubtedly hear of fatalities on both sides and that they would probably see the bodies of dead children in Iraq. Maybe I crossed the Rubicon of what is appropriate. Nevertheless, they were quiet, and not just at the front of the bus—they were all quiet.

A number of the younger ones asked me if their parents and they themselves would get bombs dropped on them. I wanted to be Santa Claus and promise them that wouldn't happen. Instead, I told them that I was sure, as I am, that that would not happen and that Iraq was far, far away. Of course, some of these children have visited family in Europe, while others come from Hong Kong and South America. They know that nothing is far, far away.

I have two runs every morning and the second was a photocopy of the first. On my way back to the storage yard I wondered if the truth wasn't just a little too tough. I rationalized that they were probably better off prepared. I still remember watching Walter Cronkite during the Vietnam war and how I used to look to Mother every time they showed something awful for the confirmation of its truth.

After I parked the bus, I walked down the aisle in my normal hunt for any forgotten mittens, lunches or—God forbid—sleeping children. I was shocked by what I saw on the windows. It's been damp lately in Southern Ontario and windows have been fogged up for days. Carved out of the fog on at least a dozen windows at the back of the bus were peace signs.

—by David Sandiford

---

16. The writer's main purpose in writing this passage was to

A. inform

B. describe

C. persuade

D. entertain

17. The word "truism," which is used in the quotation "I trudged out that old truism," is closest in meaning to the word

A. prediction

B. constant

C. proverb

D. theme

18. A synonym for the word "giddy," as it is used in the quotation "the boys were giddy with excitement," is

A. overwhelmed

B. weakened

C. excited

D. wild

19. When the narrator states that he "crossed the Rubicon," he is referring to the fact that he

A. frightened the front-row passengers

B. talked about war while driving

C. explained the realisms of war

D. lectured about dying children

20. The war discussed by the students and their bus driver took place in

A. Hong Kong

B. Vietnam

C. Europe

D. Iraq

21. The word "rationalized," as it is used in the quotation "I rationalized that they were probably better off prepared," is closest in meaning to the word

A. configured

B. balanced

C. justified

D. decided

22. As it is used in the quotation "I was shocked by what I saw on the windows," the word "shocked" means

A. traumatized

B. astounded

C. dismayed

D. unsettled

23. The main purpose of this cartoon is to
    A. make fun of television reporters
    B. warn the public about hurricanes
    C. teach people how to classify hurricanes
    D. amuse readers by poking fun at meteorologists

24. In the context of this cartoon, the word "classifying" refers to
    A. counting the occurrences of events
    B. putting school students into classes
    C. arranging and naming groups of things
    D. showing different levels of wind and rain

25. According to the images in the cartoon, which of the following categories represents the most severe hurricane?
    A. Category One
    B. Category Two
    C. Category Four
    D. Category Five

26. The character illustrated in the cartoon is best described as
    A. not very strong
    B. dedicated to his job
    C. not very interested in his job
    D. inappropriately dressed for the conditions

27. Which of the following statements best summarizes the opinion the cartoonist expresses in this cartoon?
    A. The meteorological categorization of hurricanes is easy.
    B. The meteorological categorization of hurricanes lacks technology.
    C. In order to hang on during hurricanes, reporters must be very strong.
    D. Meteorologists must continue reporting, regardless of weather conditions.

28. This cartoon's form, genre, and content suggest that it is aimed primarily at an audience of
    A. senior citizens
    B. teenagers
    C. toddlers
    D. adults

Read the following passage to answer questions 29 to 44.

COOKS BROOK

At the pool where we used to swim
in Cooks Brook
not everyone had guts enough
to dive from the top ledge
not that it would have been
a difficult dive
except for the shelf of rock
that lay two feet below the surface
and reached quarter of the way out
into the width of the pool
one by one the brave few of us
would climb the cliff to the ledge
and stand poised
ready to plunge headfirst
into the dark water below
and always there was that moment
of terror
when you'd doubt that you could
clear the shelf
knowing full well
it would be better to die
skull smashed open in the water
than it would be to climb
backwards down to the beach
so always there was that moment
when you prayed for wings
then sailed arms outspread into the buoyant air
what you feel is something
impossible to describe
as the water parts like a wound
to engulf you
then closes just as quickly
in a white scar where you entered
and you are surprised always
to find yourself alive
following the streaks of sunlight
that lead you gasping to the surface
where you make your way
leisurely to shore
as though there had been nothing to it
as though it was every day of the week
you daringly defied the demon
who lived so terribly
in the haunted hours of your sleep

—by Al Pittman

29. As it is used in the line "and stand poised," the word "poised" means

    A. fearful

    B. excited

    C. graceful

    D. balanced

30. Which of the following quotations best describes how the speaker was feeling before the dive?

    A. "one by one the brave few of us"

    B. "you'd doubt that you could / clear the shelf"

    C. "it would be better to die"

    D. "there was that moment / when you prayed for wings"

31. The speaker says "it would be better to die / skull smashed open in the water / than it would be to climb / backwards down to the beach" (lines 21–24) because the speaker

    A. likes to be challenged into doing dangerous acts

    B. would rather die than be humiliated for backing out

    C. always accepts a dare and does not want to back down

    D. is worried about getting into trouble for doing foolish things

32. The most likely reason that the poet does not use punctuation in this poem is to

    A. enhance the speed of the poem

    B. show how dangerous the action is

    C. demonstrate how free verse is written

    D. allow the readers to create their own punctuation

33. In the quotation "arms outspread into the buoyant air," the word "buoyant" means

    A. floating

    B. rising

    C. damp

    D. thin

34. Which of the following quotations contains an example of alliteration?

    A. "into the dark water below"

    B. "sailed arms outspread"

    C. "gasping to the surface"

    D. "daringly defied the demons"

35. The line "as the water parts like a wound" contains an example of which of the following literary devices?

    A. Simile

    B. Metaphor

    C. Hyperbole

    D. Personification

36. The lines "then closes just as quickly / in a white scar where you entered" contain an example of which of the following literary devices?

    A. Personification

    B. Hyperbole

    C. Metaphor

    D. Simile

37. In the quotation "where we used to swim," the pronoun "we" is used to

    A. introduce the characters

    B. established the setting

    C. build conflict

    D. set the mood

38. From before the dive to the point of coming out of the water, the speaker's emotions change from

    A. fear to indifference

    B. nervousness to dismay

    C. agitation to excitement

    D. frustration to composure

39. In this poem, the speaker's main conflict with the environment is with the

    A. "dark water below"

    B. "cliff to the ledge"

    C. "shelf of rock"

    D. "buoyant air"

40. The lines "following the streaks of sunlight / that lead you gasping to the surface" contain an example of which of the following literary devices?

    A. imagery

    B. contrast

    C. setting

    D. tone

41. Which of the following sentences best describes the main idea of this poem?

    A. People may experience many types of conflict when faced with a challenge.

    B. People should never back down from a challenge.

    C. Fears are more often than not unfounded.

    D. Diving is a brave sport.

42. The "demons" the speaker defies by completing the dive are really

    A. nightmares

    B. beliefs

    C. peers

    D. fears

43. The characteristic of Cooks Brook focused on most in this poem is its

    A. depth

    B. width

    C. coldness

    D. swiftness

44. Describe in your own words how the speaker's agony is made worse before the dive.

    _____

    _____

    _____

    _____

    _____

45. Which of the following words is a noun?

    A. Stopped

    B. Corner

    C. Near

    D. New

46. In the sentence "Some middle schools offer classes that teach students how to practise self-defence," which of the following words functions as a noun?

    A. That

    B. How

    C. Offer

    D. Self-defence

47. Which of the following words is a verb?

A. Were

B. Pictures

C. Thirteenth

D. Wonderful

48. In the sentence "After discussion regarding school uniforms, the parents decided to form a comittee," the word that is spelled incorrectly is

A. discussion

B. regarding

C. uniforms

D. comittee

49. In the sentence "My brother trys hard to do wheelies on his bicycle," the word that is spelled incorrectly is

A. wheelies

B. brother

C. bicycle

D. trys

50. In the sentence "Voters have the choice between democratic or republican goverments," the word that is spelled incorrectly is

A. choice

B. democratic

C. republican

D. goverments

ANSWERS AND SOLUTIONS—PRACTICE TEST 1

1. D	11. D	21. C	31. B	41. A
2. D	12. A	22. B	32. A	42. D
3. A	13. D	23. D	33. B	43. A
4. C	14. C	24. C	34. D	44. WR
5. WR	15. C	25. D	35. A	45. B
6. A	16. A	26. B	36. C	46. D
7. B	17. C	27. B	37. A	47. A
8. B	18. C	28. D	38. A	48. D
9. D	19. C	29. D	39. C	49. D
10. WR	20. D	30. B	40. A	50. D

1. D

The writer of this passage seeks to inform the reader about the experiences and challenges she has encountered while trying to adjust to Canadian culture.

2. D

The narrator states that she previously lived in Burma.

3. A

Since the narrator states that her homeland was Burma and her new home is Canada, the inference can be made that since the Orient refers to Burma, the Occident refers to the western world to which Canada belongs.

4. C

The narrator says, "When I got here, my sister-in-law told me that all Canadians sleep alone from childhood; therefore, to Canadianize, I had to learn to sleep bravely in my own room."

5. WRITTEN RESPONSE

The narrator describes education in Canada as a "sticky and tricky" business and mentions being challenged by increased homework demands and difficult term work.

6. A

The narrator states that when she first arrived in Canada, she would have "died of loneliness" without television.

7. B

The statement "Confronting challenges allows for progress," is suggested in both the introductory and concluding paragraphs of the passage.

8. B

Meegosh is best described as confident. She does not panic when she is captured by the stranger, but she immediately sets about trying to free herself. Once free, she is undeterred by the experience and proceeds to get even with her captor by stealing his money pouch when he is not looking.

9. **D**

A pawn is a person used to achieve someone else's objectives. The goblins are pawns because they work for Herconda, who is the antagonist. Meegosh and her companions are the protagonists.

10. **WRITTEN RESPONSE**

Meegosh complains that Telic will tease her about being caught, which suggests that she and Telic know each other and that Telic is probably one of her companions.

11. **D**

A dash can be used to clarify the meaning of a word, provide an abrupt end to a thought, replace a coordinating conjunction, or join an afterthought to a sentence. In this case, the dash is joining an afterthought that clarifies the preceding sentence.

12. **A**

Both fantasy and fairy tales use mythical creatures such as goblins, gnomes, and dwarves to tell imaginative stories in which good triumphs over evil; however, fairy tales are shorter stories aimed at entertaining young children. This excerpt is obviously part of a longer tale that could be enjoyed by both young and old; therefore, the genre of fantasy fits it best. Mythology uses fantastical elements to explore cultural stories about historical events. Science fiction is set in the future and is based on scientific knowledge.

13. **D**

Meegosh is observing a trail that she believes Herconda's goblin army is using to smuggle prisoners out of the city, which suggests that the city is under Herconda's control. This excerpt does not explain whether or not Herconda is a goblin ruler or whether the city is fighting goblins.

14. **C**

Meegosh and her companions are fighting Herconda and the goblin army. They may be paid mercenaries fighting to protect the city, but that cannot be determined from the details of this passage.

15. **C**

Telic's conversation with Meegosh's captor creates a diversion so that Traya, one of Meegosh's companions, can cut her bonds and free her.

16. **A**

The content of this passage informs the reader of the writer's experiences with the children on the school bus.

17. **C**

The word "truism" is closest in meaning to the word proverb. The quotation "the first casualty of war is the truth" is a proverb.

18. **C**

In the phrase "the boys were giddy with excitement," the word "giddy" refers to the high level of activity and excitement evident in the boys' behaviour. The word excited is a synonym for the word "giddy."

19. **C**

The narrator gives the children some information about the realities of war that probably should have come from their parents. This is why he feels that he may have crossed a line or "crossed the Rubicon."

20. **D**

The war discussed by the children and their bus driver is the war occurring in Iraq.

21. **C**

The word "rationalized" refers to the narrator justifying his reasons for telling the students about the realities of war.

22. **B**

The bus driver is astounded by the students' insightfulness when he discovers their peace signs.

23. D

An understanding of comic form and genre should include the knowledge that the main purpose of cartoons is to amuse readers. An examination of the cartoon and its title suggests that it is doing so by poking fun at meteorologists.

24. C

As it is used in the context of the cartoon, the word "classifying" means arranging or putting in a class.

25. D

The reader is shown a progression of images of worsening weather, starting with light rain for Category One, then progressing to steadily heavier rain and stronger winds as the category number increases. Following this progression, it can be deduced that Category Five is the most severe hurricane category.

26. B

The character shows his dedication by trying to do his job even in terrible weather conditions.

27. B

The title and content of this cartoon suggest that the cartoonist is critical of the methods meteorologists use to predict the weather.

28. D

This cartoon is most likely aimed at adults. Its form and genre may be understood by teenagers, but its content makes it most appropriate for adults.

29. D

To be poised is to be balanced or composed; therefore, the "brave few of us" who stood "poised" were standing with composure.

30. B

Before the dive, the speaker was concerned about clearing the shelf of rock beneath the surface of the water. The speaker knows that death is assured if the shelf is not cleared.

31. B

The reader does not know whether the speaker always accepts dares, likes being challenged into doing dangerous things, or is particularly worried about getting into trouble; however, the speaker does feel that death would be preferable to the humiliation of not performing the dive.

32. A

The purpose of punctuation is to slow down or stop the reader. The poet probably does not want the reader to slow down or stop while reading this poem. He or she probably wants the poem to be read as one continuous piece. In this way, the poem is similar in pace to the speaker's dive, which would be one quick, continuous motion from the top of the cliff to the water below.

33. B

In the context of the phrase "arms outstretched into the buoyant air," the word "buoyant" means rising. The metaphor describes the speaker as falling through air that seems to be rising up past him or her.

34. D

Alliteration is the repetition of initial consonant sounds in words that are close together.

This literary device contributes to the melody of the writing. The phrase "daringly defied the demons" contains repetition of the d sound.

35. A

A simile is a comparison between two objects using the words like or as. In the line "as the water parts like a wound," the poet compares the parting of the water as the diver enters it to the opening of a wound.

36. C

A metaphor is a figure of speech in which one thing is described as if it were another. In this quotation, the poet has followed a simile (the water parting like a wound) with a metaphor of the water closing up like a scar that remains after a wound has healed. The poet is saying that the water closes in a scar rather than like a scar, which would have been a simile.

37. A

The first three words of the line "At the pool where we used to swim" establish the setting. The use of the pronoun "we" introduces the characters who are at the pool.

38. A

The speaker is quite fearful and nervous before the dive: "there was that moment / of terror / when you'd doubt that you could." Once the dive is over, feelings of nonchalance and composure take over ("make your way / leisurely to shore / as though there had been nothing to it." The speaker forgets the fear and matter-of-factly swims back to the others.

39. C

There are various types of conflict portrayed in "Cooks Brook": human versus human, human versus self, and human versus the environment; however, the speaker's main conflict in this poem is with the shelf of rock under the water.

40. A

Imagery is a technique poets and writers use to describe things in ways that appeal to the senses. In the given quotation, the reader can create a mental image of the sunlight filtering down through the water and of the swimmer using its rays to reach the surface.

41. A

The main idea of this poem is that a person may experience many types of conflict, all of which must be overcome, when faced with a difficult challenge.

42. D

The "demons" are the speaker's fears. The speaker faces his or her fears and defies them by successfully completing the dive.

43. A

The major environmental opponent in this poem is the "shelf of rock / that lay two feet below the surface / and reached quarter of the way out / into the width of the pool." It is the depth of the brook where the shelf lies and beyond that is mainly focused on in this poem. The poet does not discuss the temperature or swiftness of the brook. The width is mentioned to point out where the brook is too shallow and how much of it (three quarters) is deep enough for the divers.

44. WRITTEN RESPONSE

The indecision the speaker feels before the dive makes the suffering worse. This is shown through quotations such as "ready to plunge headfirst," "there was that moment / of terror," and "you prayed for wings / then sailed arms outspread." The speaker vacillates between wanting to experience the thrill of diving and being terrified of the dive. If the diver had quickly climbed the cliff and dived off without any hesitation, there would have been less internal agony.

45. B

A noun is a word that refers to people, places, qualities, things, actions, or ideas. Of the words listed, corner is the only noun.

46. D

A noun is a word that refers to people, places, qualities, things, actions, or ideas. In the sentence "Some middle schools offer classes that teach students how to practise self-defence," the word "self-defence" functions as a noun.

47. A

A verb is a word or phrase that expresses an action or state of being. Of the words listed, only the word were is a verb.

48. D

In the sentence "After discussion regarding school uniforms, the parents decided to form a comittee," the word that is spelled incorrectly is "comittee." The correct spelling of the word committee contains two m's, two t's, and two e's.

49. D

The word "trys" is spelled incorrectly. To change the tense of a verb ending in y, drop the y and add ies: try = tries.

50. D

The word "goverments" is spelled incorrectly. The root of the word is to govern, hence the addition of the suffix does not change the basic spelling of the root: government.

PRACTICE TEST 2

Read the following passage to answer questions 1 to 7.

A WINTER'S WALK

It was an unusually mild winter, with so little snow that Anne and Diana could go to school nearly every day by way of the Birch Path. On Anne's birthday they were tripping lightly down it, keeping eyes and ears alert amid all their chatter, for Miss Stacy had told them that they must soon write a composition on "A Winter's Walk in the Woods," and it behoove them to be observant.

"Just think, Diana, I'm thirteen years old today," remarked Anne in an awed voice. "I can scarcely realize that I'm in my teens. When I woke this morning it seemed to me that everything must be different. You've been thirteen for a month, so I suppose it doesn't seem such a novelty to you as it does to me. It makes life seem so much more interesting. In two more years I'll be really grown up. It's a great comfort to think that I'll be able to use big words then without being laughed at."

"Ruby Gillis says she means to have a beau as soon as she's fifteen," said Diana.

"Ruby Gillis thinks of nothing but beaus," said Anne disdainfully. "She's actually delighted when any one writes her name up in a take-notice for all she pretends to be so mad. But I'm afraid that is an uncharitable speech. Mrs. Allan says we should never make uncharitable speeches; but they do slip out so often before you think, don't they? I simply can't talk about Josie Pye without making an uncharitable speech, so I never mention her at all. You may have noticed that.
I'm trying to be as much like Mrs. Allan as I possibly can, for I think she's perfect. Mr. Allan thinks so too. Mrs. Lynde says he just worships the ground she treads on and she doesn't really think it right for a minister to set his affections so much on a mortal being. But then, Diana, even ministers are human and have their besetting sins just like everybody else. I had such an interesting talk with Mrs. Allan about besetting sins last Sunday afternoon. There are just a few things it's proper to talk about on Sundays and that is one of them. My besetting sin is imagining too much and forgetting my duties. I'm striving very hard to overcome it and now that I'm really thirteen perhaps I'll get on better." ——

"In four more years we'll be able to put our hair up," said Diana. "Alice Bell is only sixteen and she is wearing hers up, but I think that's ridiculous. I shall wait until I'm seventeen."

"If I had Alice Bell's crooked nose," said Anne decidedly, "I wouldn't—but there! I won't say what I was going to because it was extremely uncharitable. Besides, I was comparing it with my own nose and that's vanity. I'm afraid I think too much about my nose ever since I heard that compliment about it long ago. It really is a great comfort to me. Oh, Diana, look, there's a rabbit. That's something to remember for our woods composition. I really think the woods are just as lovely in winter as in summer. They're so white and still, as if they were asleep and dreaming pretty dreams."

"I won't mind writing that composition when its time comes," sighed Diana. "I can manage to write about the woods, but the one we're to hand in Monday is terrible. The idea of Miss Stacy telling us to write a story out of our own heads!"

"Why, it's as easy as a wink," said Anne.

"It's easy for you because you have an imagination," retorted Diana, "but what would you do if you had been born without one? I suppose you have your composition all done?"

Anne nodded, trying hard not to look virtuously complacent and failing miserably.

"I wrote it last Monday evening. It's called 'The Jealous Rival; or, In Death Not Divided.' I read it to Marilla and she said it was stuff and nonsense. Then I read it to Matthew and he said it was fine. That is the kind of critic I like. It's a sad, sweet story. I just cried like a child while I was writing it. It's about two beautiful maidens called Cordelia Montmorency and Geraldine Seymour who lived in the same village and were devotedly attached to each other. Cordelia was a regal brunette with a coronet of midnight hair and dusky flashing eyes. Geraldine was a queenly blonde with hair like spun gold and velvety purple eyes."

"I never saw anybody with purple eyes," said Diana dubiously.

"Neither did I. I just imagined them. I wanted something out of the common. Geraldine had an alabaster brow, too. I've found out what an alabaster brow is. That is one of the advantages of being thirteen. You know so much more than you did when you were only twelve."

—by L.M. Montgomery

1. When she is 15, Ruby Gillis wants to have
   A. a boyfriend
   B. an interesting life
   C. an adult vocabulary
   D. her name in the paper

2. Describe in your own words how Anne and Diana spend most of the time on their walk to school.

   _____

   _____

   _____

   _____

   _____

3. The title of this passage refers to
   A. the girls' daily walk to school
   B. the need to be observant of nature
   C. how the girls fill their time each day
   D. Miss Stacy's composition assignment

4. Anne's composition "The Jealous Rival; or, In Death Not Divided," can best be described as belonging to the
   genre of

   A. romantic fiction

   B. historical adventure

   C. descriptive narrative

   D. information observation

5. The relationship between the two girls is shown mainly through

   A. comparison

   B. description

   C. friendship

   D. dialogue

6. The idea that Anne has a vivid imagination is most clearly shown in the phrase

   A. "'My besetting sin is imagining too much'"

   B. "'as if they were asleep and dreaming pretty dreams'"

   C. "'I just cried like a child while I was writing it'"

   D. "'Geraldine had an alabaster brow'"

7. The writer's main purpose in writing this passage was to

   A. show differences between Anne and Diana

   B. illustrate Anne's perception of the world

   C. amuse readers with teenagers' gossip

   D. illustrate the closeness of two friends

Read the following passage to answer questions 8 to 11.

BRENDA STEWART

Jill is so straight, I can't stand it.
But I need a friend who helps me touch the ground
While I chase the wind.
If I am a high-flying kite,
Jill is my string.
If I want to buy something outrageous,
She reminds me that it's not machine washable.
If I act like a complete idiot,
She tells me there is still hope.
If I have a fight with my parents,
She reminds me that it will soon blow over.
Last Saturday I wanted to go shopping with her,
But she had a game to cheer.
I went to the mall myself and
Walked through the aisles admiring everything.
Without thinking, I pulled a top off one of the shelves
And stuffed it into my bag.
A hand grabbed my arm.
A face asked me questions.
A finger dialed a phone.
I felt so embarrassed.
I kept thinking I wouldn't be in this mess
If Jill had come shopping with me.

—*by Mel Glenn*

8. What does the speaker mean when she says she needs a friend who helps her "touch the ground"?

_____

_____

_____

_____

_____

9. As she looks back on and relates her experience, the speaker is most likely feeling

   A. afraid of being caught
   B. regretful for being so impulsive
   C. angry at Jill for not going shopping with her
   D. relieved that the fight with her parents has blown over

10. The speaker mentions Jill's reminder that "it's not machine washable" to illustrate that Jill is

   A. practical
   B. concerned
   C. knowledgeable about fabrics
   D. jealous that her friend found the top first

11. The quotation "I am a high-flying kite" contains an example of

   A. simile
   B. imagery
   C. metaphor
   D. personification

Read the following passage to answer questions 12 to 17.

THE SEARCH FOR THE PERFECT BODY

I'd be happy if I could weigh 200 pounds [90 km] of solid muscle for next year in football ... instead of only 185 [83]. —Don, teenager.

Too tall! Too short! Too fat! Too thin! Too clumsy! Too weak!

Who do we say these negative things about? Not our friends. Not people we respect. Sometimes, maybe, we think or say them about people we don't like. But mostly they're said about ourselves. No matter how good you feel about your abilities and your accomplishments, it's pretty difficult to act confident if you don't feel good about the way you look.

I hate the way I look. — Darlene, 15, a typical teenager.

The present epidemic of self-dislike is related to the whole idea of "body image." Body image is really two images. One stares back at us when we look in the mirror: that's our Actual Body Image. The other is a mental picture of what we think we ought to look like: our Idealized Body Image.

Sometimes the Idealized Body Image is so firmly planted in our minds that it affects our judgment of the actual image in the mirror. We don't see our legs the way they really are—instead we see them compared to "how they ought to look." Instead of saying, "Those are my legs, not bad!" we say, "Those are my legs and they're too fat!" or "That's my nose and it's too big."

Walking away from the mirror, we feel inadequate and miserable. Unhappy with our perceived appearance, we can't relax or feel secure with other people. If you tell yourself over and over, "I'm ugly," you start to believe it and act like it's true. Self-confidence goes right out the window.

I learned the truth at seventeen / that love was meant for beauty queens / and high-school girls with clear-skinned smiles ... —Janis Ian, "At Seventeen"

Deep down, we know that there are things much more important than looks. When other people ask us what's important, we say, "Being kind," "Being friendly," or "Being loyal." But when we look in the mirror, we say to ourselves, "What's important is the way I look, and I don't look good enough."

Like our ideas about what's right or what's wrong, or about what's in or out, our ideas about ideal body image come from a number of places...starting with our parents and our friends. Even when we're very young, we see adults going on diets, working out, and worrying about the desserts they want to eat. People often apologize before eating, as if they were about to do something immoral. Have you ever made an excuse like, "I didn't eat all day," or "My blood sugar is low" before pigging out?

Kids who are overweight get teased and learn from the experience that bodies are supposed to be thin and muscular, and that there is one perfect body that everyone, especially us, must have.

The image of what that perfect body looks like hits us over and over in the media, particularly in television, movies and magazines. TV programs and advertisements tell us that women should be thin and tall with a small waist, slender thighs and no hips: while height, large biceps, and strong thighs and quads are desirable in men.

Styles change over the years and this affects what people imagine the ideal body to look like. In the forties and fifties, the pudgy (by today's standards), Marilyn Monroe look was the style. In the early sixties, everyone wanted to be blonde and tanned; the "Beach Boys" look was in. Today, blondes are unhappy because people make jokes about them, and tans are associated with older movie stars and with over-exposure to the sun, so the look has changed again.

One glance around school or the shopping mall makes it clear that in the real world people come in every shape, size, age and colour. But after looking at models and actors all day long, the fact that we don't look the way they do makes us feel inadequate.

When I was 18 years old, and did look perfect, I was so insecure that I would face the wall in elevators because I knew the lighting was bad. —Cybill Shepherd, actress.

If Cybill Shepherd is unhappy with her appearance, then what hope is there for the rest of us? We're "too fat" compared to whom? "Too short" compared to whom?

But we continue to diet, exercise and contemplate the cost of plastic surgery, trying to turn ourselves into people we can't be. Some people make themselves exhausted and even sick with starvation diets to lose weight or with drugs to improve their strength, only to discover that no matter what they do, they're still not happy with the way they look.

She ain't pretty, she just looks that way. —The Northern Pikes

With so many unhappy people lacking self-esteem and a positive self-image, sales of hair dyes, make-up, exercise equipment and diet plans are booming. People want to buy these things because they think they'll make them perfect. And perfect is happy. Well, at least the advertisers are happy!

There's some evidence that things are changing. Magazines such as Sports Illustrated are actually telling their models to gain a few pounds. Suddenly, the anorexic look is out. Not every character on television has to be perfect anymore, and some TV shows like Degrassi have made a genuine effort to portray people the way they really are. Characters from Roseanne to Uncle Buck are breaking down the false physical ideals. But there's still a lot of room for improvement.

If I spent all my life worrying about what I didn't like about myself, I'd never have fun. —Susan, 15

While we're waiting for the media to change, we can change ourselves. Not our bodies, but our attitudes. We can stop playing the Ideal Body Image game in our heads. We can accept that the way we are right now is okay. We look like us, and each one of us is different. When we start to focus on ourselves as individuals, we begin to develop the self-confidence behind the most attractive look of all.

I look like this because I want to. I like looking like this. —Sinead O'Connor

If Barbie were a person, she'd be too weak to hold her own body up. At 5'6" [168 cm], her measurements in inches would be an emaciated 31-19-27; making it tough to stay healthy or have the energy to dance at the prom.

—by Mary Walters Riskin

12. The writer uses italicized text before each section to

    A. provide antecedent action

    B. set the mood of the section

    C. establish the context of the section

    D. present various problems teens have

13. The writer's main purpose in writing this passage was to

    A. entertain

    B. persuade

    C. describe

    D. inform

14. According to the passage, a person's self-image is most affected by

    A. the media

    B. the mirror

    C. fellow classmates

    D. models and actors

15. According to the writer, a change in self-image will most likely occur when there is a change in

    A. the media

    B. advertisers

    C. self-confidence

    D. personal attitude

16. A synonym for the word "emaciated" as it used in this passage is

    A. ill

    B. gaunt

    C. evasive

    D. exaggerated

17. This passage leaves the reader with a sense of

    A. control

    B. realism

    C. direction

    D. acceptance

Read the following passage to answer questions 18 to 24.

SETTING A SNARE

Melanie struggled to twist the fine fishing line into rounded snares, her fingers numb from the cold. The thin glove liners were no match for the bitter cold of late January.

"Five times lucky," she muttered as she pulled the slipknot tight. This was her fifth snare, her fifth attempt at catching something to eat, and her fifth guess at where to set the snares and how to build them. Although she'd grown up camping and hiking near Fort Smith, she'd never hunted, fished, or trapped—skills she desperately needed now.

Melanie blew on her hands to warm them. This was a long shot at best, but it was the only chance she had. She couldn't live on boiled willow broth for much longer. Her pants were already hanging off of her. Every rib stuck out. She wasn't in the city anymore, and there was nothing she could do about her weight, or lack thereof, until she learned how to catch food.

"It's do or die now, Mel," she said. The sound of her voice echoed in the quiet of the woods. "You brought this situation on yourself. Now you have to get yourself out of it."

Brushing away the dried leaves, she lowered the bottom of the loop so that it was resting a hair's width off the ground. The trick was to get the loop big enough so that the rabbit's head would go through, but not its body. As it ran forward, the snare would pull tight, killing it, or at least that's what she hoped would happen. It all depended on setting the snare in the right spot in the first place.

Rabbits were prey animals. They relied on speed and agility to outmaneuve their predators. She knew from past experience watching the time-honored game of chase between her husky and the rabbits back home that rabbits liked to travel through narrow trails between gnarled thickets of willows and shrubs. They fit; the dog did not. In no time at all, the dog was miles behind and hopelessly out of the game. If she could just guess the right tunnel network …

The problem was snow—there was no snow anywhere. She couldn't use rabbit tracks to set the snare because there were none. There were no clues to tell her where the rabbits lived, where they traveled, or even if there were any rabbits here at all.

Climate change, the great scapegoat for all environmental changes, was not helping her out. Less winter snow meant less water in the spring. It meant less protection for the plants and animals. Sub-zero temperatures were killing off the mice and other small rodents that normally lived under the snowpack, throwing shockwaves back up the food chain as carnivores like foxes, wolves, and weasels struggled to find new food sources. Plants, normally insulated by thick layers of snow, were dying, their cells rupturing in the intense cold.

The world around her was changing. Each time one link came undone, others strained to compensate, only to find that something else further down had given way. It was a cascading effect with no end in sight, and now she was caught up in that game, as hapless as the rabbits she was hunting.

She brushed the leaves back over the fishing line. Please work this time. Please.

Humans were never meant to live in this godforsaken place, Melanie wrote. The fact that native people had survived for so many thousands of years was mind boggling to her now. They had been able to live off the land for centuries, and she was not going to survive one winter. Of course, they had communities and traditional knowledge of the land to help them. She, on the other hand, had nothing.

I take back my arrogance. I thought I could survive here. I thought I knew enough about gathering edible plants and berries, drying herbs, and all that. I thought I was better than all those people lining up for food stamps and water rations. Instead, I'm the fool. If these snares don't work, my arrogance may cost me my life.

18. The phrase "This was her fifth snare, her fifth attempt at catching something to eat, and her fifth guess at where to set the snares" contains an example of

    A. metaphor

    B. repetition

    C. alliteration

    D. exaggeration

19. Fort Smith is most likely

    A. a northern community

    B. a southern community

    C. an aboriginal community

    D. an old-fashioned community

20. The ellipsis in the sentence "If she could just guess the right tunnel network …" represents

    A. an omission

    B. a pause in speech

    C. the end of an idea

    D. an incomplete thought

21. The dash in the clause "The problem was snow—there was no snow anywhere" is used to

    A. end a thought

    B. explain a word

    C. replace a comma

    D. connect two ideas

22. Climate change is referred to as a "scapegoat" because

    A. no one understands it

    B. it is a very complex issue

    C. it is often blamed for environmental disasters

    D. the science surrounding it is uncertain and inconclusive

23. Melanie describes herself as being "as hapless as the rabbits" because she is

    A. now living as part of nature

    B. powerless to change her situation

    C. impacted by environmental change

    D. depending upon her own resourcefulness to catch food

24. The italicized text in this passage represents Melanie's

    A. written thoughts

    B. internal dialogue

    C. past conversations

    D. imagined conversations

Read the following passage to answer questions 25 to 32.

FROM THE WEALTHY PAPER CARRIER, ANDREA'S STORY: HOCKEY NIGHT IN CANADA

IN THOSE DAYS, the Ottawa Senators certainly weren't a force to be reckoned with. In fact, to put it crudely, next to the Anaheim Mighty Ducks, they were the doormat of the league. They were still a good dozen years away from making a decent showing, and a full 15 years away from their first of two consecutive Stanley Cup victories. On that momentous evening in February, 1995, when Uncle Bill took Logan and myself to our first game together, their fabulous goalie, Claude Dupont, was just barely out of diapers. For Logan and me, it was a momentous evening because, looking back, we got our first taste of what was to become our work ethic. It took us a little time, though, to appreciate Uncle Bill's concept of working smart not hard—but
I guess I'm getting a bit ahead of myself in this story.

That afternoon, Uncle Bill came into the kitchen at the stroke of 4:00 wearing his red and yellow 'Flaming C' jersey. Logan groaned.

"You weren't really serious, Uncle Bill, about wearing that jersey tonight?"

"You betcha," Uncle Bill exclaimed.

"They're gonna stone us."

"Don't tell me the Ottawa Senators really have fans," Uncle Bill said in a mocking tone. "In fact, if the Prime Minister is smart, the government will abolish the darn Senate anyway and then your miserable excuse for a hockey team will have to change its name."

Uncle Bill didn't realize it at that time, but he had actually uttered in jest what almost turned out to be a prophecy. In fact, the Senate wasn't really abolished until eight years later and then, in one of the first computer referendums, the citizens of the Ottawa region voted narrowly to retain the name of their hockey club. By that time, the team was starting to emerge as a powerhouse and was becoming a force to be reckoned with, although they were beaten that year in the quarter-finals by the Stockholm Timberwolves. (As you may have guessed, I'm a big hockey fan—even more so than my brother. I often wonder if it weren't for Uncle Bill, whether I could've afforded my season's tickets on the blueline—a small indulgence??)

"I'll make the hot chocolate today," Uncle Bill said. "It's starting to snow out there and I think we should try to leave in about an hour or so. Maybe we'd be better off getting some hot dogs at the game, rather than trying to go out for dinner."

"Are you trying to increase your personal wealth at our expense?" Logan asked with mock seriousness.

"At the price they charge for hot dogs—highly unlikely," replied Uncle Bill. "Besides you should never look a gift-horse in the mouth."

"You know I'm only joking," Logan said.

"Of course," Uncle Bill replied. "Anyhow, let's get down to work. In the last couple of days, we've talked about saving and investing but perhaps the most important question is: where is your money going to come from in the first place? Obviously, the two of you need to explore your opportunities to earn income."

"I think we should get part-time jobs, Uncle Bill," I said, and Logan nodded his head in agreement.

"For now," Uncle Bill acknowledged with a chuckle, "I think, that's a good idea, although, I suspect within a short period of time you're going to want to look at something a little bit more creative."

"Creative?" I asked

"Yep," replied Uncle Bill. "There are better ways to make a living than working for somebody else. But just to get your feet wet, let's look at a job, at least for the short-term."

"I've got an idea," said Logan.

"Hang on to it," I replied. "It doesn't happen too often." Uncle Bill reached in to intercept Logan's jab.

"Let's hear it, Logan," he said.

—*by Henry B. Cimmer*

25. The phrase "the doormat of the league" compares
    A. two hockey teams with each other
    B. a hockey team with a doormat
    C. the Stanley Cup to a doormat
    D. the brother and the sister

26. The eventual success of the Ottawa Senators demonstrates the idea that
    A. it is awful being humiliated
    B. organizations can change dramatically
    C. the Stanley Cup is not within every team's reach
    D. they can at least beat the Anaheim Mighty Ducks

27. What does the quotation "Claude Dupont was just barely out of diapers" mean?

_____

_____

_____

_____

_____

28. Logan most likely groans when his Uncle wears the "Flaming C" jersey because
   A. Logan hates the Calgary Flames
   B. they are going to a Senators home game
   C. his sister Andrea likes the Calgary Flames
   D. the Calgary Flames are competing in the Stanley Cup

29. In your own words, describe what the phrase "uttered in jest" means as it used in the passage.

_____

_____

_____

_____

_____

30. In the context of this passage, the word "prophecy" means
   A. realization
   B. prediction
   C. hope
   D. joke

31. This particular February evening stands out in the narrator's memory because
   A. she got to sit on the blue line at a Senator's game
   B. the Senators began their run for the Stanley Cup
   C. she learned a lesson about working and finance
   D. it was the night that the Senate was abolished

32. Explain in your own words the writer's main purpose in writing this passage.

_____

_____

_____

_____

_____

Read the following passage to answer questions 33 to 35.

THE GUEST

Clomp, clomp, clomp. Booted feet echoed off the stairs leading up to the house. To a person, the sound was barely noticeable, just a soft thump announcing the arrival of the guests, but for Jetta, it was as loud as a freight train rolling up the stairs.

With one bound, she leapt off her chair and dove at the door. "RrrrRouff. RrrrrwarowWoof. RrrowRrrrowRrrrow!" She let off a tremendous series of growls and barks, enough to shake the roof right off the house. She might be little, but she was going to make sure no strangers trespassed in her house.

She was at the door now. Her little paws burrowed into the floor mat, ready to greet a friend, stand her ground, or run away; she would decide which option was best once she saw who was on the other side of the door.

"Jetta, hush," it was Donna, her human. Donna was nice, but she really didn't understand the importance of a good first line of defense. If guarding the house was left up to humans, there would be no accounting for how many strange and crazy people, and animals for that matter, snuck in. No, humans were just too trusting for their own good. That was probably why they kept dogs, Jetta reasoned, to protect themselves from their own follies. Well, she was one dog who took her guarding duties very seriously. With her pearly white teeth showing and her front legs braced, she waited for the door to open.

All was going according to plan. Jetta was ready to attack—attack first, ask questions later, that was her motto—when suddenly, at the last possible second, Donna reached down, slid one hand under Jetta's small belly, and scooped her up off the floor.

Jetta squirmed and twisted in Donna's arms, trying desperately to free herself. "Rrrfff, rrrrfff," she barked. Don't let them in! They will wreck the place, steal food and toys. They might even be worse. They might go after the jelly beans. She twisted and turned, but Donna's arms held firm. No matter how loud she barked or how much she squirmed, Jetta could not get Donna to listen. She could not get her to understand the perils that were lurking on the other side of the door.

The door handle slide down with a sickening clunk. Then, ever so slowly, the door screeched open, sending shivers racing down Jetta's spine. It was as if a million alarm bells were going off, but she was the only one who could hear them. She tensed. It was coming. Any second now, the door would open and …

"Hello, Jetta." She knew that voice. It belonged to … One more bark, and then she remembered. It belonged to Anita.

Jetta's tail started to wag first, and then her back and her ribs started to move. Soon her whole body was shaking. Put me down! Put me down! She squiggled and squirmed until at last she was free. With a big woof of excitement, she leapt into Anita's arms. It was so good to have company over to visit.

33. The quotation "She let off a tremendous series of growls and barks, enough to shake the roof right off the house," contains an example of

   A. simile

   B. metaphor

   C. hyperbole

   D. onomatopoeia

34. The word "follies" means

    A. errors

    B. foolish acts

    C. relationships

    D. performances

35. Jetta's favourite food is most likely

    A. steak

    B. cookies

    C. dog food

    D. jelly beans

Read the following passage to answer questions 36 to 41.

THE SQUAD OF ONE

Sergeant Blue of the Mounted Police was a so-so kind of guy;
He swore a bit, and he lied a bit, and he boozed a bit on the sly;
But he held the post of Snake Creek Bend in the good old British way,
And a grateful country paid him about sixty cents a day.
Now the life of the North-West Mounted Police breeds an all-round kind of man;
A man who can finish whatever he starts, and no matter how it began;
A man who can wrestle a drunken bum, or break up a range stampede—
Such are the men of the Mounted Police, and such are the men they breed.
The snow lay deep at the Snake Creek post and deep to east and west,
And the Sergeant had made his ten-league beat and settled down to rest
In his two-by-four that they called a "post," where the flag flew overhead,
And he took a look at his monthly mail, and this is the note he read:
"To Sergeant Blue, of the Mounted Police, at the post at Snake Creek Bend,
From U.S. Marshal of County Blank, greetings to you, my friend:
They's a team of toughs give us the slip, though they shot up a couple of blokes,
And we reckon they's hid in Snake Creek Gulch, and posin' as farmer folks.
"Of all the toughs I ever saw I reckon these the worst,
So shoot to kill if you shoot at all, and be sure you do it first,
And send out your strongest squad of men and round them up if you can,
For dead or alive we want them here. Yours truly, Jack McMann."
And Sergeant Blue sat back and smiled, and his heart was glad and free,
And he said, "If I round these beggars up it's another stripe for me;
And promotion don't come easy to one of us Mounty chaps,
So I'll scout around tomorrow and I'll bring them in—perhaps."
Next morning Sergeant Blue, arrayed in farmer smock and jeans,
In a jumper sleigh he had made himself set out for the evergreens
That grow on the bank of Snake Creek Gulch by a homestead shack he knew,
And a smoke curled up from the chimney-pipe to welcome Sergeant Blue.

"Aha!" said Blue, "and who are you? Behold, the chimney smokes,
But the boy that owns this homestead shack is up at Okotoks;
And he wasn't expecting callers, for he left his key with me,
So I'll just drop in for an interview and we'll see what we shall see!"
So he drove his horse to the shanty door and hollered a loud "Good day,"
And a couple of men with fighting-irons came out beside the sleigh;
And the Sergeant said, "I'm a stranger here and I've driven a weary mile,
If you don't object I'll just sit down by the stove in the shack a while."
Then the Sergeant sat and smoked and talked of the home he had left down East,
And the cold and the snow, and the price of land, and the life of man and beast,
But all of a sudden he broke if off with, "Neighbours, take a nip?
There's a horn of the best you'll find out there in my jumper, in the grip."
So one of the two went for it, and as soon as he closed the door
The Sergeant tickled the other one's ribs with the nose of his forty-four;
"Now, fellow," he said, "you're a man of sense, and you know when you're on the rocks,
And a noise as loud as a mouse from you and they'll take you home in a box,"
And he fastened the bracelets to his wrists, and his legs with a halter-shank,
And he took his knife and he took his gun and he made him safe as the bank,
And then he mustered Number Two in an Indian file parade,
And he gave some brief directions—and Number Two obeyed.
And when he had coupled them each to each and set them down on the bed,
"It's a frosty day and we'd better eat before we go," he said.
So he fried some pork and he warmed some beans, and he set out the best he saw,
And he noted the price for the man of the house, according to British law.
That night in the post sat Sergeant Blue, with paper and pen in hand,
And this the word he wrote and signed and mailed to a foreign land:
"To U.S. Marshal of County Blank, greetings I give to you;
My squad has just brought in your men, and the squad was Sergeant Blue."
There are things unguessed, there are tales untold, in the life of the great lone land,
But here is a fact that the prairie-bred alone may understand,
That a thousand miles in the fastnesses the fear of the law obtains,
And the pioneers of justice were the "Riders of the Plains."

—by Robert Stead

36. The type of poem presented here is best categorized as a

A. ballad

B. sonnet

C. lyric poem

D. narrative poem

37. Sergeant Blue can best be described as

   A. mediocre

   B. negligent

   C. perceptive

   D. innovative

38. As it is used in the phrase "In his two-by-four that they called a 'post'," the word "post" means

   A. mail

   B. fence

   C. office

   D. dispatch

39. The season in which this poem is set is

   A. fall

   B. spring

   C. winter

   D. summer

40. Which of the following words best describes the sergeant's behaviour at the shanty?

   A. Cruel

   B. Shrewd

   C. Impulsive

   D. Trustworthy

41. The word that best expresses the meaning of the word "fastnesses" as it is used in the line "a thousand miles in the fastnesses" is

   A. permanences

   B. strongholds

   C. boldnesses

   D. locations

Read the following passage to answer questions 42 to 51.

WINDS THROUGH TIME

On a warm spring evening in 1996 I listened as a frail, white-haired man, his wheelchair pushed up against a small table, spoke to several hundred people in an auditorium in Winnipeg. As he talked his voice faltered, but his words were sure and strong. He told of being a child in the 1920s, of being kept out of school because he had tuberculosis which had settled in the bones of his wrist. He wore a protective cage on that wrist, he told us, but it didn't prevent him from spending his days out on the prairies, watching the gophers as they popped up from their homes to stare curiously at him, listening to the harsh cries of the crows. He spent many hours alone on the prairie, the dust and the smell of dry grass thick in his throat, the empty sky arching above, the wind all around him.

In Canada, he said, a young person has "no medieval cathedrals with soaring Gothic arches to comfort him with ancestor echo."

Those words made a great impact on me. In the darkened auditorium I rummaged for my notebook and a pencil and wrote them down. I realized that Canadians do not need to walk on ancient Roman roads or touch crumbling castle walls to reach our past. We hear our "ancestral echoes" in mountain streams, in rustling prairie grasses, in the songs of our oceans. We hear our echoes in the wind.

When the speech was over the audience stood. They applauded for a long time; many cried. Finally it grew quiet and W.O. Mitchell was wheeled from the stage.

Bill Mitchell knew well the sound of the wind which blows across this Canada of ours. He heard it first, he wrote about it first, that wind which carries in it the echoes of our ancestors, the voices of people long since gone. The contributors to this anthology have also heard that wind and those echoes. These authors wonder at the vast emptiness of the Canada of yesterday, and they write with great empathy about those who were Canadians before us.

The wind blows. Listen. In a small New Brunswick town, two sisters sit in a sunny doorway, whispering stories to a doll with cornsilk hair. The wind changes and, in another century in another province, medals clink together in a duffel bag as a weary father returns home from war to find that his son is no longer a child.

Listen again. A train whistle wails mournfully. From one ocean to the other train tracks stitched Canada together. As this train crosses a high trestle bridge in Northern B.C. a boy sits on a hard wooden seat, his mind and stomach uneasy, while a fellow traveller tells of the Gold Rush. In another train in Ontario, a young man imagines he hears the crackle of flames engulfing a cheese factory and wonders if he will be able to solve the mystery of how the fire began. Near a coal mine on Vancouver Island, the earth rumbles. An underground rail car moves slowly upwards towards the light where a desperate son waits for news of his father.

The wind blows through the years. It brings with it, loud in the midnight cold, the whine of a bush pilot's engine.
The northern lights blaze; there is laughter. As the wind changes, more laughter comes from a tiny community where a solitary family celebrates Hanukkah in the midst of their neighbours' Christmas festivities.

Listen to the wind. Can you hear the music spilling from a Vancouver mansion where, beneath a candle lit Christmas tree, a masquerade party begins? Can you hear the splash as a whale rises from the sea, and two boys standing on the slippery rocks beneath a lighthouse watch in awe? Can you hear, from a burning shed in the Red River settlement, the panicked whinny of a frightened horse as a young Metis girl struggles to save its life and also to change her own?

The wind's power intensifies. The stiff branches of a dying orchard creak; pages flutter as a difficult letter is written to a grandfather in England. Another shift of wind and a harmonica's tune is carried up to a flock of migrating geese, while on the Saskatchewan prairie below an unhappy boy watches, envying the birds' freedom.

It is the wind which turns the pages of this book, releasing the soft voice of a Japanese grandmother as she tells of being imprisoned in an internment camp during the war; the determined voice of young Nellie McClung protesting in Manitoba years before her suffrage debate; the terrified voice of a mother screaming to protect her child from the cougar who crouches in a tree's shadow.

The wind gusts. As it moves across the land and through the decades, we are blown from island to prairie, from the Maritimes to the far north, from mansions to shacks, from farm to city. We hear shouts of joy, cries of grief, the howls of wolves and the whispers of ghosts.

Listen to the echoes as you read. Listen to the wind.

—by Ann Walsh

42. The quotation "sisters sit in a sunny doorway, whispering stories" contains an example of which of the following literary devices?

A. Contrasting imagery

B. Alliteration

C. Hyperbole

D. Allegory

43. The man described at the beginning of the passage is most likely

A. an architect

B. a historian

C. an author

D. a farmer

44. The reason the man wore a protective cage on his wrist when he was a boy was

A. to shield it from animals like gophers and crows while he was on the prairie

B. so that other people could not see his deformed wrist

C. because his wrist had been weakened by disease

D. to keep his wrist straight

45. As it is used in the phrase "this train crosses a high trestle bridge," the word "trestle" means

A. rickety

B. precarious

C. suspension wire

D. supporting framework

46. The image of fluttering pages in the quotation "pages flutter as a difficult letter is written" calls to mind

    A. a forgotten memory

    B. the passage of time

    C. cold afternoons

    D. a winter storm

47. The "ancestral echoes" referred to in this passage symbolize

    A. forgotten relatives

    B. the voices of ghosts

    C. answers to questions

    D. a sense of belonging

48. Which of the following events was most likely documented in the "difficult letter"?

    A. A grandson who sought his fortune in a new country has died.

    B. A son has gambled away his father's fortune.

    C. Insects have decimated a family's farm.

    D. A flood has destroyed a town.

49. Which of the following quotations does not contain an example of parallel structure?

    A. "As he talked his voice faltered, but his words were sure and strong."

    B. "He heard it first, he wrote about it first"

    C. "We are blown from island to prairie, from the Maritimes to the far north, from mansions to shacks, from farm to city."

    D. "We hear shouts of joy, cries of grief, the howls of wolves and the whispers of ghosts."

ANSWERS AND SOLUTIONS—PRACTICE TEST 2

1. A	13. D	25. B	37. A	49. A
2. WR	14. A	26. B	38. C	50. B
3. D	15. D	27. WR	39. C	51. D
4. A	16. B	28. B	40. B	52. C
5. D	17. A	29. WR	41. B	53. D
6. D	18. B	30. B	42. B	54. C
7. B	19. A	31. C	43. C	55. B
8. WR	20. D	32. WR	44. C	56. A
9. B	21. B	33. C	45. D	57. D
10. A	22. C	34. B	46. B	
11. C	23. A	35. D	47. D	
12. C	24. A	36. D	48. A	

1. A

According to Diana, Ruby Gillis wants to have a beau, or boyfriend, as soon as she turns 15.

2. WRITTEN RESPONSE

Anne and Diana spend most of their time on the walk gossiping. They are uncharitable about Ruby Gillis, they have nothing nice to say about Josie Pye, and they comment on Alice Bell's physical shortcomings. They are supposed to be observing their surroundings and thinking about their compositions, but they are too busy gossiping.

3. D

Miss Stacy has assigned the girls a composition entitled "A Winter's Walk in the Woods." The writer has shortened the title to "A Winter's Walk" to show how the girls' daily walk to school ties in with the essay they are required to write. It is possible that the girls pay little attention to their environment as they walk to school (as is shown in this excerpt), and the teacher wants them to become more observant.

4. A

From the description Anne gives to Diana of her completed composition, it appears to be very much in the genre of romantic fiction. Anne has exaggerated the looks of her two heroines by giving one of them "a coronet of midnight hair and dusky flashing eyes" and the other "hair like spun gold and velvety purple eyes" with "an alabaster brow." These fanciful descriptions are typical of romantic fiction.

5. D

The girls' relationship is illustrated mainly through dialogue. Anne and Diana converse throughout their entire walk to school. They talk about assignments, Mrs. Allen, and their schoolmates.

6. D

Alabaster is a fine-textured, milky white material that is often carved into vases and ornaments. Anne's imagination is evident when, at barely 13 years old, she uses descriptions like "alabaster brow" in her writing.

7. B

The passage consists mainly of Anne expressing her wonder at being a teenager, her views on various people in her life, and her exuberant imagination.

8. WRITTEN RESPONSE

The speaker describes herself as a flighty or impractical person who needs a logical, practical friend to keep her in touch with what is reasonable.

9. B

When the speaker relates her experience, she mentions Jill, who represents all that is reasonable and practical. Her last statement, "I wouldn't be in this mess / If Jill had come shopping with me," supports the idea that the speaker wishes she had been reasonable, like Jill, instead of impulsive.

10. A

Jill is down-to-earth and logical. She thinks things through before she does them; for example, she checks to see how easy or difficult it will be to clean something before she buys it.

11. C

The quotation contains a metaphor, which is a direct comparison between two unrelated subjects, usually using the verb to be. The quotation is not personification because personification is when an inanimate object is referred to as though it had human qualities.

12. C

The italicized text introduces the focus that each section develops.

13. D

The writer's main purpose in writing this passage was to inform. The article increases awareness of where self-image originates and discusses the importance of being self-confident.

14. A

The writer states directly in the third section of the passage that the media affects self-image most dramatically.

15. D

In the last section, the writer states directly that people can change themselves by accepting who they are now.

16. B

The word "emaciated" is used in reference to Barbie's measurements of 31-19-27, which would make her body gaunt or skeletal.

17. A

The passage leaves the reader with the sense that his or her self-image is within his or her control. The writer states, "While we're waiting for the media to change, we can change ourselves. Not our bodies, but our attitudes."

18. B

Repetition as a literary technique repeats a word or concept to increase emphasis. The word "fifth" is repeated to emphasize how many times Melanie has tried to set the snares.

19. A

There are several clues in the passage that indicate that Fort Smith is most likely a northern community, for example, the descriptions of the cold weather and the mention of Melanie's husky, which is a breed of dog associated mainly with northern communities.

20. D

The ellipsis in this sentence represents Melanie's incomplete thought about where to lay her snare.

21. B

A dash can be used to connect an explanation to a word. In this case, the dash is explaining that the problem with the snow is the lack of snow.

22. C

Climate change is referred to as a scapegoat because it is often blamed for environmental disasters. The reader could use prior knowledge or context clues to select the correct alternative.

23. A

Melanie describes herself this way because in this situation, she feels as pitiful as the rabbits she is hunting. She recognizes the relationship between herself and her setting.

24. A

Italicized text is used to identify special text that is not a part of the normal narration. In this passage, the italicized text is used to identify thoughts that Melanie writes down.

25. B

The phrase is a metaphor that compares a hockey team, the Ottawa Senators, to a doormat.

26. B

The Ottawa Senators were a team that went from the bottom of the league to winning the Stanley Cup, which is a dramatic change.

27. WRITTEN RESPONSE

The quotation contains a typical sports hyperbole that refers to the fact that Claude Dupont is a young, inexperienced player. The expression creates an image not to be taken literally.

28. B

Uncle Bill and the children are going to a Senators game, and Uncle Bill's Flames jersey is likely to attract negative attention. The other alternatives may be true, but they are not supported by context.

29. WRITTEN RESPONSE

To "utter" something means to say it; "Jest" means to tease or joke. Uncle Bill said something in a joking manner; he did not really mean it. From the passage, it can be inferred that Uncle Bill has a sense of humour and a jovial personality. It is also clear that the specific comment is not meant to be taken seriously.

30. B

In the context of this passage, the word "prophecy" means prediction. The word is used in connection with a story about something that eventually comes true.

31. C

The night stands out in the narrator's mind because it was the night Uncle Bill began to teach her the principles of finance.

32. WRITTEN RESPONSE

The chapter opens with a hockey story, but continued reading reveals that the purpose of the article is to encourage financial intelligence. The hockey is a hook to set the context, engage the reader, and make the characters seem warm and human.

33. C

A hyperbole is a deliberate exaggeration or overstatement that helps the reader create a mental image of an event, person, or object. Describing Jetta's barking as "enough to shake the roof right off the house" conveys how loudly and excitedly she is barking.

34. B

The word "follies" describes foolish acts or ideas based on poor judgment.

35. D

For Jetta, stealing jelly beans is the worst thing a stranger could possibly do, which suggests that jelly beans are probably her favourite food.

36. D

This poem can best be categorized as a narrative poem. A narrative poem is an extended poem that tells a story.

37. A

The first line of the poem states that Sergeant Blue is a "so-so kind of guy" and provides evidence for the quality of mediocrity attributed to his character.

38. C

The "two-by-four that they called a "post" is Sergeant Blue's command post or office. This is the literal meaning of a colloquial term that would have been used in the past.

39. C

Since "the snow lay deep," and Sergeant Blue uses a sleigh to get himself to his destination, it can be concluded that the poem is set in winter.

40. B

The sergeant's behaviour is entirely premeditated—from his disguise in farmer's clothing, to his claim to be a stranger, to his diversion of asking one of the men to liquor—to enable him to overpower and capture the criminals. It is his shrewdness that allows for his ultimate success.

41. B

The reader must infer the literal meaning of a figurative term. The fear of the law provides a stronghold for those alone in the vast prairie: it offers security for them and is upheld by the North West Mounted Police, the "Riders of the Plain."

42. B

Alliteration is the repetition of initial consonant sounds in words that are close together. In this example, the s sound is repeatedly stressed. This is alliteration, and it also suggests the sound the girls might make when they whisper.

43. C

The man described at the beginning of the passage is a writer. This is made clear by the statement "He heard it first, he wrote about it first."

44. C

The man explained that disease "had settled in his wrist." The protective device was necessary so that he would not further injure his weakened wrist.

45. D

The word "trestle" refers to a frame used as a support. This was once a common way to support a train bridge high over a river valley.

46. B

The imagery of the fluttering pages calls to mind the passage of time.

47. D

When readers hear or imagine the voices and words of those people who came before them, it ties them to a greater history. A sense of collective history among a society or community gives people a sense of belonging.

48. A

Canada is a relatively young country. Much of its population is made up of immigrants, especially from Europe. The dying orchard symbolizes death, and the most difficult thing to report back to relatives back home is death.

49. A

Parallel structure means using the same pattern of words to show that two or more ideas have the same level of importance. The sentence "his voice faltered, but his words were sure and strong" does not contain parallel structure.

50. B

The writer repeats words like "wind," "blows," and "listen" in order to establish a mood of storytelling. The writer also repeats structures throughout the passage, evoking the voice of a storyteller who has told a tale many times.

51. D

The word intern means to confine or imprison. A synonym for the word "internment" is confinement.

52. C

The word weather refers to climate. When used as a conjunction, the word is spelled whether.

53. D

"Dissiness" should be spelled with a double z: Dizziness.

54. C

A verb is a word or phrase that expresses an action or state of being. In this sentence, the word "played" functions as a verb.

55. B

An adjective is a word, phrase, or clause used to modify a noun or pronoun. In this sentence, the word "sore" describes the state of the "eyes."

56. A

An adverb is a word, phrase, or clause that is used to modify a verb, adjective, or another adverb. In this sentence, the word "frequently" modifies the verb "buries" by telling how often the dog buries the toys.

57. D

A preposition is a word that shows the relationship between a noun or pronoun and some other word in the sentence. In this sentence, the word "by" functions as a preposition.

Appendices

GLOSSARY OF RELEVANT TERMS

abstract	Abstract terms and concepts name things that are not knowable through the senses; examples are love, justice, guilt, and honour. See CONCRETE.
alliteration	Repetition of initial consonant sounds
allusion	Indirect or passing reference to some person, place, or event; or to a piece of literature or art. The nature of the reference is not explained because the writer relies on the reader's familiarity with it.
analogy	A comparison that is made to explain something that is unfamiliar by presenting an example that is similar or parallel to it in some significant way
anecdote	A brief story of an interesting incident
antecedent action	Action that takes place before the story opens
assonance	Repetition of similar or identical vowel sounds
ballad	A narrative poem that tells a story, often in a straightforward and dramatic manner, and often about such universals as love, honour, and courage. Ballads were once songs. Literary ballads often have the strong rhythm and the plain rhyme schemes of songs. Songs are still written in ballad form, some old ballads are still sung, and some literary ballads have been set to music. Samuel Taylor Coleridge's "The Rime of the Ancient Mariner" is an example of a literary ballad.
blank verse	Poetry written in unrhymed iambic pentameters
chronological	In order of time
cliché	An overused expression; one that has become stale through overuse
colloquial	Informal, suitable for everyday speech but not for formal writing
concrete	A concrete thing exists in a solid, physical way; it is knowable through the senses; trees, copper, and kangaroos are all examples of concrete things. See ABSTRACT.
connotation	Implied or additional meaning that a word or phrase imparts. Such meaning is often subjective. See also DENOTATION.
denotation	The explicit or direct meaning of a word or expression, aside from the impressions it creates. These are the meanings listed in dictionaries. See also CONNOTATION.
discrepancy	Distinct difference between two things that should not be different or that should correspond
fantasy	A literary genre; generally contains events, characters, or settings that would not be possible in real life
foreshadowing	A storytelling technique; something early in the story hints at later events

free verse	Is usually written in variable rhythmic cadences; it may be rhymed or unrhymed, but the rhymes are likely to be irregular and may not occur at the end of lines
hyperbole	A figure of speech that uses exaggeration for effect
imagery	Language that evokes sensory impressions
imitative harmony	Words that seem to imitate the sounds to which they refer; buzz and whisper are examples of imitative harmony; also called ONOMATOPOEIA.
interior monologue	Conversation-like thoughts of a character
irony	The difference—in actions or words—between reality and appearance. Authors use irony for both serious and humorous effects. Irony can also be a technique for indicating, through character or plot development, the writer's own attitude toward some element of the story.
jargon	Special vocabulary of a particular group or activity; sometimes used to refer to confusing or unintelligible language
justification	The giving of reasons or support; for example, giving an argument or reason that shows that an action or belief is reasonable or true
juxtaposition (or contrast)	The deliberate contrast of characters, settings, or situations for effect; the effect may be a demonstration of character or heightening of mood
lyric	A poem that expresses the private emotions or thoughts of the writer; sonnets, odes, and elegies are examples of lyric poetry
metaphor	Comparison without using the words like or as
monologue	A literary form; an oral or written composition in which only one person speaks
mood	In a story, the atmosphere; when a writer orders the setting, action, and characters of a story so as to suggest a dominant emotion or patterns of emotions, this emotional pattern is the mood of the story. Also a person's state of mind or complex of emotions at any given time.
ode	A poem expressing lofty emotion; odes often celebrate an event or are addressed to nature or to some admired person, place, or thing; an example is "Ode on a Grecian Urn" by John Keats
onomatopoeia	Words that seem to imitate the sounds to which they refer.
oxymoron	A combination of two usually contradictory terms in a compressed paradox; for example, "the living dead." An oxymoron is like a metaphor in that it expresses in words some truth that cannot be understood literally; truthful lies is an oxymoron that describes metaphors.

parable	A short, often simple story that teaches or explains a lesson: often a moral or religious lesson
paradox	An apparently self-contradictory statement that is, in fact, true
parallelism	The arrangement of similarly constructed clauses, verses, or sentences
personification	The extension of human attributes to objects or to abstract ideas
point of view: first person	The story is told by one of the characters in the story ("I"). The narrator is in the story. First-person narrators only know what they think, feel, do, see, and hear.
point of view: objective	The story is told without telling any characters' thoughts and feelings. Only the characters' actions and words are told. This point of view is a lot like the camera's point of view in a movie. Objective narrators only know what a camera can record. This story-telling form suffers from the limitations of film but at the same time can produce a film-like effect.
point of view: third person	The story is told through the eyes of one or more characters ("he, she, and they"). The narrator is outside the story, and tells what the characters think, feel, and do. Omniscient narrators know about everything that happens and what any character thinks and feels. Limited omniscient narrators only know about one character and the things that one character knows, thinks, feels, and does.
prologue	An introduction to a play, often delivered by the chorus (in ancient Greece, a group, but in modern plays, one actor) who plays no part in the following action
pun	A humorous expression that depends on a double meaning, either between different senses of the same word or between two similar sounding words
ridicule	Contemptuous mocking or derision (contempt and mockery); ridicule may be an element of satire
satire	A form of writing that exposes the failings of individuals, institutions, or societies; to ridicule or scorn in order to correct or expose some evil or wrongdoing
simile	Comparison using the words like or as
sonnet	A lyric poem 14 lines long and usually written in iambic pentameter. The Shakespearean sonnet consists of three quatrains (four-line stanzas) and a couplet (two lines), all written to a strict end-rhyme scheme (abab cdcd efef gg). The development of the poet's thoughts is also structured. There are several methods: one method is to use each quatrain for different points in an argument and the couplet for the resolution of the argument. Because of the complexity of the sonnet, poets sometimes find it a suitable form for expressing the complexity of thought and emotion.

symbol	Anything that stands for or represents something other than itself. In literature, a symbol is a word or phrase referring to an object, scene, or action that also has some further significance associated with it. For example, a rose is a common symbol of love. Many symbols, such as flags, are universally recognized. Other symbols are not so universally defined. They do not acquire a meaning until they are defined by how they are used in a story. They may even suggest more than one meaning. For example, snow might be used to symbolize goodness because of its cleanness, or cruelty because of its coldness. Symbols are often contained in story titles; in character and place names; in classical, literary, and historical allusions and references; in images or figures that appear at important points in a story; and in images that either receive special emphasis or are repeated.
thesis	A statement that is made as the first step in an argument or a demonstration
tone	A particular way of speaking or writing. Tone may also describe the general feeling of a piece of work. It can demonstrate the writer's attitude toward characters, settings, conflicts, and so forth. The many kinds of tone include thoughtful, chatty, formal, tragic, or silly; tone can also be a complex mixture of attitudes. Different tones can cause readers to experience such varying emotions as pity, fear, horror, or humour.

DIRECTING WORDS	
The following list of directing words and definitions may help you plan your writing. For example, a particular discussion might include assessment, description, illustrations, or an outline of how an extended argument could be developed.	
Directing Word	**Definition**
Agree or Disagree	Support or contradict a statement; give the positive or negative features; express an informed opinion one way or the other; list the advantages for or against
Assess	Estimate the value of something based on some criteria; present an informed judgement. The word "assess" strongly suggests that two schools of thought exist about a given subject. Assessing usually involves weighing the relative merit of conflicting points of view; e.g., negative vs. positive, strong vs. weak components, long-range vs. short-term.
Compare	Point out similarities or differences; describe the relationship between two things; often used in conjunction with CONTRAST
Contrast	Show or emphasize differences when compared; see COMPARE
Describe	Give a detailed or graphic account of an object, event, or sequence of events
Discuss	Present the various points of view in a debate or argument; write at length about a given subject; engage in written discourse on a particular topic
Explain	Give an account of what the essence of something is, how something works, or why something is the way it is; may be accomplished by paraphrasing, providing reasons or examples, or by giving a step-by-step account
Identify	Establish the identity of something; establish the unique qualities of something; provide the name of something
Illustrate	Give concrete examples to clarify; provide explanatory or decorative features
List	Itemize names, ideas, or things that belong to a particular class or group
Outline	Give a written description of only the main features; summarize the principal parts of a thing, an idea, or an event
Show (that)	Give facts, reasons, illustrations or examples to support an idea or proposition
State	Give the key points; declare
Suggest	Propose alternatives, options, or solutions
Support	Defend or agree with a particular point of view; give evidence, reasons, or examples
Trace	Outline the development of something; describe a specified sequence

CREDITS

Every effort has been made to provide proper acknowledgement of the original source and to comply with copyright law. However, some attempts to establish original copyright ownership may have been unsuccessful. If copyright ownership can be identified, please notify Castle Rock Research Corp so that appropriate corrective action can be taken.

Some images in this document are from www.clipart.com, © 2013 Clipart.com, a division of Getty Images.

Excerpts from *The Diamond Necklace*, by Guy de Maupassant. New York: Random House, Inc., 1950.

"I Am A Native Of North America," from *My Heart Soars*, by Chief Dan George, Hancock House Publishers Ltd., 1992. Reprinted by permission of Hancock House Publishers, Ltd.

The Highwayman, by Alfred Noyes. Oxford University Press.

"Ex Basketball Player," from *Collected Poems: 1953–1993*, by John Updike. Copyright ©1993 by John Updike. Used by permission of Alfred A. Knopf, a division of Random House, Inc.

"Father Calls Hockey Game of Butchery," by The Canadian Press.

Excerpt from To Touch a Mammoth, by Patricia Nikolina Clark. http://www.highlightskids.com/Stories/Fiction/F0197_mammoth.asp.

The Blind Men and the Elephant, by John Godfrey Saxe. Public domain.

On the Way to the Mission, by D.C. Scott. Public domain.

"The Coming of Mutt," from *The Dog Who Wouldn't Be*, by Farley Mowat. McClelland & Stewart, Ltd., 1957. Reprinted by permission of McClelland & Steward, Ltd.

Hector the Stowaway Dog, by Captain Kenneth Dodson. Angus & Roberson, 1959. Reproduced by permission of Pollinger Limited and Captain Kenneth Dobson.

Mulga Bill's Bicycle, by A.B. "Banjo" Paterson. Public domain.

Warren Pryor, by Alden Nowlan. Stoddart Publishing Co. Limited, 1989.

Excerpt, "An Unexpected Announcement," from *Drift House*, by Dale Peck. Allen & Unwin Book Publishers, 2005.

Excerpt, "They Didn't Know Hockey," from *Leslie McFarlane's Hockey Stories*, by Brian McFarlane. Key Porter Books, 2005. Reprinted with permission of Key Porter Books. Copyright © 2005 by Brian McFarlane.

In Search of Santa, by Matthew Frederick Davis Hemming. Cosmos Magazine, Issue 6, December 2005/January 2006, Luna Media Pty Ltd.

Excerpt from *Jabberwocky*, by Lewis Carroll. Public domain.

"Skating," excerpted from *Prelude–Book First, Introduction–Childhood and School-Time*, by William Wordsworth.

"Sport," by Kirk Wirsig, from *Who Owns the Earth?* Alberta Heritage Learning Resources Project, 1979.

Never Look a Baboon in the Eye, by David Suzuki.

On His Blindness by John Milton. Public domain.

To Autumn, by John Keats. Public domain.

"Insolence," by Nanci Neff. *Literary Cavalcade*, May 1972. Copyright © 1972 by Scholastic, Inc. Reprinted by permission of Scholastic, Inc.

The Tell-Tale Heart, by Edgar Allan Poe. Public domain.

Excerpt from *Island of the Blue Dolphin,* by Scott O'Dell. Houghton Mifflin Company, 1990.

Excerpt from *A Tale of Two Cities,* by Charles Dickens. Public domain.

Excerpt from *Soaked in Seaweed,* by Stephen Leacock. Public domain.

Excerpt from "I'm So Lonesome, I Could Cry," by Hank Williams.

"Nothing Gold Can Stay," by Robert Frost.

"How Long Have I Known You, Oh Canada?" published as "The Lament for Confederation," from *The Best of Chief Dan George,* by Chief Dan George. Hancock House Publishers Ltd., 2004. Reprinted by permission of Hancock House Publishers.

Storyboard based on the story *The Gift of the Magi* by O. Henry.

Dragon Night, by Jane Yolen. Copyright © 1980 by Jane Yolen. Currently appears in *Here There Be Dragons*. Harcourt Brace and Company, 1993. Reprinted by permission of Curtis Brown, Ltd.

Fork in the Graveyard, by Julie V. Watson.

Challenges, by Jodie Chen, Wall & Emerson, 1993. Permission has been granted for its reproduction by Wall & Emerson, Inc.

Letter by David Sandiford, by David Sandiford. Published in *The Fourth Moriningside Papers*, by Peter Gzowski. Toronto, McClelland & Stewart, 1993.

"Cooks Brook," by Al Pittman, from *An Island in the Sky: Selected Poetry of Al Pittman*, eds. Martin Ware and Stephanie McKenzie. Copyright © 2003. Published by Breakwater Books, Ltd.

"A Winter's Walk," from *Anne of Green Gables*, by L.M. Montgomery.

"Brenda Stewart," by Mel Glenn. Published in *Class Dismissed! High School Poems*, by Mel Glenn, Clarion Books, Ticknor & Fields, a Houghton Mifflin Company, 1982. Reprinted by permission of the author.

The Search for the Perfect Body, by Mary Walters Riskin, AADAC/Information Management Services, reprinted with permission of the Alberta Alcohol and Drug Abuse Commission (www.aadac.com). "The Search for the Perfect Body" by Mary Walters Riskin, http://www.aadac4kids.com/doiknowme/perfect_body.asp.

"Andrea's Story: Hockey Night in Canada" from *The Wealthy Paper Carriers,* by Henry B. Cimmer, Calgary, Springbank Publishing, 1993.

"The Squad of One," by Robert Stead, published in *Crime in a Cold Climate—An Anthology of Classic Canadian Crime*, ed. David Skene. Simon & Pierre. Poem reprinted with permission from The Dundurn Group. Copyright 1996.

"Introduction," from *Winds Through Time*, by Ann Walsh. Beach Holme Publishing, Vancouver, 1998. Excerpt reprinted with permission from The Dundurn Group, copyright © 1998.

SOLARO Study Guides
Ordering Information

The SOLARO Study Guides are specifically designed to assist students in preparing for unit tests, final exams, and provincial assessments.

SOLARO Study Guide—$29.95 each plus applicable sales tax

SOLARO
Study Guides

Ontario SOLARO Titles	
Mathematics 12, Advanced Functions, University Prep (MHF4U)	Civics 10, (CHV2O)
Mathematics 12, Calculus and Vectors, University Prep (MCV4U)	English 10, Academic (ENG2D)
Mathematics 12, Mathematics of Data Management, University Prep (MDM4U)	OSSLT, Ontario Secondary School Literacy Test
Physics 12, University Prep (SPH4U)	Mathematics 9, Academic, Principles of Mathematics (MPM1D)
Biology 12, University Prep (SBI4U)	Mathematics 9, Applied, Foundations of Mathematics (MFM1P)
Canadian and World Politics 12, University Prep (CPW4U)	Science 9, Academic (SNC1D)
Chemistry 12, University Prep (SCH4U)	Science 9, Applied (SNC2P)
English 12, University Prep (ENG4U)	Geography of Canada 9, Academic (CGC1D)
English 12, College Prep (ENG4C)	English 9, Academic (ENG1D)
World History 12, University Prep (CHY4U)	Science 8
Mathematics 11, Foundations for College Mathematics (MBF3C)	Mathematics 7
Mathematics 11, Functions and Applications, U/C Prep (MCF3M)	Science 7
Mathematics 11, Functions, University Prep (MCR3U)	Mathematics 6
Biology 11, University Prep (SBI3U)	Science 6
Chemistry 11, University Prep (SCH3U)	Language 6
English 11, University Prep (ENG3U)	Mathematics 5
World History 11, University/College Prep (CHW3M)	Science 5
Mathematics 10, Academic, Principles of Mathematics (MPM2D)	Mathematics 4
Mathematics 10, Applied, Foundations of Mathematics (MFM2P)	Science 4
Science 10, Applied (SNC1P)	Mathematics 3
Science 10, Academic (SNC2D)	Science 3
Canadian History 10, Academic (CHC2D)	Language 3
Canadian History 10, Applied (CHC2P)	

To order books, please visit
castlerockresearch.com or call
1.800.840.6224
Volume pricing is available. Contact us at
orders@castlerockresearch.com

Student Notes and Problems
Workbook
Ordering Information

Student Notes and Problems (SNAP) Workbooks contain complete explanations of curriculum concepts, including examples and practice exercises

SNAP Workbook—$29.95 each plus applicable sales tax

Ontario SNAP Titles
Physics 12, University Preparation (SPH4U)
Physics 11, University Preparation (SPH3U)
Math 10, Academic, Principles of Mathematics (MPM2D)
Math 9, Academic, Principles of Mathematics (MPM1D)
Math 9, Applied, Foundations of Mathematics (MFM1P)

Total Cost	
SOLARO Study Guides Ordered	_____
SNAP Books Ordered	_____
Cost Subtotal	_____
Shipping and Handling Please call for current rates	_____
GST	_____
Order Total	_____

Payment and Shipping Information

Name _____

School _____

Telephone _____

SHIP TO:

School Code _____

School Name _____

Address _____

City: _____

Postal Code: _____

PAYMENT OPTIONS:

☐ By Credit Care VISA/MC

Name on Card: _____

Number: _____

Expirely Date: _____

☐ By Enclosed Cheque

☐ Invoice School

PO Number: _____

To order books, please visit
www.castlerockresearch.com

Volume pricing is available. Contact us at
orders@castlerockresearch.com